What Others Think Of Nail it!

"Nail it! is a spell book from a good witch about nail care. It is easy to understand and apply, with mind-blowing fast behavior transformation for canine and human alike. Nail it! helped me get the confidence to do Bruno's and Daisy's nails without breaking a sweat or having an elevated heart rate. Betty's respect for dogs is a brand new way to look at providing services to animals."

~ *Nancy, Dog mom of Bruno and Daisy*

"As a professional groomer, I was shocked (and honestly very envious) to learn about Betty's incredibly low rate of quicking dogs (cutting the nails too short to the point of bleeding), so I put my pride aside and got a copy of her book. The details of the nail anatomy section and the impact of the environment and exercise on the dogs' behavior opened up a brand new perspective for me about nail care. I haven't had to use my Kwick Stop Powder ever since I am using Betty's method. Grooming schools should teach Nail it! and it's a must for already practicing groomers as well!"

~ *Kim, Professional dog groomer*

"This book is the Bible of Dog Nail Trimming."

~ *Julie, Professional dog groomer*

"Nail it! should be a part of the curriculum of every veterinary technician training! It is a hard-to-swallow pill to realize how little professionals in the pet care industry currently know about nail care, but it is one issue that we must face and work on intensely. The tiny cut per nail and praying method so many of us use still has a higher error rate than I'd like to admit. Betty's book and video combo is the most detailed literature available and I highly recommend it to colleagues, and anyone really who wants to avoid a bloody scene, painful looks from canine clients, upset owners, and aim for a fun experience for all."

~ *Josh, Veterinary technician*

"Penny passionately hated nail care, so did we. Her hiding and loud screaming broke our hearts and ears every time I teamed up with my husband to cut Penny's nails. The Nail it! book combined with Betty's videos helped us understand why our baby behaved the way she did and how we could change her experience to keep her comfortable (and cooperative). I was surprised to see her tolerate nail filing almost instantly and nail trimming by like the third try. Looking back we did a few ridiculous mistakes that after them being eliminated, it was a day and night experience for all of us. Now we can trim and file her nails without the need of both of us present, in about 10-15 minutes. This book is worth every penny, costs way less than hearing aids, and helps us skip the sometimes day-long "silent treatment" from Penny after a nail trim of the past."

~ *Sharon and Tim,* Pawrents of Penny

This Nail care course was PAWSOME!!! I was surprised to find the depth of knowledge this course offers, absolutely nothing is left out or left to chance. I completed this course after having a nasty nail incident with my puppy and didn't actually feel confident to continue nail trims at home. However, I now safely and confidently keep my doggies' nails in tip-top condition, with the recommended tools, knowledge, and lifetime access to the course notes!!! - what more could you ask for, thank you so much, Betty! :)

~ *Dana,* Sydney's Dog mom

Nail it!

A Step-by-Step Guide To Wholesome Dog Nail Trimming

BETTY PETO

NAIL IT! - A Step-By-Step Guide to Wholesome Dog Nail Trimming
Copyright © 2021 Betty Peto. All rights reserved.

Printed in the United States.

FIRST EDITION

This book contains advice and information relating to dog nail trimming. It is intended to be a supplemental aid rather than a replacement of a trained pet service provider's advice. If your dog shows symptoms of distress for nail care or handling in general, seek a dog trainer's or a veterinary behaviorist's advice before applying the methods detailed in this book. All efforts have been made to ensure the accuracy of this book's information as of the publication date.
The publisher and the author disclaim liability for any medical or behavioral outcomes due to applying the book's methods.

No part of this book may be used or reproduced without written permission, except for brief quotations embodied in critical articles and reviews. For information, contact the author directly: betty@wholesomegroomingacademy.com.

ISBN 978-1-7340203-2-8 (hardback)
ISBN 978-1-7340203-9-7 (paperback)
ISBN 978-1-7340203-5-9 (ebook)

Ordering information: amazon.com or contact the author: betty@wholesomegroomingacademy.com

Credits
Name: Peto, Betty, author.
Cover image: Peto, Levente - LeviPetoPhotography.com
Cover Design: L1graphics - 99designs.com
Editing coordinator - Bailey, Shannon
Proofreading - Strecker, Susan
Interior design: Spears, Brent - BrentSpears.com
Nail Anatomy Illustrations - Szabo, Brigitta TheBridgeWoodArt.com
Other Illustrations: Peto, Betty
Full Page Posters: Uvarov, Mykhailo
Images - Peto, Betty WholesomeDoodleSpa.com and Peto, Levente LeviPetoPhotography.com
Subjects: Dog Nail Trimming - Compassionate Dog Nail Trimming - Dog Grooming - Gentle Dog Handling - Compassionate Dog Training - Compassionate Dog Grooming.

> "I have done some things I wouldn't have done in case I knew then what I since have learned."
> ~ Marshall B. Rosenberg

For you, who cherish the soul behind bare teeth, let it be because of joy, worry, or warning.

With tremendous gratitude to my husband, Levi, for believing in me and understanding my passion for dog nail care. For tirelessly encouraging me with compassion and phrases like: "It might seem like you are going against the traffic, but it does not mean you are going in the wrong direction!"

I am very grateful to you for picking up my pieces when I felt overwhelmed and helping me get back on my feet again to make two of my doggy-related dreams come true. The first is helping dogs and care providers with nail care and the second for publishing valuable knowledge to leave behind on this planet after I'm gone.

Contents

Chapter 1
Introduction 1
- How and Why This Book Came Around 1
- Reality Check About Dog Nail Care 3
- Who's This Book for? 4
- The Four Significant Parts of Dog Nail Trimming 5
- In This Book, You Will Learn 5
- How to Use This Book 6
- Order of Practice 6
- Top 10 Nail Care Secrets 7

Chapter 2
Paw and Nail Care Needs of Dogs 17
- What are the Dog's Pawdicure Needs in General? 17
- Harmful, Painful, Uncomfortable Nail Care Procedures 21
- Harmful, Painful Nail Accessories 21
- Miscellaneous Paw Clues 27

Chapter 3
The Calm and Cooperative Dog 29
- The Magic of Cooperation is Preparation 29
- The Importance and Power of Pain-Free Experiences 35
- Comfort Measures 36
- Reading Dog Minds 39
- Dog Love Languages 41
- Medical Restraints 58

Chapter 4
The "Thinking Outside the Box" Mindset 63
- Why Compassionate Nail Care and Dog Grooming? 63

Chapter 5
Training Dog Minds 79

Chapter 6
Nail Care Tools 87
- About Nail Care Equipment in General 87
- Nail Care Equipment in Details 88

Chapter 7
Canine Anatomy in a Nutshell 100
- The Structure of the Nail 105
- About the Nail Structure in General 106
- Nail Types by the Visibility of the Sole 116

Chapter 8
Positioning Options for Nail Care 127
- Positioning 101 for Canine Pawdicure 127
- Location Ideas for Nail Care 128
- Positioning 133

Chapter 9
Holding Techniques of the Canine 145
- The Goals of Holding Techniques 145

Chapter 10
Nail Care Preparations Way Before Trimming 151
- Finding Possible Triggers 151

Chapter 11
Nail Care Preparations Right Before Trimming 156

Chapter 12
Nail Trimming 166
- Paw-di-cure™ Method - Clip the Tip, Bit by Bit 171
- Holding the Nails for Nail Trimming 172
- Trimming Step-by-Step 173

Chapter 13
First Aid for Nail Trimming 183
- Injury at the Time of the Nail Care (Hitting the Quick) 183
- The Efficacy of the Paw-di-cure™ Method 186
- How to Tell When the Quick Got Hit 187

Chapter 14
Nail Filing 189
- Nail Filing Tools 189

Chapter 15
Nail Care Plans After Pawdicure 197

Chapter 16
Exercises 200

Attachments 205
- Guidelines - Before Trimming the Nails 205
- Checklist for Nail Trimming 206
- Nail Tissue Cheat Sheet 207
- Nail Types 208
- Nail Layers 209
- Nail Length 210
- Paw Positioning 211
- Top 10 Nail Secrets 212

References 213
Resources 214
- FREE Nail it! Course 214
- Free Printable Downloads 214
- Recommended for Further Education 215

Appreciation 217
Afterword - Be the Change! 218
Your Notes 223
Glossary 225
Acknowledgments 229
About the Author 233

Letter From Betty

I think we have a few common goals we share that are the foundation of your and my philosophy in canine care. The top ones are probably safety and comfort for dogs and care providers, closely followed by connection and progress.

Just the fact that you are reading this book tells me you're not trying to become Cruella de Vil with the "let's get over with this no matter what" mentality. I hear your dog sigh in relief in the background. :)

You are about to read a book that brings unprecedented understanding and endless creativity to the next level in dog nail trimming.

Paws down, there will be times you'll smile because you are already using the technique. I bet there will be also times when you'll raise your eyebrows in surprise high enough it almost becomes an impromptu facelift.

I encourage you to keep an open mind for the things you'll see here and after you grasp the whole concept, give the method a try and see the results for yourself!

I'm looking forward to meeting you in the online Nail it! course to supplement the contents here with videos and in the Nail it! Community and the monthly live roundtables to hear your milestones, resolve any roadblocks, and answer any questions of yours!

Belly rubs to the dogs in your care!
With love,

Betty

Chapter 1

Introduction

How and Why This Book Came Around

Back in the day when I was a kid, our pets never got their nails done professionally.

We lived in the countryside, and they were outside dogs and cats. I did not think about nails, nail colors, shapes, etc. There were just dog nails that magically took care of themselves. Then, when I became a groomer in 2010, I was still confused about nail care.

The groomers who taught us talked about only two nail colors, black and white, and the European grooming literature mentioned the same thing. (I graduated from grooming school in Europe, then moved to the United States.)

There were only a few sentences about trimming nails and one or two black and white drawings—if at all—as guidelines.

There were a few images here and there in hairstyling books, mostly showing one or two doggy positions for nail care, shot from a distance so that you could not see any details about the nail trimming itself.

Long story short, even the leading American best-selling grooming books ($50-$100 each) "the grooming bibles" and grooming videos did not offer the answers I was seeking.

Not much detailed help existed for learning about safe nail trimming, let alone how to have a wholesome nail trimming experience with more cooperation and less restraint.

I felt puzzled because I've met a wide variety of nail shapes and nail colors in practice. I needed systematic, logical, and trustworthy guidelines and suggestions I could count on.

When I was hesitating at the beginning of my career i.e. Should I trim one more piece off or not? I often left the nails a tad longer, rather than cut them too short, and asked the pawrents to bring the doggy back for an extra nail filing session within a week or two to stay safe yet getting that quick to recede. With the multiple nail care appointments combined with natural wearing off the dog's nail, we made the quick to recede pretty fast, without bleeding, and pain-free. That was when I was still figuring out distinguishing between the layers of powdery layer and Jelly sole. Once I got the hang of it, I was able to confidently get to the tip of the Jelly sole and know that's the farthest I can go without causing bleeding.

I was desperate to see nail types and shapes and all kinds of details in a book so that I explain nail layers and nail filing to pawrents faster. The doggy owners wouldn't have to bring their pups back to see me as often to get the quick to recede, and I'd be able to educate the owners so that the quick would have never grown down with the nails in the first place.

I wanted to find a safe and accurate nail trimming method that would help me figure out where to stop trimming so that the dog would be protected 100 percent of the time.

After detailed research on the American market (veterinary, grooming, pet care books, videos, etc.) yielded no proven, logical, reliable explanations on the dog nail trimming topic I had to figure out the rules myself.

I explained to my husband how puzzled I felt, and he encouraged me to follow through with my wish and find answers independently. I took a deep breath, pulled up my sleeves, and made a plan to create that book myself.

I got a new phone with a good camera and started shooting dog nails with it. Then I collected the dog nail clippings I cut off for further observation.

I ziplocked them and showed off my collection to clients when they had questions about nail care. They are still a big hit, especially among kids or "kids" who outgrew their kid bodies, like me, but their curious kid soul is still there.

I was not satisfied enough with the first close-up images. They did not represent the details I could see on the nails with the naked eye. I figured I needed a macro lens to make the photos higher resolution, easier to zoom in and analyze the layers, and to pass on the knowledge to others in the easiest and most detailed way.

I asked professional photographers and ended up getting a 10x and 20x zoom macro lens that I could attach to my phone to start documenting dog nails on the next level. I finally achieved the quality I was looking for: sharp, macro, HD, and even 4K resolution.

Over the years, I ended up owning a pretty decent collection: over 3000 nail images (still counting) and several dozen nail clippings in different nail colors, shapes, and sizes.

By this time, I distinguished between two major nail types and got my hands on many images of nail colors, shapes, and sizes. Nail trimming became a calculable, safer, more comfortable, and faster process. I was able to get closer to the tip of the "quick", which meant fewer trips for doggy owners to get the quick to recede. I distinguished between two layers of the sole and had a clear structure in my mind about dog nail layers, their location, thickness, color, texture, etc. to identify them quickly.

Then I went wild and asked an artist friend, Brigitta Szabo, to draw dog nails for me, since I needed some help to explain the layers to curious doggy owners and for my curious peers. The only thing I can draw when I attempt to draw dog nails is happy little flat potatoes, so I truly needed Brigi's help.

She made over ten letter-size colored nail drawings to make my life easier when explaining nail care secrets to others. You will see those beauties throughout the book.

They became an enormous help, though it raised another need: 3D nail models so people can easily convert the 2D images and layers to 3D reality.

Brigi had moved to Australia by then, so I had to get creative alone. I got some sculpting clay from the local craft store. I sculptured, baked, and painted over a dozen nail shapes in different nail colors to make it easier to explain the critical details. With a kitchen table, two seasons of Call the Midwife, clay, paint, some water, and abracadabra, the dog nail models were ready for the show.

With the sculptures' help, everyone can familiarize themselves with how dog nail types look in real life so that they will be able to find those layers on their dogs much faster and deliver injury-free nail care.

The 3D nails are also an enormous help for me to explain the holding techniques. It's now even easier to imagine the layers' location in a dog nail, in reality.

I made notes about the process. The result is what you are reading right now.

Reality Check About Dog Nail Care

I look like my cat, Luna (on the right) when she demonstrates a princess yawn every time I hear dogs getting their nails trimmed to the point of bleeding.

Luna's princess yawn

I believe that accidents can happen. But how often is too often to be considered an accident? Isolated incidents happen very far apart, right? Like once a year. Multiple nails quicked several times a day, week, or even months are not considered accidents in my book. The situation cries for help and revision since the victims cannot defend themselves verbally but only physically, if at all. And even if they try, they get labeled as "mean", "evil", "biter", or "high maintenance", to say the least, so lots of restraints are added to the paw care session to get over it. And it's like a snowball effect. Dogs become even more reactive due to their lack of autonomy to move around and their emotional state not being addressed and eased.

I worked for "factory grooming facilities" at the beginning of my career and I went home devastated and crying almost every day. I could not handle my colleagues' and bosses' lack of knowledge about nail care nor their use of the same faulty method day after day, expecting a different outcome somehow. I find it deeply disturbing and unacceptable to see dogs restrained and nails cut so that they bleed as a routine procedure.

For me, doggy feelings and needs are just as an important part of the picture as their need for nail care. I do not just want my doggy clients to do what I prefer them to do; I deeply care about WHY they do it—whether they cooperate or not. I enjoy providing an environment where my furry clients do not feel forced to do something. Instead, they feel safe, respected, and they cooperate willingly. When I worked/"did my time" at big box grooming facilities, I saw the dogs' need for comfort, calm, and compassion, so I trimmed their nails in corners or empty rooms by myself, without muzzles and restraints, even on previously labeled "aggressive" dogs. It often took a while because I connected with them first, built trust, and once we clicked, I took the clipper in my hand. I cut off tiny, tiny pieces, multiple times on each nail, and then filed them with a hand nail file designed for dogs. It was safe and comfortable for the dogs and me as well.

Those dogs who showed late sensitivity signs (growling, biting) with my colleagues were snuggling with me for nail care. The magic was this: they felt comfortable around me, with my techniques, how I handled them, and the way I chose and used nail trimming equipment around them. I listened to them; they listened to me. They felt respected and heard, and the pawdicure got done.

My employers did not tolerate the way I did dog nails. I sensed they were envious of the bond and connection I created, and they told me, "I was working too slow" or "You should make one cut per nail and just use the Kwick Stop Powder if you 'need' it, and go on to the next dog/task. You have more dogs to work on, so speed it up." I am talking about upscale grooming shops in California where they did not tolerate "slow work". Sad, sad story.

Their single-mindedness, for-profit orientation, and ignorance for the dog's comfort woke up the snoring little rebellion in me, so one day I could not bear it anymore and I quit. I decided to swim upstream, gather and analyze nail trimming data, and learn to put my method into words to share with professionals and dog enthusiasts to learn about an error-free nail trimming method.

We moved to Texas and the joyride began. I opened my grooming salon and have worked by myself from home ever since in a low-key atmosphere (3-4 dogs tops a day). More like how mobile groomers work, but with a location, one doggy in the spotlight at a time, where dogs feel at home, safe, and are not distracted or rushed. We take time, include breaks, and have some serious fun.

I felt deeply motivated to help care providers and pet owners understand nail trimming because of those traumatic experiences with highly educated, facility-owning professionals.

This book offers a much wider perspective and a different approach than corporate grooming provides to make sure we will keep our furry friends safe and happy for nail trimming.

I want to help professionals, dog owners, and doggies enjoy nail trimming to the fullest.

Whether you are a dog owner, pet service provider, or a curious soul, I want you to know how to provide safe nail care and gain the confidence to step up for the dog's and your safety for joyful and wholesome nail care experience.

In this book, I would like to give you all the tools and knowledge I have to offer so that all doggies and care providers on Earth will be super happy before, during, and after the nail trimming. That's my dream.

Who's This Book for?

I dedicated this book to actively practicing, soon to be or wannabe:

- Groomers
- Bathers
- Veterinary Technicians
- Veterinarians
- Breeders
- Pawrents
- Dog Trainers
- Curious dog lovers who want to learn how to trim dog nails safely and gently

This book is for everyone who agrees with the following quote:

> "You do the best you can until you know better. Then, when you know better, do better."
> ~Maya Angelou

The Four Significant Parts of Dog Nail Trimming

1. Training yourself about anatomy, nail trimming methods, dog behavior, etc.
2. Training, preparing your dog/client, including:
    a. Behavior assessment
    b. Exercise before paw care
    c. Training/Desensitization
    d. Socialization
3. Performing a full pawdicure
    a. Trimming eye area hair and paw hair if needed
    b. Trimming nails
    c. Filing nails
4. Factors for a calm environment and experience

In This Book, You Will Learn

1. To keep your dog comfortable and still for nail care (without muzzling or restraining)
2. To trim paw hair to help dogs get a good grip and file nails more effectively
3. To trim dog nails without causing discomfort, pain, or bleeding for anyone on either end of the nail clipper
4. To figure out your dog's nail type
5. To get the right type and size of equipment, customized to your dog's nail size and needs
6. To tell whether your dog needs a nail care session or not yet

7. To make nail care plans for dogs with too long nails
8. To help your dog LOVE nail trimming—train and desensitize your dog to nail care

How to Use This Book

Nail care may sound complicated, but it is a pretty straightforward task once you have the needed information. With clear suggestions, equipment, and a bunch of cashew nuts to practice before bringing a volunteer canine in for a pawdicure, your confidence will show up lightning-fast, and it's here to stay.

If you want to get the most out of this book, just read it from cover to cover. If you are curious, take a peek at different parts, but promise your dog and me that you will go through it at least once before you try to trim your dog's nail, all right? It will be worth it, I promise.

For further education, watch the free online course that this book comes with! Coupon link and code for free access are at the end of this book by the Resources section.

Order of Practice

This book is the most comprehensive "recipe" today to help you achieve a pain-free pawdicure for your canine friend or client. Just as with a recipe, we benefit if we read through it first—at least once—before we go grocery shopping or fire up the stove.

Once you are done reading it all, you can start practicing the positions and comfort measures on your canine, memorize the nail structure, and get the equipment.

When you first practice the positionings with your canine do it without using any nail trimming equipment. (You can have them around if doggo does not get triggered.)

Without the dog, you can play around with cashew nuts to get the hang of the nail trimming procedure.

FUNNY STORY

One day I was eating some nuts, and I had an epiphany. I was grabbing a cashew nut and realized at that very moment that it looked like a dog nail. I got so excited that I instantly took the bag into my salon and started playing with food. Yes. This experiment would likely not get much encouragement from parents, but luckily mine were not around to comment on my actions.

Ever since I connected the dots between cashew nuts and dog nails, people burst out laughing when they see my face brighten up as I pull out a bag of cashew nuts in our training. It was an incredible realization, and it brings massive relief to my students in the early stages of practice, trimming "dog nails" without blood vessels and nerve endings around.

As a quick guideline, once your dog stays still long enough for you to take sharp, close-up images of its nails with a 20x zoom lens on your phone (or a professional camera), then the dog is comfortable and ready for you to try nail care for real.

Once you have familiarized yourself with the nail structure and practiced on enough cashew nuts to get experience and confidence around nail trimming, you can merge that with the nail care positioning you were practicing separately, with your dog. Then, you can start cutting real dog nails safely.

The "take an image challenge" is the test for both you and your dog. It is pretty tricky to zoom with a 20x zoom lens. Once you can keep your dog still long enough to focus on taking the image of his nails, it means your dog is all set to give it a try in reality. Once you can comfortably identify which nail layers you see in the photos, that's a good sign that you are both ready for a safe nail trimming experience.

Top 10 Nail Care Secrets

Secret #1: White or Clear Nails are Not Easier to Trim Than Black Nails

Taco (left) and Hot dog (right) nail types

When we look at the nails from the paw pad side, tons of information about the soft nail tissue is revealed. This information is, literally, right at our fingertips to help us make a precise game plan of cutting lines while making the nails shorter. We can identify the layers of the nail and find our stop signs easily to prevent injury. The way you hold the paw and toes, and the way you angle the clipper are much more critical for safety than the nail colors. If you take a look at the image on the left, you will see what I mean. The left image shows a black nail with a taco nail type, and the right one shows a black nail with the hot dog nail type. It's the matter that you can distinguish between the two and understand how to trim them or not, making it easy or hard. Often, care providers get lucky when trimming white nails because seeing part of the soft tissue gives them a better chance to avoid the quick. However, it does not make the method logical or 100 percent trustworthy. Furthermore, just because you did not hit the quick does not mean you trimmed the nail short enough. It is especially important in those cases when the quick has grown down with the nail to the tip and we want it to recede so we need to go as close as possible without hitting the quick.

Secret #2: The Safe Holding Technique to See the Layers is the "Paw Pad View" Holding

The horny nail tissue that protects and hugs the sensitive parts of the nail prevents us from seeing exactly where the quick is when we take a look at the nails from any other direction other than from the paw pad side (bottom of the nail). We might be able to see some part of the soft tissue as a pink/black/gray cloud in the nail from the outer sides, but we can't precisely locate the tip of the soft tissue.

Many people make this mistake and think they see the tip of the quick from this angle, but when I ask them if they would bet their lives on it, most of them say no. If we take a closer look at this issue, we will realize it'd be awesome if we could see the soft tissue precise enough to avoid cutting in it, but it is not the case. We can't be sure we are cutting into only horny tissue from that perspective.

Don't be fooled by clear nails! Avoid injury by taking a detailed look at the nail's bottom to see the layers and determine the stop sign with accuracy.

Examples of safe positionings to hold *paws for nail care (See below!)*

The safest position is to take a look at the nails from the paw pad side. That way, we can see some of the layers under the horny tissue to get the information we need. The safe holding technique for nail trimming is to look from the paw pad side while the dog stands on all fours (top left image) and while the dog is on its side/back (top right photo). The dog can also be in the owner's or helper's arms for this position (bottom left photo) or standing/sitting (bottom right image).

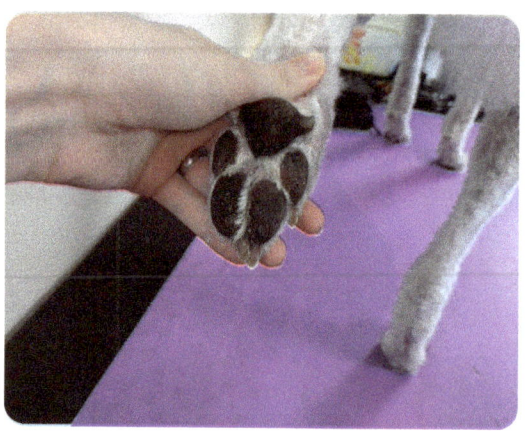
Positioning that enables you to see the nail layers

Close up of the nail layers (taco nail type)

Close up of the nail layers (hot dog nail type)

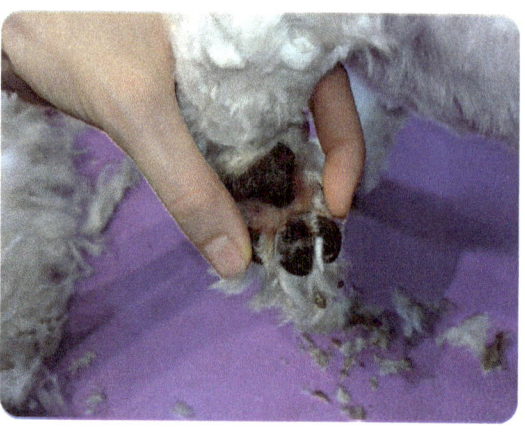
Searching for foreign objects between pads

Examples of "prone to error" positionings to hold paws for nail care (See below!)

If you have been trimming dog nails with the holding technique shown below, count your blessings if you haven't cut them too short yet. And please forgive yourself if you indeed trimmed too short. You did the best you knew how, the culprit was the method you used that led the trim to go south. Keep your curiosity alive, understand that you had good intentions and that you used the best possible knowledge you had at the time.

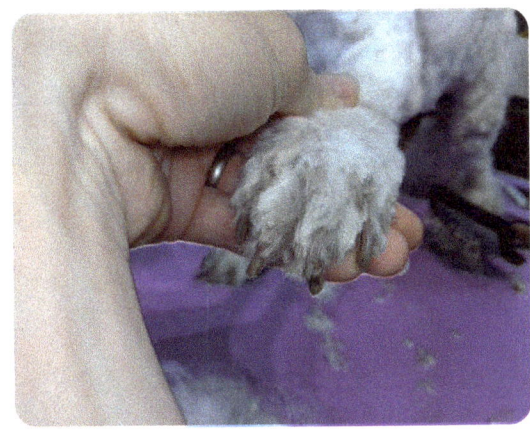

Warning! This positioning is prone to error. Horny tissue is blocking the view to see the soft tissue underneath, even on light colored nails.

Warning! This positioning is prone to error. Horny tissue is blocking the view to see the soft tissue underneath, even on light colored nails.

> *"I've done some things I wouldn't have done in case I knew then what I since have learned."*
> ~Marshall Rosenberg

By learning a logical and trustworthy method, you will make nail care a safe and fun experience for all participants. You will make your dog's and your life safer, more comfortable, not only for nail trims but also for any paw-related grooming steps.

If you are a pet care provider, and you are holding your doggy client's paws like any of the two examples above for nail care, I recommend you revise your method to one that enables you to see all layers of the nail, not the horny tissue only.

Hitting the quick with this holding method is almost guaranteed. It will also exponentially decrease friendship points from your furry clients and make each nail care session more difficult for all of you. Plus, the dog will not be happy about any paw-related grooming steps, making it more difficult for groomers to care for your doggy and for pawrents to brush, wash, or do just a general check-up around the feet.

If you would like to trim your dog nails yourself, please educate yourself from a logical and trustworthy source before clipping nails to ensure everyone is protected. It takes way less time to learn about nail care before attempting it than to desensitize a dog after a painful experience. See the demonstration of the prone-to-error holding methods below! By looking at the nails from the top/side when the paw is horizontal and below the care provider's eye level, the horny tissue blocks the view to see the soft tissue under it. Injury is guaranteed.

Secret #3: Quick Stop/Styptic Powder Helps to Stop the Bleeding, But it Won't Eliminate the Pain

Think about a cut on your skin. You sanitize it and put a bandage on it to stop the bleeding and prevent infections. If it's serious, you might get some painkillers. Painkillers do block pain, but they wear off. It's the same with dogs. The bleeding will eventually stop due to the coagulant styptic powder. If we used a styptic powder that did not contain pain blockers, the pain would remain. If we used a quick stop powder that had pain blockers in it, the pain would resurface after the pain blocker wore off. So the dogs would experience pain sooner or later if we hit the quick. And they would highly likely defend any further attempts to work on the feet, be it brushing, combing, or a simple paw wiping on a rainy day. Often, due to the lack of logical and trustworthy information on nail trimming methods, care providers conveniently go for the backup plan, and they use the quick stop powder. ("You just put the quick stop on it, no big deal.") While I am absolutely for immediate injury management when nail care goes south, I would love to see people be more interested in prevention instead of being a frequent buyer of styptic powder. I'd love care providers—whether pawrents, groomers, vet techs, or veterinarians—to immerse themselves in learning a safe method to trim nails so the dog will be comfortable and cooperative. Along with tricks on keeping the dog still for nail care, what are some environmental tricks we can put into practice to create a relaxing room, render gentle and compassionate care, and have a calm dog?

Secret #4: Most Dogs are Sensitive to Nail Care Because the Method is Uncomfortable or Painful for Them

There are no evil dogs, biters, or crazy ones. But dogs do remember and react. Growling and biting are late discomfort signs. There are MANY early discomfort signs that they show us. We just need to be aware of them and customize the dogs' care plan around their comfort levels until we up our game to level with the doggy's needs. The more fun pawdicure sessions they experience, without approaching the threshold (see in a later chapter), the more trusting and the more easy-going they'll become. If a doggy reacts, we need to find his triggers, take a few steps back, and work with him in smaller steps to connect the doggy pawdicure with fun and joy. Then he will be calm, he will cooperate with a big smile. Literally.

Secret #5: You CAN Desensitize a "Feet Sensitive" Dog

Like humans, there are parts of a doggy that vary in their sensitivity. (In general, the more sensitive parts are the face, ears, feet, or private areas; less sensitive areas are the back and sides.) It's good to remember, however, that we can desensitize dogs to be okay with, and even enjoy the grooming steps on all body parts, even if they've had a rough start. We can do a LOT to keep them comfortable. Finding their triggers, as mentioned above, and working on them will help you turn a doggy who is pulling feet away like Fred Astaire or biting like a "sewing machine" into a cooperative, smiling cutie pie even while getting his/her nails done. (Note: I use the "sewing machine" phrase to humorously describe the sensitivity's intensity, not to frighten anyone. Furthermore, I am not using it as a label.)

A Solution in a Nutshell

Step #1
   Stop those traumatic, painful, and unpleasant experiences from happening again, regardless of where they have occurred, i.e. a DIY nail trimming, at grooming facilities, or vet offices. It is key.

Step #2.
   Get serious about desensitizing. Watch tutorials, hire a dog trainer or a dog groomer to help you with this. And practice, practice, practice!

Step #3.
   Take the time to find a caring care provider/trainer or learn to trim nails yourself in a safe and gentle way!

Secret #6: Dogs Need Their Nails Trimmed and Filed Customized to Their Needs

The frequency of nail trims depends on a lot of things such as:

- Nail type—toenails vs. dewclaws
- Paw/leg structure differences and deformations—Shih-Tzus, dachshunds vs. dogs with straight legs
- Pain—arthritis, hip dysplasia, etc.
- Age—puppies and elderly pups move less than adult dogs move
- Surgery—restriction - in moving
- Energy level—dogs with low energy levels often need more frequent pedicure sessions
- Injury—cut on the feet
- The doggy's weight
- The doggy's body/leg/paw shape, the general structure
- Doggy's activity level

These and many other circumstances influence the frequency of nail care. Some doggies do not need nail care, only regular checkups, which can be done by a knowledgeable owner. Some dogs need only their dewclaws trimmed or filed frequently. Some canines need regular pawdicures on some or all of their nails for a lifetime. For more information, see the chapter about nail care plans.

Secret #7: One Nail Trim Appointment, in Some Cases, Might Not Be Enough to Get the Nails to the Proper Length

Nail lengths from normal to severely overgrown
1. Normal – 100 percent comfortable dog, pawrents
2. Normal, a bit scratchy. - 99 percent comfortable dog, 70 percent comfortable pawrents
3. Too long, nail is touching the ground. – 100 percent uncomfortable dog
4. Too long, touching the ground, and lifting up the toe. – 100 percent painful dog
Dog neglect below:
5. Too long, touching the ground and lifting up the toe and about to grow in the skin.
6. Too long, touching the ground and lifting up the toe, and rubbing against the skin on the side.
7. Too long, touching the ground, and lifting up the toe, and pushing against, about to open up the skin due to rubbing and pressure. (Can be trimmed to the proper length in one appointment.)
8. Too long, touching the ground, lifting up the toe, and pushing against, about to open up the skin due to rubbing and pressure. (The quick has grown down together with the nail, it cannot be trimmed to the proper length without bleeding.)
9. **Too long, touching the ground, and lifting up the toe, and nail grew into the skin already.**

One Nail Trim Appointment, in Some Cases, Might Not Be Enough to Get the Nails to the Proper Length.

If the quick has grown down together with the nail, we can't trim the nail to the proper length in one doggy pawdicure appointment. It might take several nail care sessions to make the quick to recede the fastest possible way without causing significant pain and bleeding. See the chapter about nail care plans for more information or a variety of options beyond trimming.

The image on the left is about the cycle of the toenail growing too long. Notice the red layer in the middle—the quick—on all drawings. That's the part of the nail that is rich in nerve endings and blood vessels. Drawings 1 and 2 show optimal nail length. In some cases, the horny part grows way longer than it should be, but the quick stays in the same place as if the nail were the desired length and not overgrown. See drawing 7. In this case, we can achieve the optimal nail length even on extremely long nails within one pawdicure session. Lucky for everyone, right? In cases such as 4, 5, 6, 8 and 9 several nail care sessions are needed to get the quick to recede and to get the nails to the proper length without making them bleed.

We will detail what's going on in the other drawings in a later chapter, and we will also discuss what we can do about each situation to get the nails to the proper length.

Secret #8: Tiny-tiny Cuts on Nails are the Safest, most Comfortable, and Fastest Way to Trim Nails

The one-cut per nail method may seem to be a pretty fast-working way of shortening dog nails; however, there are two reasons I prefer the tiny cuts method over it. In the end, this will work safer and faster for you than the one-cut method. Plus, the dog will feel more comfortable due to the lack of pressure on the soft tissue ensured by the tiny cuts and tool angling and will be significantly more cooperative. The one-cut-per-nail method puts a lot of pressure on the nail's horny tissue, which directly presses on the soft tissues underneath. That sensation will put dogs in alert mode, even in attack mode in the case of dogs that had been "quicked" in the past.

Dogs will react differently based on their present comfort level, plus their previous experiences around nail trimming. If they got hurt because of nail care, they might tolerate it, cooperate with it, wiggle away, kick or bite, etc. but they won't enjoy it due to the fear of history repeating itself. When we use the one-cut-per-nail method on the hot dog nail type, we won't see what we are doing, even when using the right holding method for the nails and paws. The horny tissue encircles the soft tissue, and we need to go tiny by tiny cut to stay safe. You see why the one-cut method can, and will, result in a too short cut, tremendous pain for the dog, and increasing the risk of us getting bitten. Many, tiny cuts will enable us to see the stop sign in time, and it reduces pressure on the dog's nails. Combining that with aligning the clipper to put even less pressure on the dog's soft tissue while making the cut, dogs go sensation-free and we'll be surprised how cooperative the doggy is for us, without bites, sweating, or swearing.

Secret #9: Dogs Can Be in Any Position They Want for Nail Trimming, as Long as You Can Get a Paw Pad View, Enough Space to do a Safe Angle for the Clipping

Doggies can be in any position where they and we are comfortable as long as we can see their nails from the paw pad side and our body is relaxed, too. We can even change our position throughout the pawdicure session. For the dogs, sitting, standing, lying on their sides or backs is perfectly fine. Being in the pawrent's/other care provider's arms is also acceptable, though I prefer different positions since doggies tend to wiggle a lot there; plus, there is always a bigger chance of getting bitten by a more reactive dog since a bigger human surface is presented.

Secret #10: Dremels or Grinders Might Promise a Fast and Safe Alternative to Make Nails Shorter but at the Expense of the Dog's Comfort and Safety.

While the Dremel might seem to offer a faster and safer way to shorten nails, I would like to raise awareness of how it adversely affects the dog's behavior, comfort, and grooming experience.

- It makes a thunderous amount of noise
- It vibrates
- The drum blocks our vision
- It works way faster than we want it to, to be able to perform a precise, safe, and comfortable pawdicure
- The sandpaper drum tears out any hair that gets close enough to tangle up on the drum. The "safety cap" makes it less likely, but the chance is still there and puts your dog's hair (or yours!) on the line
- The drum heats up to burning hot in no time

All these are extremely triggering, unpleasant, and painful for dogs, as you can imagine. No wonder they become super sensitive about us messing with their paws, or get stuck at the "I freeze until it's done" phase when we are trying to use Dremels or even the brush for grooming, right? Based on the above reasons, and since my highest priority is safety and comfort for a joyful experience, I do not recommend Dremels, and I never use them. For nail filing, I use a dog nail file. See my favorite in the tool list later!

Often people get a Dremel and shorten nails without educating themselves first about nail care, thinking that they can't hurt their dog with a Dremel. It's not only the tool you are using, but it's also your knowledge about nail trimming, positioning the dog, the instrument, yourself, and using a cutting method that eliminates pressure and discomfort; all that makes trimming nails safe and joyful.

I find that the Paw-di-cure™ method I designed helps dogs stay calm and cooperative and enables us to work just as fast and even more precisely than the Dremel. I find it much safer, even on reactive dogs.

Secret +1: The Scratchboard Will Not File All Nails Evenly

Think about the curve of the front legs and the back legs and the presentation of the legs, feet, toes, and nails. Some dogs have tighter feet, some more massive, flatter paws. Some have O legs, and some have X. (See dog anatomy section later) Even a genetically excellent foot won't enable a dog to file his nails evenly on each nail on a scratchboard. Why? Because the shape of the foot is round. Not like ours, where most of the toes are kind of aligned. Dogs have four toes and a dewclaw on the front legs. The two middle toenails will get worn off way more than the outer two on the scratchboard. Just from that one example, you'll see that you will end up with some follow-up care on the two nails on the sides and the dewclaws for sure.

On top of that, the pads can get worn off with this method faster than the nails. Regardless of which tools you use, I think it is crucial to recognize the nails' layers in order to know when to stop. Why not train yourself to understand how to trim dog nails safely and desensitize your dog to nail care at the same time? Once the nail care is pain- and pressure-free, comforting, and fun, your dog will forgive and forget the past experiences. Those who had a rougher start might take a tad longer before they will fully trust the method, nevertheless, it's in the picture and will happen. I am happy to help you and accompany you and the dog(s) you'll work on on the journey.

Secret +2: The Safety Guard on the Nail Clipper Will Not Keep You from Hitting the Dog's Quick

The safety guard on the clipper might sell better with the slogan suggesting you won't hit the quick that way, but the fact is you need to learn about the layers of the nail to be safe. That little tongue-like thing will not help you avoid the quick by itself. Plus, adding some common sense to the equation, you need to see which layer you are working on between the clipper's jaws. When the guard is in the way, it is blocking your vision; you have no idea which layers you are cutting. It's as precise as someone putting a cutting board between a surgeon and his patient in the OR and expecting the surgeon to cut in the right spot at the proper depth. The only thing the safety guard does is stop you from chopping the whole toenail off at the base. But there are many other ways to prevent that from happening, so why not see what we are doing instead and make precise decisions on the cut line and angle rather than gambling with dog nails based on a false promise?

Secret +3: Using the Quick Stop Finder Type Clippers and Nail Grinders Will Not Keep You From Making Your Dog's Nail Bleed

The quick finder nail clippers are a blockbuster idea for sellers, combined with unreliable engineering. There, I said it. They are incredibly unpredictable, and I cringe just at the thought of using them. While they sound like a sweet promise to our worried souls, I've seen them fail in so many hands. When we combine good intentions with a lack of knowledge about nails and cutting techniques along with a faulty tool, it leads to a bloody scene and a very sad dog in pain for days.

Secret +4: Trimming the Nails Needs to be Followed up with Filing Them

Trimming the nails (without following up with filing) is neither safe nor recommended. After cutting nails, filing them is a must to avoid scratches on the dog's skin, cornea, or on our person. Notice the sharp edges on the left image below after trimming nails. If we leave the nails sharp like that, those edges will draw blood with one jump, let it be your thigh, or your kid's or colleague's skin. Also, you quadruple your chances to win a ticket to the vet for a scratched cornea, bleeding ears and deal with weeks of medication, and hands-on care for your dog. So, I think it's safe to say it is easier and safer to trim AND file.

Trimmed nail tip (no filing)
Notice the sharp edges that can seriously injure the dog or people around him.

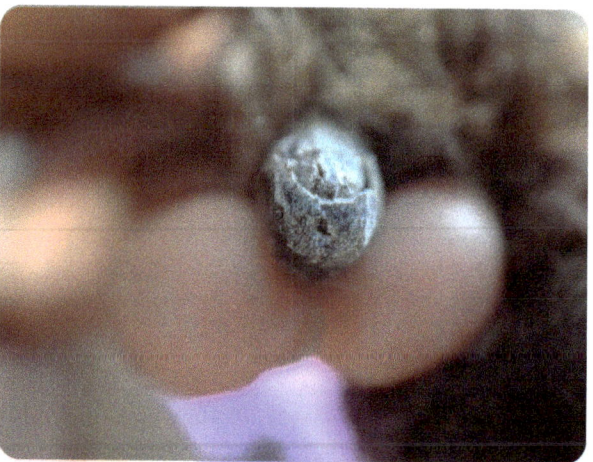

Trimmed and filed nail tip.
Notice how rounded it is, smooth to the touch. Injury is very unlikely, even when the dog scratches himself or paws at us asking for a belly rub.

Chapter 2

Paw and Nail Care Needs of Dogs

What are the Dog's Pawdicure Needs in General?

What do doggies need beyond nail trimming? The more fluff they have around their feet, the more work they'll need before the nail care. Beyond a nail trim, dogs often need one or more of the following:

- Excess hair shortened on the bottom of the pads, around the paw, and between toes. It helps them get a good grip and prevents them from sliding on slippery surfaces such as tile or hardwood floors. This is especially important for puppies and elderly dogs. It also helps prevent mats between toes and among the pads
- Mats trimmed out between their toes and paw pads if present
- Nails trimmed and filed to the proper length without pain or bleeding. Filing nails is critical after cutting so dogs won't hurt themselves (skin, cornea, etc.) or scratch their pawrents' legs and arms when they get excited
- A care plan worked up for cases when the quick has grown down together with the nail. That prevents us from trimming the nails to the proper length without cutting the nails to the point of bleeding, but we can make the quick to recede over time

You may think, *Holy smokes! How on Earth do they keep up with that in the wild?* Well, they do have to walk, dig, run, chase animals to get food, water, and shelter, so an average wild dog, fox, or wolf travels several miles a day. Compare that to our pets, who take a few blocks long walk once a day, on a leash, mostly on super soft precious sod. Plus, they have short hair in the wild, making it more efficient to wear off their nails. Think about a Poodle, Maltese, or a Doodle. Believe it or not, that fluff in front of the nails makes it much harder for pups even for adults to file their nails down. On the other hand, if a dog, wolf, etc. is born with a malformation on his feet, he is doomed to experience life-long discomfort or pain due to his inability to file his nails naturally to the proper length unless we intervene and save the day. That's the very painful product of Mother Nature's natural selection. But, our domesticated pets are enjoying the alternative of relief when needed provided by us humans when needed.

Paw Pad Boomerangs

I came up with the grooming term "paw pad boomerang". These matted, muddy monsters have such a significant impact on the dog's comfort level, yet they did not have a name, other than being referred to as "matted hair around the feet". I felt the need to name them and give them a little bit of stage time to know them better.

They are boomerang or banana-shaped; they develop when mud, water, saliva, dirt, and long dog hair converge at the right time. Doggy has some fun in a puddle (or in water, and you walk on a dirt road after that), then when you go home, it gets dry and hard as a rock. It irritates the paws big time, can make the skin between the pads raw and bleed.

Three elements need to happen simultaneously or right after each other, followed up with a fourth for paw pad boomerangs to develop. Paw hair, dirt, and water/saliva need to mix; then air dries it. The longer the hair, the more dirt gets stuck in it, so the larger the paw pad boomerang that will develop. It comes with the most discomfort.

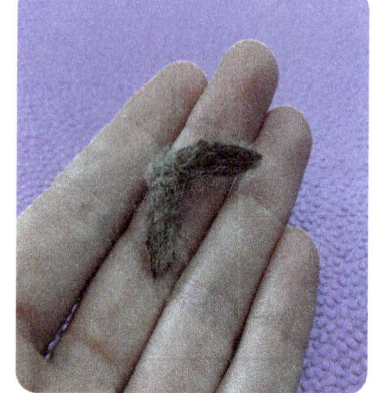

Paw pad boomerang
(Matted hair nestled in by the paw pad and the toe pads.)

Paw Pad Boomerangs do not affect doggies with super short hair underneath their paws. Naturally, short-haired dogs and "Poodle feet" hairstyle have a significant advantage here, so even when those dogs get exposed to mud, they will likely be able to clean it off themselves.

Know the feeling when a tiny rock gets in your shoes? That's how toe mohawks and paw pad boomerangs feel. Constant discomfort and irritation. Yikes. Until removed or, better, prevented in the first place.

Foreign Objects Among Paw Pads

Before a doggy pedicure, I like to make sure that there are no foreign objects among the toes and paw pads. If there is something in there, the doggy won't stand still, and later in the process, we might get bitten due to not addressing this in time, so it is worth it to "take a look" with your eyes and fingers deep in between the pads. I've found many things stuck in there such as sticker burrs, grass, other plant parts, dirt, cereal, popcorn, rocks, acorns, chewing gum, ticks, glue, paint, dried baby food, painkillers, vitamins, candy, and more....

Toe Mohawks

Toe mohawk
How they are hiding between the toes

Toe mohawk
How they are hiding between the toes

Toe Mohawk is another term I came up with so learning is fun and descriptive. Same scenario: a significant impact on the dog's comfort level, with no name yet for these little (sometimes not so little) monsters. These guys are one of the ultimate reasons why dogs hate getting their feet brushed or even touched. (The other one is a painful nail care experience, hint hint.) They are invisible unless you spread the toes. Since they did not even have a name, barely anyone knows they exist, so we all just jump right in and brush the feet! Boom! We encountered a wiggly dog. Surprise! The pins of the brush or comb get stuck in the toe mohawk, which means direct pulling on the skin (on a super-sensitive part). No wonder doggies pull their legs away, bounce, growl, bite and, in general, just fight with us in this case! But now we know why. It won't happen anymore because we will check for toe mohawks from now on and will prevent it!

How Can We Keep Toe Mohawks Away?

We can keep the toe mohawks away with regular brushing for dogs with longer than a ¾" coat on the feet area. For short-haired dogs, you just need to keep an eye on the feet for foreign objects. Short-haired dogs do not develop toe mohawks.

Nail Socks

Nails socks are smaller or bigger bunches of tightly matted hair that got stuck on the nail.

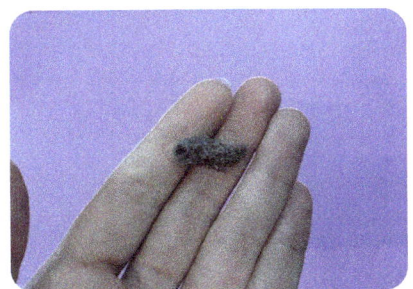
Nail sock - side view
(Matted hair that got caught up on the dog's nail.)

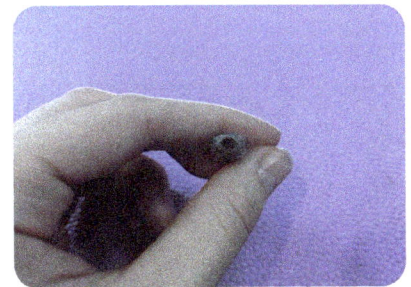
Nail sock - nail bed side view
(The hole is where the nail was. Like a glove for nails.)

They develop when the side of the nail splits, and the nails start to work like fishing hooks, catching all kinds of stuff and fluff such as dog hair and carpet fluff, and they won't let go.

If you take a look, nail socks look like the rounded beehives you see in Winnie the Pooh.

If you get lucky and remove a toenail sock in one piece, you'll see a hole in the middle, hence the name, nail socks. They can develop on toenails and dewclaws. Based on their location, I refer to them as toenail socks or dewclaw socks.

On the three images below, you see white toenail socks circled with yellow. Notice how the other nails' full length is visible, while only the tip of the nail is poking out of the toenail sock on the nails that have them on. When it comes to removing nail socks, I use a rounded tip shear. See the tutorial on how to deal with nail socks in the online Nail it! Course!

www.WholesomeGroomingAcademy.com/page/nail-it-book

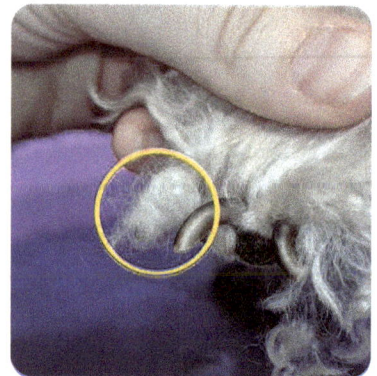
Toenail sock - top view

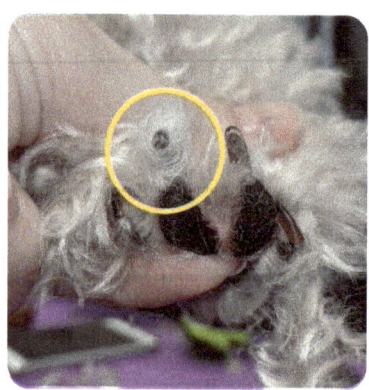
Toenail sock - frontal view

Toenail sock - bottom view

Spreading the Toes for Checking

I have two favorite positions for this. I'll explain one and the other is its reverse. Depending on what position the canine client is comfortable with, I use either or.

Method 1.

We need to keep in mind two layers. The first is the top layer between the toes, where we check for toe mohawks. The second layer is the bottom, where we manipulate the pads to spread the toes apart. Let's detail the pad side first. With the pinky, ring, or middle finger, we put mild pressure between the two pads located below the two toes we'd like to examine. With our thumb on the top, we apply a tiny amount of pulling on the closest toe's inner side toward the outer side. And voila, we can see between the toes and check for toe mohawks, foreign objects, mud, injuries, etc. Can you see the fox tail's butt hanging out in the hair between the toes? Looking deep

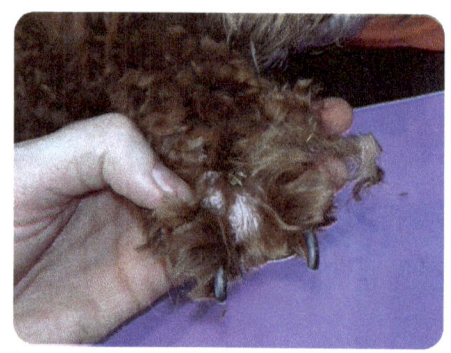
Spreading the toes - method 1

enough will help you find them before they would dig in/under the skin. One peek will save your dog lots of discomfort, a huge vet bill, and a surgery experience to get them out.

Method 2.

On large dogs, this second method will work a bit better. We will need two hands. The left hand's pinky-ring finger or ring-middle finger combo goes on the toe pads that we would like to work on. This will stabilize the paw from going up/down. Using the right hand from the top of the foot, we spread the toes apart with the thumb-index or index-middle finger combo.

It helps to get a bit more room between the toes for the shears (for trimming) or your fingers (for checking) if

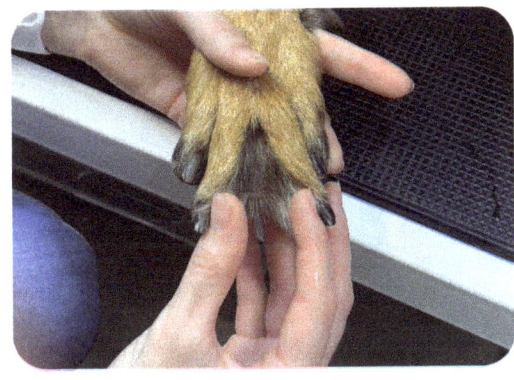

Spreading the toes - method 2

you spread the pads with your fingers. Place your thumb and index finger just before the nail bed (angled a bit so it won't slide off) and gently spread them apart. You'll be amazed at how much more room you can get with this quick technique. It also works on a lying dog. Just rotate the image as needed.

That's it! See the tutorial videos for more specific tips, tricks, and exceptional cases at:

www.WholesomeGroomingAcademy.com/page/nail-it-book

Harmful, Painful, Uncomfortable Nail Care Procedures

Trimming the Nails Without Filing

Dogs can hurt (scratch) themselves, their skin, their cornea, etc. or you. Not recommended.

Nail Grinding

The machine is loud and it vibrates. It is painful if hair gets caught up in the drum; it works too fast to do precise work, and it heats up. To keep dogs calm and cooperative, I like to avoid nail grinders/Dremels.

Harmful, Painful Nail Accessories

Soft Claws (Nail Caps)

They prevent the dog from wearing off his nails. They can contain loosely regulated or unregulated chemicals; they cause discomfort. They prevent a good grip and will result in the quick-growing down together with the nail, causing constant pain for the dog due to continuous pressure on the toes and paws. A lot of maintenance and upkeep is needed to get the soft tissue of the nail to recede.

A well-trimmed and filed nail will keep furniture safe without the use of soft claws.

Toe Grips (Rubber Rings)

Toe grips' supposed purposes are to support the dog in getting a better grip and to keep leather furniture safe from scratches. Toe grips create constant pressure on the dog's nails. When the dog walks on soft surfaces, his nails will dig into the soil/grass/carpet, which will push the rubber rings up into the nail bed, adding even greater pressure around the nail and ongoing discomfort. In some cases, they even cause the dog constant pain. The worst thing about these is that once doggy owners put them on their dog, they often forget about them, and under the fluffy paws, the pressure on the nail beds goes unnoticed, leaving the dog with raw skin in severe cases.

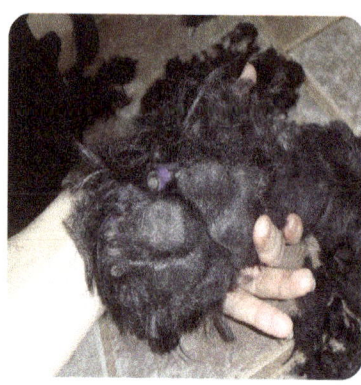
Toe grips - purple ring on nail

When we keep the hair on the paw pads short, and the nails the proper length, dogs can get a good grip on the ground. For elderly dogs, when this is combined with health issues, we can get a cooling mat for summer, rugs for colder days out in places where the doggy likes to sleep or hang out so he can get up easier. This is a less intrusive, more effective way, in my opinion, and it certainly satisfies the dog's needs for comfort and mobility.

Dog Nail Polish

They are a decorative way to apply harmful chemicals to dog nails. Dogs instinctively want to blend in, not sparkle. I don't think any more needs to be said, but given the number of people buying this, please don't. Admire the wolf in your dogs and let them blend in and be what they are, dogs.

When the Nails are Too Long

There are a few situations when the nails grow super long and they are considered a health/safety hazard for the dog and others. Nail trimming is the highest priority in those severe situations. There is no room for desensitization, the nail care has to happen urgently, no matter what. Even in those cases, we can choose less triggering strategies as solutions honoring the dog's comfort as the second-highest priority. And make the next nail care session a tad easier rather than more triggering.

Cases when the dog desperately needs an urgent nail trim are:

1. When the nails are long enough to lift the front part of the toe pad

2. When the nails curl close to the skin and rub against it
3. When the nails curled and grown close to the skin and is irritating the skin
4. When the nails have grown into the skin

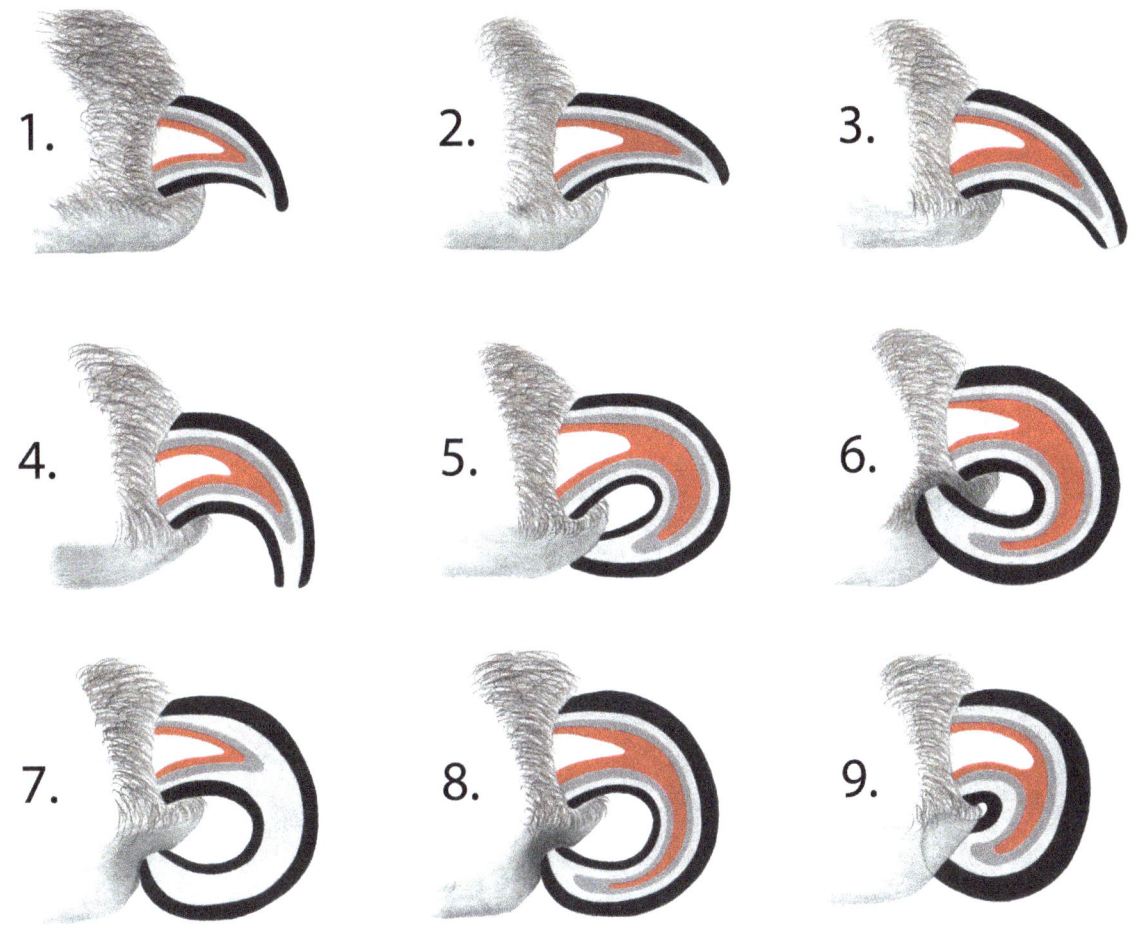

Nail lengths from normal to severely overgrown
1. Normal – 100 percent comfortable dog, pawrents
2. Normal, a bit scratchy. - 99 percent comfortable dog, 70 percent comfortable pawrents
3. Too long, nail is touching the ground. – 100 percent uncomfortable dog
4. Too long, touching the ground, and lifting up the toe. – 100 percent painful dog

Dog neglect below:

5. Too long, touching the ground and lifting up the toe and about to grow in the skin.
6. Too long, touching the ground and lifting up the toe, and rubbing against the skin on the side.
7. Too long, touching the ground, and lifting up the toe, and pushing against, about to open up the skin due to rubbing and pressure. (Can be trimmed to the proper length in one appointment.)
8. Too long, touching the ground, lifting up the toe, and pushing against, about to open up the skin due to rubbing and pressure. (The quick has grown down together with the nail, it cannot be trimmed to the proper length without bleeding.)
9. **Too long, touching the ground, and lifting up the toe, and nail grew into the skin already.**

Nail Shortening Options for Comfortable (Less Reactive) Dogs

Activity

Walking, hiking, running, digging, etc. are Mother Nature's way of shortening and smoothening nails. If the dog gets enough of those fun runs, they can even wear off most of their paw hair enough to get a good grip on the ground. It works for dogs with standard body builds. See the chapter about anatomy to learn more!

Trimming

I find trimming nails with clippers a great way to get the nails short, fast, and sensation-free when done right.

Filing

We can smooth dog nails with doggy nail files, Dremels, grinders, and human nail files. I find dog nail files the most loved and practical. See the chapter about tools to learn why!

The Power of Positive Distractions

To get dogs to cooperate for urgent nail care in less severely reacting cases, we can use positive distractions. Positive distractions can be watching chickens, squirrels through the window; seeing kitty cats in the backyard; licking a Kong toy filled with frozen goodies, etc. They can be used in all four extreme nail situations, as long as we are very skilled in reading dog body language. We need to know the dog and be able to predict his behavior with high accuracy. The dog needs to be highly interested in these entertainments to make it work. Be aware that it is a risky business, though. Take it with a grain of salt and analyze your situation thoroughly before making a decision or going with it. And remember, if you or the dog is not comfy, there is always room to try another plan!

Scratchboards

Helping/teaching your dogs to wear off the nails himself on a scratchboard can be an option. If they are not fast learners nor you are a dog trainer to get super-fast results, you can alternatively move their paws on the scratchboard to make the nails shorter. I suggest these options for less severe cases, such as when the nails are not long enough to lift the toepad's front part. And, like in all reactive cases, doing counter conditioning and desensitization (CCDS) to improve the dog's reactions as an addition to the nail care plans and afterward. See the Training Dog Minds chapter for more information on this topic!

Note for Care Providers, Vets/Vet Techs, and Groomers

When pawrents are not aware of or do not want to disclose/acknowledge/work on their dog's behavior

If you are a care provider reading this, chances are, there will be times when you will be the one breaking the news to the pawrents how their dog is acting for nail trims. If you can present it with a solution tied to a clear observation, they will be way more understanding, cooperative, and more likely to take the necessary steps to change the dog's behavior.

Often dog behavior for nail trims is not revealed to pawrents by professionals. It can happen due to lack of time, lack of awareness, willingness, desire to give good/happy news and hope for a better chance for a good tip, or whatnot, so it might come as a massive surprise to the owners. Most of the time, they are understanding. However, there can be times when you will want to take big breaths before you respond.

They might try to push you into doing the nails by saying, "But, my dog's nails are so long. They need to be trimmed NOW!" or "He did fine at the (other) groomer!" So we, as care providers, need to hold a safe space for our furry, less furry clients, and ourselves. We need to deal with the symptoms the dog showed us, leaving out judgments such as "bad dog", "aggressive", "mean", etc. Laying out a few options for solutions that are at your disposal to transform behavior. Discussing risks and benefits goes a long way to keep the dog along with the care provider(s) safe and pawrents informed. We will talk about options and action plans in detail; for now, let's just take a brief look at what some options are.

Exploring Less Invasive Options for Reactive Dogs Who Desperately Need a Nail Trim

Dogs like their freedom and will protect it. After we have decided that it is crucial to do a nail trim, but the dog is not responding well enough to our adjustments to perform one safely, we need to use protection to keep the dog and ourselves safe and make the nail trim happen. The less invasive the treatments we use to meet our safety needs are (keeping the most freedom possible for the dog), the more cooperative the dogs will be now and in the future. Let's take a look at a few possibilities!

Note #1. Dogs that have been traumatized before might need more time to feel comfortable enough to cooperate. Just like one therapy session will not solve all our childhood traumas, for severe cases, we'll need to give more time to the dogs to forgive and forget.

Note #2. Keep in mind that these options are again for less reactive dogs and for the initial urgent appointment only to succeed with nail trimming. If you keep doing these methods without any training, counter-conditioning, or desensitization, the dog will likely be more reactive after each nail trimming session.

Using Grooming Loops

Grooming loops are a practical tool in the groomer's hands to prevent the head from reaching the care provider when doing nails on a dog who is showing late sensitivity signs (snapping, attacking, etc.). It works best for working on the hind feet. For large dogs, the front nails can be done with this method, too, if the legs are long enough to ensure the dog won't reach us even when we lift the paw to work on it. Grooming loops are very trustworthy; they won't break or snap. Use one with heavy padding under the dog's neck so it won't dig in the skin or make the dog choke.

Using Muzzles and/or Cones

From a safety perspective, we can face situations where we have exhausted all other options, such as using a more experienced care provider, having a new trainer, new location, food, toys, positioning, etc. except for sedation or anesthesia.

There can be cases when we see the dog is not comfortable; however, there is a dire need for a nail trim, and we sense the dog would do somewhat okay without anesthesia.

It is worth entertaining a muzzle/cone/grooming loop(s), or a combination of those resolutions to avoid anesthesia or to resolve an urgent nail care issue.

Carefully analyze whether the stress of doing nails with grooming loop, muzzle, and/or cone without sedation or the stress coming with using sedation/anesthesia will mean a higher impact for the dog.

If the dog shows body language that supports he would be less stressed by the restraining tools above than the anesthesia, or there is no care provider available to assist with sedation, we can give the nail trim a go using those types of equipment one by one or their combination.

It will be a substantial setback for the dog and pawrent training-wise, so please use this as an absolute last resort. Like cases when there is no availability for a vet/professional within a reasonable time and the dog's nails grew to the skin, or if a broken nail piece is hanging there lifeless and causes discomfort to the dog by pressing against the toes—in a rural environment, etc.

Again, please use the grooming loop, muzzle, or cone methods, or a combination as a method as before the last resort (sedation/anesthesia). And please promise to do/suggest serious counterconditioning and desensitization afterward to improve the dog's behavior. Muzzling dogs for nail trimming should not be a routine procedure.

Medical Restraint - Sedation or Anesthesia

Sedation or general anesthesia can make nail trims work for the highly reactive/anxious/traumatized dogs who have long nails, grown close to or grown into the skin. Talk to your vet about options. You don't have to put your dog under general anesthesia right off the bat. Taking the edge off the stress might be just enough for safe nail trimming. I highly recommend monitored sedation by a veterinarian on-site if sedation is needed. Anxious dogs can have complications, and having a skilled care provider who can act fast and have the tools ready to revert a complication will save lives. Additionally, doing lots of CCDS training at home or with the help of a trainer will transform the dog's behavior. Often pawrents get relief after the nails get trimmed and do not follow recommendations for CCDS for their dogs. That will result in the same stressful nail care for all—if not more so.

Make sure the dog does not get quicked under sedation/anesthesia! Just because the dog is not conscious, doesn't mean they don't deserve the same standard of care.

Not so Fun Fact

It is common to have students learn to trim nails on sedated dogs due to the benefit of a "still" and "non-biter" dog. For clarity, nail trimming can absolutely happen under anesthesia. However, you need to be highly skilled to determine how far you can trim back to avoid an injury. In my opinion, the dog's reactions—if they are mild—are excellent indications of when to stop, so I welcome it and prefer to work on conscious dogs. Plus, seeing the dog stand on all fours is also very helpful because it allows you to see how far back you need to trim and can work up a better care plan if needed after the nail care to getting the quick to recede. You can adjust the care plan based on these parameters.

The pain will remain after hitting the quick, just as it does when your nail curls back up or something goes under it. I know. Goosebumps. Be mindful, and stay safe. Ask your vet about the safety and the type of sedatives he recommends.

Miscellaneous Paw Clues

Paw Hair Discoloration, Hair Loss, Licking, Chewing on the Paws

Hair discoloration or loss can occur mostly from infections or licking, but the reasons can vary widely.

Possible Causes for Licking

- sticker burrs stuck in the hair (paw pads, between toes, etc.)
- matted hair
- insect bite
- allergies
- joint/malformation pain (see leg/feet positioning)
- physical injury (nick, cut, burn, bruise, etc. on nails, toes, paw, paw pads, legs, upper body, other body parts)
- dry skin
- yeasty skin

- grass treatment on the skin (chemicals irritating the skin)
- chemicals in coats (left in shampoo, conditioner, etc.)
- etc.

Our task is to try to figure out the cause of the irritation. The best way to do it is to consult with a veterinarian who will physically examine the dog, run some tests if needed, and find the root cause by our statement. An allergy test often helps speed up the research and the owner can monitor the dog daily for any triggers or allergens.

If there are any signs of discomfort beyond licking, it is better to postpone the nail care session until after the dog heals, if at all possible.

Limping

Limping or favoring a leg can occur when a more profound issue is going on, such as a more significant cut, burn, physical injury, joint pain, muscle injury, ligament injury, etc. Grooming a dog who is limping is not advisable at any time without a diagnosis and green light from a veterinarian. There can be more significant issues going on and dogs can get injured further. Dogs are more reactive due to discomfort or pain, meaning they will use late discomfort signs sooner, rather than start with early discomfort signs, placing all of us in direct danger.

Chapter 3

The Calm and Cooperative Dog

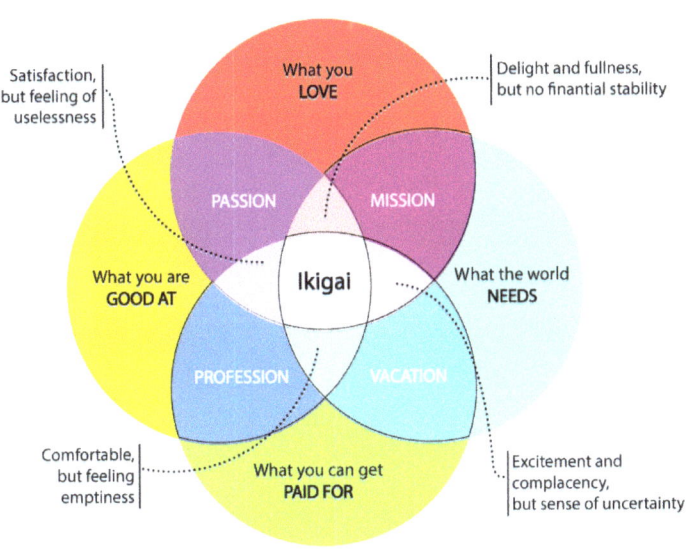
Ikigai

I wanted to introduce this chapter with a cool concept I came across a while ago called Ikigai. It originated in Japan, and this is how the Japanese people see "a reason for being". Ikigai is when you balance what you love, what the world needs, what you can get paid for, and what you are good at. Once you manage to get all four elements in harmony, you reach Ikigai. It inspired me to come up with a similar figure about canine and human behavior. To better understand what brings us closer to a joyful and cooperative spa day also to understand what makes it more challenging. Enjoy this image and once you are ready, let's look at what makes dogs and humans behave in ways we prefer or ways we'd like to change!

The Magic of Cooperation is Preparation

Like humans, dogs are born with some instincts, but not with a full stack of skills; we learn those. Consequently, dogs need to experience, get used to being handled, get nail care done; it won't just happen that they'll be textbook perfect on the table for anyone and for everything. I created the following two figures to help you get a taste of what we will be cooking. How can we transform dogs from "No, thank you" to "Hmmm, yes, please". In this chapter, we will talk about the aspects of cooperative canine-human teamwork; what makes dogs still/squirmy, and what makes humans compassionate/sympathetic. In the next chapter, we will dig deeper into how you can translate your dog's behavior and come up with custom plans to get the results you both desire.

Check out the following images about the five core components of the biggest influencers of behavior!

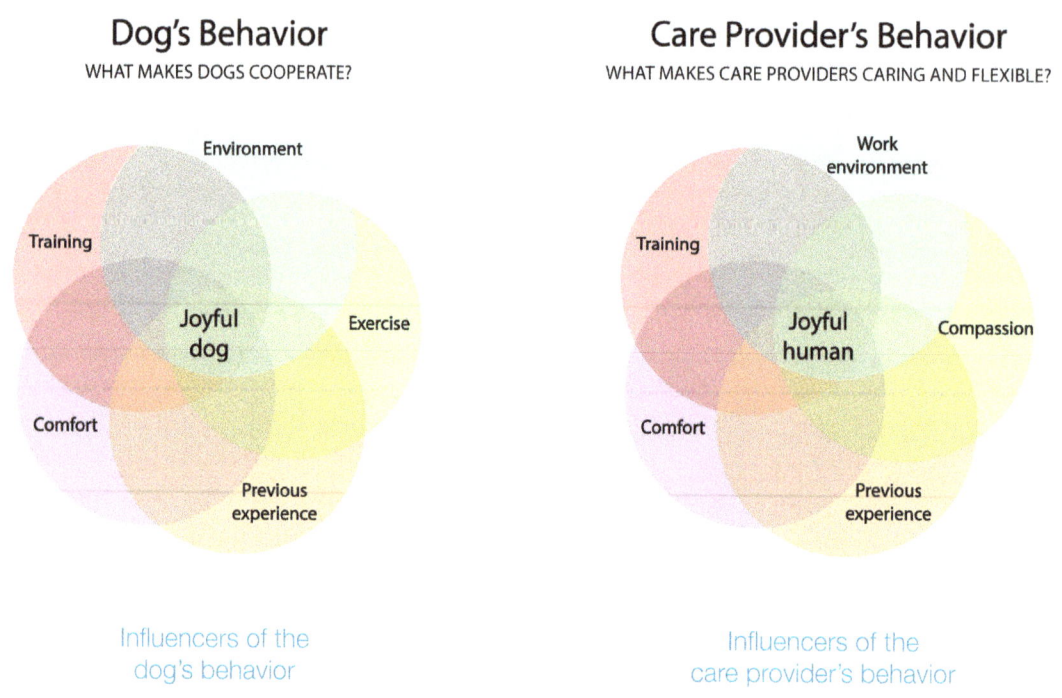

Influencers of the dog's behavior

Influencers of the care provider's behavior

Dog Behavior Influencers - The 8 Es

How does all this translate to a cooperative canine? Here are the eight core elements of a cooperative dog. The 8 Es if you will.

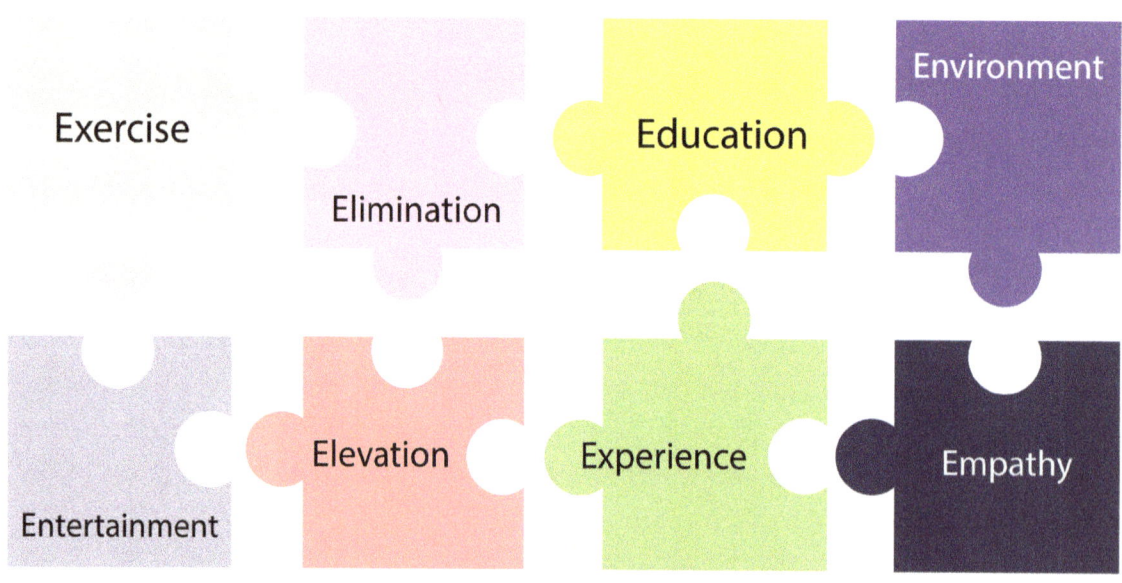

Dog behavior puzzle - What makes a dog cooperate for nail care?

1. Exercise

To satisfy one of the most substantial needs of dogs, especially high-energy dogs, exercise is a golden strategy for calm and cooperative nail care.

Tired dog vs. one that is full of energy.

So take a big walk, hike, play chase indoors or outdoors depending on the weather, have a doggy playdate, swim in the pool/lake, whatever comes to mind that your dog enjoys doing will help you take care of that excess energy.

2. Elimination

Peeing and pooping (for all participants) are highly recommended before a nail trim for comfort and a longer-lasting cooperation.

3. Education

There are many things dogs need to be trained to do and get used to so that they are confident and curious rather than unsure or afraid. We can see there are many things to practice beyond actually trimming nails. And this is only one section of the five. There are lots of things to practice to keep your dog comfortable, aren't there?

To keep dogs confident and cooperative for nail care, it is beneficial to get them:

1. Exercised (Tired dog vs. one that is full of energy) Used to people
2. Used to other dogs, other pets
3. Used to sounds (weird, loud)
4. Used to sensations (cold, metal parts)
5. Used to grooming positions (paw holding techniques, jumping up and down from the table, staying on the table, turning around, sitting down on the table, etc., and doing so when we request it.)
6. Used to examination
7. Used to transportation method to get to the service location
8. Used to being elevated (to be on a sometimes moving grooming table)

Checkmark the bullet points above that your dog is confident doing/around and circle the ones you feel you both need to work on!

4. Environment

Think about one of the most critical sections of becoming an animal film star. It's cool that your dog can do a handshake or a handstand in your living room, but can he do it in a new, busy environment as well? The same applies to dog grooming, and even for nail care. It's great that dogs are comfy in your home, but we want to make sure they are just as comfortable and confident in other environments, such as a vet office or a grooming salon as well. Other places probably have more distractions to lure the doggies' attention elsewhere, so we need to work on a bulletproof focus, eye contact, and connection to make confidence and cooperation happen outside of that living room. A low-key environment is a fantastic aid for a smooth experience. Veterinarians, vet techs, and pawrents are in an advantageous position given that their setting suits higher energy level dogs. Groomers need to adapt to a low-key environment setting to reform dog behavior in the fastest possible way.

To keep dogs confident and cooperative in different environments, we'll need to get them used to:

1. Strange sounds (shears, clippers, etc.)
2. New smells (room, table, surroundings, care provider, etc.)
3. Movements/activity around (see table manners for care provider!)
4. Presence of other people and animals (for a smooth waiting room experience and to avoid dogs getting pumped up before the nail care session)

Checkmark the bullet points above where your dog is confident and circle the ones you feel you will need to work on.

If you use a table for nail trimming, its location is a critical part of the dog's behavior. Dogs feel more comfortable when the table is pushed back toward a wall or a shelf. Plus, it's a great way to keep him safe and avoid a surprise flying off the table or off the other, hard-to-reach end. I keep my grooming table located right in front of a window that faces the backyard. My clients enjoy watching squirrels, my cats, my dog, birds, whoever is out while getting their nails (and other grooming steps) done, and so do I. Their calm demeanor is totally worth the brainstorming needed to reorganize a room.

5. Entertainment

Treats and toys instantly come to mind to focus the dog's mind and help them get busy while they get their nails done. I started to recognize the impact of other entertainments such as watching squirrels or my chickens or cats while getting nails done. It is a huge hit among my clients and I highly recommend this as a special addition to the tool list to use to keep dogs still.

6. Elevation

The elevation is one of the key components of keeping the dog still. A grooming/non-slip exam table is a great way to elevate the dog from the ground and get them into the "grooming mode". On the ground, they are close to other distractions and are used to running around or playing with other dogs or humans. On the table, they get used to focusing on the care provider and at the treats, I mean tasks at hand. Haha. In my experience, most dogs become way more still on the table than on the ground.

Side note, if a dog is traumatized and sees the table as a trigger, skip the table and find a cozy place to do the nail care either while the dog is standing or is on his side or back.

7. Experience

Previous Experience

Previous experience plays a significant role in how the dog will react to nail care right now. If the dog's experience was great, he most likely won't make a big deal out of it; he will cooperate willingly. If the previous experience was overwhelming, uncomfortable, painful, or even traumatic, dogs will likely use everything in their power to prevent it from happening again—understandably. The slightest triggers will set off the dog, and the reactions will most likely be on the upper end of the sensitivity spectrum. To get dogs to enjoy and cooperate during nail care, preventing injuries is vital. Avoid overwhelming them (approaching their threshold or going over it) to make the most significant progress in the fastest possible way. But that's a topic of a later chapter.

The dog's previous experience is similar to when people lie to us. We most likely won't be able to fully trust them after the initial apology for a while. They will need to earn our trust back. And that takes time and actions that speak for themselves. And if they lie to us again, the leftover faith will vanish for even longer.

To desensitize dogs, we will need to keep painful experiences from happening again. Now add another layer to it: lies won't hurt us physically, but nails cut too short will, for days.

The dog's previous experiences and happenings in life that happen around nail care time can significantly change the dog's behavior. Consider the dog's previous experiences with:

- grooming
- a specific care provider
- care providers in general
- other people
- the location
- grooming and grooming steps
- brushing paws (toe mohawks)

- moving to a new place
- rehoming/adoption
- boarding for several days
- a vet visit
- a dog attack
- a new baby/member in the family
- a new dog in the family
- the loss of a family member (canine/human)

Checkmark the bullet points above that your dog does not have a problem with. Then highlight the ones you feel you both need to work on! For example, if your dog had to have a cast due to an injury, then examinations or touching legs or paws will likely need to be worked on to rebuild the dog's comfort level because of the pain he experienced before.

Current Experience

The way the dog is experiencing the happenings around right now is also a huge part of how he will react.

The dog's comfort is based on many of the above-mentioned pillars, but there are other layers to it, so it has its own section as well. In later chapters, we will discuss how these influence the nail care session and what we can do to provide the most comfort for the pawdicure sessions.

The dog's comfort is based on the following perspectives:

- elimination (pee, poop)
- health/illness/injury (ear infection, diarrhea, UTI, sore spot, etc.)
- the comfort of the grooming method/tool (pressure on the nail while cutting, electric nail grinders, etc.)
- handling by the care provider (how considerate and compassionate the care provider is compared to the dog's threshold)
- being alone without other pack members (separation anxiety)
- energy level
- age
- breed
- physical flexibility
- hunger/thirst (hungry rescue, the thirsty guy right after a summer run, etc.)
- comfort with the environment (chance to sniff around and get comfortable)
- comfort with care provider (chance to sniff the care provider, understand body language)

A high-energy level dog without exercise or a pee break, especially when he is in a high-distraction environment setting will likely not cooperate and will wiggle a lot. Adjusting the prep-work and the environment will help us keep the dog calm and cooperative.

Customize the list above to your dog's needs and see how he reacts and what can alter the difficulty of the nail care session!

More on step-by-step guidance and troubleshooting in the Nail it! Community in the Nail it course. Come and join us there!

8. Empathy

Celebration and Clear Observation

When we learn to make clear observations about canine behavior, we open the door to celebrate behavior that we desire and are already shown by the dog in front of us, so we can see it more often. Or we open up to changing the ones we see and we rather want to avoid. Either way, all participants' experience is joyfully fluid, not static like with labels. We work in collaboration and express what we like and what we'd like to happen. With clear communication and empathy toward all participants, we help nourish a wholesome collaboration. The second we label dogs as aggressive, shy, good, or bad, we've already entered a mindset where our need to get stuff done overrides the dog's need for comfort and safety. Even if the dog has to be muzzled to cut ingrown toenails out safely for everyone, we still need to think about how it's done so we can keep the dog as comfortable as possible to prepare him for the next nail care. Keeping dogs comfortable is an experience not only for the moment but for the future as well. It will fuel the dog's behavior and will pivot their response either toward more cooperative or more fighting. Considering everyone's perspective and needs brings a new level of understanding, flexibility, creativity to the equation and results in a calmer dog and a more respectful and respected care provider.

The Importance and Power of Pain-Free Experiences

One of the most significant and surprisingly most overlooked reasons why dogs hate nail care is because they had an undesired experience. That can vary from the dog feeling overwhelmed by the physical restraint while performing pain-free nail care through a full-on three-person restraint with muzzles topped off with multiple bleeding nails.

Many people are in a rush or do not have the knowledge, tricks, or patience to prevent them from hitting the quick. I'm talking about well-meaning but overworked professionals and owners. Often, rather than making a care plan with the owner/coworker about how to desensitize the dog for paw care, they proceed, the dog wiggles, or fights back, and they hit the quick. The dogs remember those cases—even one will suffice and they'll take action to keep it from happening again. They will use more and more powerful tools after each traumatic experience. Who can blame them, right?

And what is our reaction most of the time? We label the dog who tries to communicate discomfort or pain as aggressive or a biter. They get banned from salons and get sedated at vet clinics without emphasizing the dire need for training and desensitization.

The good news is that we CAN DO MANY things to keep them safe and comfortable so they'll stay still for us.

Again, there are cases when sedation is the only safe way to go for both dog and care provider. I'd like to encourage us all to graduate from that being the norm for "tricky dogs" and teach that dog-human team to evolve to a stage of collaboration.

Transitioning From "Not Collaborating" to Cooperation and Joy

Once we see the importance of the canine needs, we can start working on fulfilling them to score trust and joy points in our relationship. When we build our connection on these premises and not on the "Sit means sit, or else!" approach, dogs will be interested in working with us. If we can provide an atmosphere where they feel comfortable, and the method we use is pain-free as well, they will cooperate willingly. After we have scored enough points in the bank to balance out previous lack of training or uncomfortable experiences to get a solid trust and have practiced the drill together a few times, dogs will understand we listen to their needs and will relax more and more. That's the cherry on the top, the transformation from uncooperative, to cooperative, then joyfully cooperative.

Still vs. Cooperative

When a dog is still, it does not necessarily mean he is comfortable as well. Often dogs show discomfort or fear by freezing. Considering the dog's facial expressions, the tail's movement and position, the body's position, heart rate, and breathing, we might come to the surprising conclusion that the "good girl" we thought was cooperating was in fact still due to fear and not from joy. I find it helpful to distinguish between the two, and I urge care providers to share details of the dog's behavior for nail care with pawrents beyond saying, "Oh, she was a good girl/boy." Taking a dog to the back and doing the nails with two other people's help without urging the client to take action to train that dog will come back and bite someone in the tush. Transparency pays off for everyone—care providers, pawrents, and dogs as well.

Comfort Measures

It is tremendously helpful to understand a bit of canine body language to precisely translate the dog's message, based on his feelings and needs. That will enable us to make adjustments accordingly to keep both parties comfortable and safe.

Below you will find two groups: comfort and discomfort signs. Discomfort signs further break down into early and late discomfort signs to better understand the dog's situation. Let's dig deeper to better understand our pets and clients. We'll start by gathering some canine linguistic knowledge, and we'll sharpen our eyes to learn to detect minor behavior signals in the tutorial videos in real doggy cases.

If we wanted to translate these three into colors, we could say signs of comfort are green. You can go ahead, the dog is comfy.

Orange would be the early discomfort signs. Stop, analyze, and proceed with caution!

Red would be the late discomfort signs. It's dangerous to proceed. We need to make a plan to keep the dog comfortable enough to cooperate!

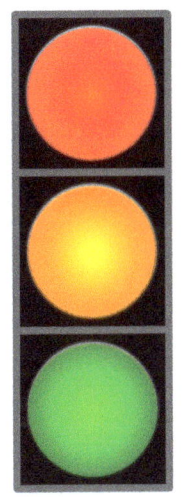

Comfort measures
Stop!
Proceed with caution!
Proceed!

Signs of Comfort

This means we have the green light, it's clear to go ahead with the grooming step we're trying to do. The dog is comfortable.

- wagging tail (happy wagging, sweeping movements, can be either slower or faster)
- relaxed posture
- relaxed muscles
- not putting pressure on the leg when you lift the leg
- no kicking or pulling of the leg away from us
- the dog does not visually check what we are doing
- normal breathing
- no drooling
- no excessive licking
- no excessive drinking
- no excessive eating
- a combination of any of these

Proceed!
Dog is comfortable

Signs of Discomfort

Early discomfort signs are not as well-known and understood by the general public as the late discomfort signs, such as growling and bites. However, they are tremendously helpful signals that, once noticed, help us easily figure out the dog's comfort level. That, in turn, enables us to predict the dog's next move and prepare a care plan for doggy desensitization, when necessary. Most of the time, with the right nail care technique, it is possible to work around early sensitivity signs without having to resort to restraints.

Early Discomfort Signs

Detecting early discomfort signs in time will be our best bet for getting a super cooperative dog and preventing injuries to dogs or humans. Here are some examples. The more early discomfort signs dogs show, the closer we get to the late sensitivity signs.

- pulling away from the grooming shop's door
- tail tucked in
- head-turning
- softening the eyes
- turning away
- wagging tail (the anxious type of movement with the tail, narrow wagging, the tail is either very low or very high, fast movements mostly)
- yawning
- pulling feet away
- moving away with the whole body
- curled up posture (angry cat style or donut style on the sides, hiding paws, and protecting face) when standing or lying
- sniffing on the site where we are working
- nose licking
- licking our hands/tools where we are working
- play bow
- sitting down
- lying down
- sniffing "away" (not a tool, not care provider, but something else, such as the ground)
- kicking/pushing our hands away
- kicking back or out when messing with their feet
- putting weight on the leg you're trying to lift up
- not coming to us when invited to get a pawdicure
- not getting up (from a lying position) when asked
- not jumping up on the grooming table when asked
- pricked/pinned ears
- panting
- drooling
- shaking

Proceed with caution! Dog is showing early discomfort signs.

- excessive drinking
- muscle twitching
- pulling their legs away when we are trying to hold the leg/paw
- stiff muscles
- frozen posture
- slow movements
- curving (walking in a curve, out of the way of the trigger)
- barking
- nibbling (on our hands or equipment)
- hiding under the bed after the sight of nail care tool(s)
- splitting up (physically putting one's body between dogs or people or tools)
- paw lift
- a combination of any of these

Late Discomfort Signs

Late discomfort signs are easier for the average eye to notice since they are more direct. By the time the dog in our care chooses to show the big guns, pulling the trigger is right around the corner. It is worth making sure that we are not only familiar with the late discomfort signs, but that we adjust our care plan accordingly when we notice any of the following:

- hyperventilating
- raised hackles
- lip lifting, exposing teeth
- growling
- snapping (at our hands or equipment)
- biting (at our hands or equipment)
- or a combination of these

Stop!
Dog is showing late discomfort signs, a new plan needs to be created.

Reading Dog Minds

Threshold

To better we understand what might be going on in our client's/canine's mind, we need to understand the term threshold. **The threshold is the point at which your dog is starting to show sensitivity signs of getting triggered.** When the dog is **below the threshold,** the dog's body language shows the dog feels relaxed. When the dog is **at the threshold,** the dog is starting to show early sensitivity signs. When the dog is **over the threshold,** the dog shows early or late sensitivity signs, and everyone is at a higher risk of getting injured.

Being relaxed is a feeling, an emotion. It is not a behavior.

Just because a dog is not moving or is not actively biting does not necessarily mean he is relaxed. Learn to read your dog's body language signs to understand where the dog is on the threshold scale.

My goal—and hopefully yours—is to keep dogs below threshold while under our care. It's good to keep in mind that every time we work on dogs at or above the threshold, they build up experiences that will make them lose trust in us and the process. They will react increasingly to similar situations over time if we do not develop and practice a desensitization plan. So when we proceed, disregarding the canine's signals that indicate distress or pain, we are building a ticking time bomb. When I see dogs with early or late discomfort signs, I bring it up and start a conversation with the pawrents to find a resolution for everyone—proceeding without an action plan for desensitization and training places everyone in danger—the dog, the pawrents, and the current and future care providers.

I find it incredibly important to be aware of this and make custom homework plans or refer the pawrents and dog to a trainer for fast behavioral transformation.

Let's look at what kind of signs and symptoms we might see from the threshold perspective!

Threshold and Canine Body Languages

Body Language Indicating Being Below the Threshold = Dog is Comfortable

- loose body, soft muscles, mouth, and ears
- dog's attention gained easily and quickly
- normal breathing
- relaxed body posture
- shows no early or late discomfort signs of fear, anxiety, or worry
- tail untucked
- doesn't over monitor you; watches you or the environment with casual curiosity without licking, snapping, or attempting escape
- can lie down or rest calmly

Body Language Indicating Being at the Threshold

! showing one or a few early (mild) discomfort signs (see list above)
! you can get the dog's attention, but it is more challenging with voice only, often requires deliberate distractions, such as treats or funny sounds
! You are able to do the nails, but the dog needs very frequent or constant distractions with food/toys/rubs, etc. to do so. (The dog might leave when there are no positive distractions to keep him close by.)

- "supervising what you are doing, where you are going" shows increasing concern with you, the environment, or the tool
- ears up, focused eyes, jumpy, tail often wagging anxiously
- The dog often turns his head away from you. "I can't see what you are doing to me" while in a frozen/curled up position.
- fidgety, yawning, nose licking
- licking the tool, self, or you
- moving away from you, hiding paws

Body Language Indicating Being Over the Threshold

- showing a few or several mild or severe early discomfort signs (see list above)
- showing late discomfort signs (see list above)
- must be held, physically moved into place, or restrained to make nail care happen (using slings, the help of coworkers, family members, etc.)
- tense, stiff body, flinching, gets startled easily, ears pinned back
- trying to escape by moving/running away, pulling leg away
- showing/using teeth
- panting
- heart rate increase
- dilated pupils, whale eyes
- will refuse to eat treats
- yelping, whining, howling
- mouthing/snapping at hand or tools
- "fooling around" (stealing items, rolling around, playing chase, dead, etc.)
- squinty eyes
- becoming frozen or immobile, "submissive"
- trembling
- being a "drama queen" or "stubborn" or "aggressive" or simply "bad dog" (But remember, these are only labels, not a life sentence!)

Dog Love Languages

Remember the doggy needs list at the beginning? Here, I grabbed five of the most frequent needs aka "Love languages" doggies prefer. The name "Dog love languages" is an inspiration after Gary Chapman's book: 5 Love Languages. Let's see the five dog love languages!

Dog Love Languages

1. Treats
2. Toys
3. Physical touch and comforting
4. Quality time
5. Closeness, connection

#1. Treats

Some doggies go nuts for treats (they have **a high food drive**); some dogs won't move a muscle for them (possible **high prey drive**). For a multipurpose dog, trainers often look for a canine who has both drives, and depending on the type of work they'll do, they can be precisely trained (and faster) with treats and/or toys.

Most of the time, dogs show at least a little bit of an interest in food, especially when using powerful treats. That's great news for us since it is easier to reinforce a food-driven dog and master timing when it comes to nail care rather than a prey-driven one. (Imagine giving a piece of food to a dog and then imagine throwing a ball or a squeaky toy to one as a reward. Lots of movement there at the second one and it takes significantly longer to calm the dog down, get in position, and continue work.)

We can still get useful information out of the cases when the dog doesn't show any interest in food at the beginning or at all. In those cases, we may need a more powerful treat and training/socialization/desensitization tricks to help them feel more comfortable in the environment and accept treats. What do I mean by a **"powerful" treat**?

Powerful Treats

From the dogs' and the trainers' perspective, powerful treats have many superpowers. Let's see what those superpowers are!

- **Moist**, so it will not "dry the dog out", resulting in a lot of drinking and a lot of peeing
- **Soft**, so the dog won't need to chew on it for too long and can swallow it fast.
- **Intense Smells**, so the pure smell of it will focus the dog's attention on us and will bring joy for the dog. A good smelling treat helps to keep the dog's focus on us, not on any other distractions or boredom.
- **Nutritional and organic** (or at least non-toxic, i.e. no additives, no preservatives, no colors, etc.).
- Cut up into **tiny pieces,** or at least it is **easy to break** into pieces (so we won't fill the dog's belly up in the first minute). Prepare the treats and break them up into tiny bits before playtime.

The Irresistible Baked Chicken Liver Recipe

Preparation: 5 mins
Baking time: 40-45 mins
Yield: about 2-3 trainings

Storage: Refrigerate. (Freezes well.) You can keep it in the fridge for a few days, and you also can portion them and even freeze them in zip locks for summer treats or thaw them later on for "quick fix" treats for training.
Try to keep them apart in one layer if you want to freeze them so they won't stick together.
Note: I usually make at least 2 lbs of liver for my pup (100 lbs Malinois), so it'll last.

Ingredients:

- Organic chicken liver 1 lb
- Salt
- Water
- Glass, stainless steel, ceramic, cast iron, etc. (avoid Teflon) baking pan

Steps:

1. Preheat the oven to 350 F
2. Put the livers in the pan
3. Add some water so that you can make the most of it and flavor the dog's dinner/breakfast for a few days
4. Bake for about 40-45 mins
5. Cut up in small pieces
6. Put in the fridge the portions you won't use right away

Fruits and **veggies** (raw, dried, frozen) can work great. Several clients bring snacks such as raw blueberries, cucumbers, carrots, or dried/frozen bananas to their grooming session. (My dog's favorite fruit is blueberries, and his favorite veggies are carrots and pumpkin. Keep an eye on the sugar intake for doggies! Bananas, apples, and pears, for example, are pretty high in sugar, so you want to give them less of these two or mix with low sugar veggies/fruits or give only a moderate amount.)

Two of my favorite treats are **pulled organic chicken breast** and **organic, baked chicken liver**. They work by themselves in about 98 percent of the cases. (I prefer organic in general, but especially organic liver. The reason for that is the liver is a very nutritious food, but it is a cleansing organ that filters and stores some toxins.)

Dry treats such as Milk Bones or an average quality kibble **do not work well** for most dogs and grooming situations, and they are not very healthy either. They smell not so interesting, take forever to chew, are dry, which makes the dog thirsty, doggy will drink, then needs to pee, ergo the nail care session will last for two weeks.

Our task is to find the treat that works best for us. There are many out there, so **keep being a label detective** and synchronize your dog's taste with nutritious and training-friendly bites.

Treat Bags

Keeping the treats in a container that is easy to get stuff out of is crucial from a timing perspective. To get the doggies to understand what we want them to do, we need to grab and deliver the treats super-fast. If we give the treat too late, dogs may not connect things precisely the way we want them or it takes longer.

As an example, one of my clients took her pup to the vet for regular puppy shots. The doggy got the injection, and just when the owner started to put the harness on the dog, the spot of the shot began to sting, and the pup connected the harness with the stinging sensation. It took him a long time and lots of treats to help him understand the harness means walkies, not the stinging.

Timing is essential to move our "grooming dance" forward and improve the dog's cooperation, so having great treat bags is super important. Depending on the dog's food drive, you may need to keep the treats out of sight in a waist-style treat bag or, better yet, teach the dog to leave it before proceeding. For less interested pups or highly trained dogs who understand "Leave it!", you can have a wide-mouth container on the table or around the dog as a treat bag. It is pretty straightforward to teach dogs this. Check out the following video about "Leave it" by Emily Larlham, an exceptionally great, gentle, clinker trainer (https://www.youtube.com/watch?v=pEeS2dPpPtA)

Criteria

A handy treat bag will enable you to easily reinforce the dog's behavior and do so fast enough to make progress in training.

- **Easy to open/close, wide enough mouth** for your hands, so it won't get stuck on your hand when you're getting out some treats.
- **Large enough** to keep one training's treats inside
- **Washable** (food grade silicone) **or easy to clean fabric liner** so it won't get too stinky or moldy (a plastic sour cream container will do for DIY-ers)
- **Clip** for smaller-medium size, lightweight bags
- **Waistband** for large bags to keep it on your waist or buckle or a clip to keep it in your pants (optional)
- For high food drive beginners, a **closeable mouth** can be convenient.

My favorite treat bag is the Royalcare silicone dog treat pouch. It is a small training bag that is portable, has a magnetic closure and a waist clip. It is incredibly easy to take off or put on, can withstand wet treats, and won't make a mess on your clothes. It is super easy to clean and is BPA Free.

https://www.amazon.com/RoyalCare-Silicone-Training-Portable-Magnetic/dp/B07C4V2GG3

#2. Toys

Just as with the food, some dogs love toys, and some couldn't care less. Our task is to figure out whether the pup we are working on likes to play with toys or not and which type their favorite might be. Plastic? Wood? Leather? Plush? Silicone? Squeaky? Soft? Hard? Undestroyable? Balls? Prey-like appearance? Squishy?, etc.

Sidenote: The more the dogs like to play with toys, it's likely the wilder they'll become near one. For this reason, toys are not necessarily the most comfortable option for reinforcement for trimming nails. However, they are a fantastic "jackpot" for the beginning, before a break, and the end of the nail care session or to signal a break and take five.

With dogs who love to play with toys, seeing one is often a "turn on" for fun and focus, so they'll do anything and everything to get that toy. We'll discuss body language and moving with mindfulness to keep them still enough for long enough in a separate section.

The Best Toys (from the dog and care provider's perspective)

- **Non-toxic material**
- Often overlooked but essential criteria is whether you can tolerate it for ~15-20 mins. (think about squeaky toys)
- **Soft** (we do not want to get a right hook from a large, hard toy when the doggy gets excited and shakes it. If you have a Maligator (Malinois), then you're probably used to it by now.)
- **Proper size** compared to the dog's size (as long as the dog is happy with it, won't swallow it, and can play with it, it's all good.)
- **Preferably not squeaky**, since it'll end up right by your ear and will eat up your neurons pretty fast at least it would do it with mine. Earplugs might be the golden middle as an alternative solution for squeaky toy enthusiastic woofers.

Toys and Treats Combined

A Kong toy filled with food is a magical combo. If you use frozen goodies inside, it'll last for a good while. I had a Labrador retriever client a couple of years ago with some unpleasant nail care experiences from the past. At the time of his first appointment with me, he was not fond of the pawdicure, which he desperately needed. The first time, we needed a whole hour to succeed and do all four feet; paw hair trim, nail trimming, filing using treats, and belly rubs. We talked and made a plan for next time.

The second time, the owner took a Kong toy stuffed with frozen goodies, which kept the dog busy for nail care and cut the time in half. That is a considerable improvement and it got further reduced by the mom practicing at home and us performing comfortable nail care. We were down to the normal 15-20 min time for a paw hair trim and nail trim and file from the third meetup on.

#3. Physical Touch and Comforting

Some doggies do not care about either treats or toys but cannot resist a good belly/butt/ear rub. For those pups, we present belly rubs and massage and spoil them rotten. A friend, partner, a colleague can be a huge help to deliver the rubs while you do the nail care.

Rubs and Massage
Be it a belly/butt/leg/neck/ear or base of the tail rub; it is heaven itself for the puppies who enjoy physical touch. Most of the time, we can satisfy them with rubs only throughout grooming with no need to think about treats or toys.

Doggies can get a literal massage while getting their nails done and often they just forget about the pawdicure part and doze off. A cat could even curl right by their heads, and they wouldn't care because they fell into a "rub trance". I've seen this in action countless times with Mr. Chips curling up near a doggy client getting a pawdicure.

#4. Quality Time

Breaks
Breaks are a magic wand tool when the doggy is running low on "patience credit" and moving like Fred Astaire on the table. It'll probably be useful for the care provider to take a few deep breaths as well when feeling overwhelmed and give a break to the exhausted patience production part of the brain. Letting the dog go in the room or proposing a run in an open area usually gets all participants back on the right track, and it is faster and safer for all of us than if we proceeded with force.

Exercise
Exercising a dog before any grooming session is as important as taking the dog to the grooming appointment, and I am not kidding. :) The #1 solution for a cooperative dog (and the easiest one as well) is to work all the pent-up energy out of the dog. Puppies and elderly dogs are exceptions because they get tired super/fairly fast.

Generally speaking, a moderate amount of exercise for puppies and a small amount of activity or no activity is ideal for elderly dogs, so they will have the energy to move around.

Playing fetch or running in the park or the backyard will do pure magic when it comes to precise work such as nail trimming on dogs.

Rest

Sleep, peace, and quiet, or alone time are sometimes what a dog needs to get all its nails done. It can be especially true for elderly dogs with a new puppy addition to the family or adult dogs with toddlers in the household. They will be the most relaxed after a rejuvenating nap and their nerves nurtured with a quick snooze.

#5. Closeness, Connection

For some dogs, just being around us means the world. They get very anxious in crates, away from us, and are super chill when we let them hang out with us freely, whatever we may be doing. It's excellent to double-check what our dog is trying to tell us with "misbehavior" such as whining, barking, scratching, escaping, etc. Often a tiny tweak will satisfy both humans and canines.

Sexual Expression

Since urban dogs, in general, do not get to practice and express their sexual needs much—they get corrected for it—their need for satisfaction often does not get met. Dogs that show signals of the heightened need for sexual expression benefit from freedom about it. And, as a result, they will be even calmer for nail care as well. What do I mean?

Some dogs have an admirable sexual appetite, and they constantly try to hump whatever they can reach; legs, plush toys, other dogs let it be male or female, from the front or the back, etc. We've all seen it at the dog park or been to that relative's house with the frisky woofer. A heightened sexual appetite is especially true for those dogs who are intact and have their family jewels dangling between their hind legs. For them, having a go-to plush toy that can help them express their passion freely will bring much-needed relief. And chances are there will be fewer embarrassing events in public for the pawrents watching their dogs humping legs and dogs as well.

I have doggy clients who have their dedicated "plush bitches" that pawrents frequently throw in the washing machine for rejuvenation. Other dogs figured out the magic of masturbation. Yep, that was one eye-opening experience for me when I saw one of my furry clients go down on himself to the point of pleasure.

Per the American Kennel Club's suggestions for studs, both humping and masturbation can be encouraged by a designated plush toy, or just by not "correcting" the behavior. "Allowing a dog to practice masturbation on a favored object or toy is a good idea."

https://www.akc.org/expert-advice/dog-breeding/what-to-expect-when-you-collect/

It is not only fun for them but will keep the sperm pool fresh.

If dogs can get relief from sexual tension it will result in a calmer, happier, more cooperative dog, even for nail trimming.

Turns out, my grandma's suggestion, "The secret to a happy man is to keep their belly full and their testicles empty " is true not only for humans but dogs as well.

Now that all of us have gotten over a surprise blushing and our eyebrows are back to the normal position reading through this, let's take a look at other comfort measures to keep dogs cooperative!

Environmental Comfort Measures

Depending on your dog's confidence and training, he either can tolerate and be comfortable in a broader range of distractions or can get easily triggered by anything and everything.

Sounds/Noises

Fun facts first. Scientists say dogs can understand the tone of your voice and the meaning of your words. https://qz.com/769400/dogs-understand-tone-of-voice/

Doggy hearing is a mesmerizing feature. The frequencies that dogs hear are much higher and much lower than what humans can hear. Dogs hear a frequency range of 40 to 60,000 Hz, while the human range is between 20 and 20,000 Hz. Because of this, dogs have a much more difficult time around loud noises. They get more distracted, even uncomfortable at times. And from a nail trimming perspective, we need to be careful with noises in general. Thus, it is super important to reduce noise triggers when it comes to precise grooming steps, such as nail care.

What kind of noises can steal the dog's attention and make him startle or wiggle? In one word; any. It depends on what the dog is used to and what triggers the dog. Distraction can be your voice, other human voices, TV, radio, music, doorbells, sirens, other dogs barking, cats meowing or scratching in the litter box, other pets moving around (parrots, ferrets, etc.), the noise of a car door, collar, carabiner on the leash, fireworks, alarms, treat bag, cookie jar lid where you keep the dog food or treats, squeaky toys, sounds of you putting the "dog walking pants/shoes" on, and the list goes on. I bet you can fit in quite a few of the things that your dog loves to hear and goes nuts for and those that he hates or gets scared of. And that's awesome because the more you are aware of, the more stuff you can do to get your dog prepared and eliminate the triggers and enjoy calm and relaxing nail care.

Many sounds can more/less trigger a dog, depending on their upbringing. Our challenge of the day is to figure out which noises impact our pup, whether it encourages desired or not desired behavior, and how intensive that impact is. Once we know that, we can rank those that positively influence the doggy, and we can try eliminating those which are "not beneficial" for us around grooming time for now.

Observing your dog's behavior and how he reacts to those mentioned above and other noises will help you lay out a plan to keep him still for the pedicure session.

Generally, I eliminate all possible noises so that the doggy won't be distracted by them.

Movements are another big trigger, and we'll cover that next.

Movements/Visual Distractions

When the doggy's vision is intact, visual distractions can significantly impact the behavior. Movements or lack of movements can keep doggies still or invite them to move around.

The care provider's body language is crucial, and the surrounding happenings are almost equally as important. This chapter will cover those as a second and third layer, which will work as fantastic support to get a doggy to stay still for nail care.

Care Provider's Movements

When you are around doggies, I bet you already know a few tricks. For example, when you run or make fast movements most of the time, some dogs take it as a "Let's play and run" sign, but others will be super frightened and scared and they freeze. I bet you had tried to pet a pup who got shy when you reached down to let the dog sniff your hands. Some of us may even have gotten bitten for one reason or another related to this. The most important take-home message is that our behavior and movement significantly impact how doggies behave around us and with us. Often our behavior will determine whether we'll get bitten or not. The fear of getting bitten causes the most sweating among care providers (and owners), hence the overuse of muzzles.

Many care providers and dog owners with high-energy level dogs are having such a hard time because they don't know the following tips on how to behave around a high-energy level dog.

Guidelines About Movements: (Will Talk About Them in Detail Later)

1. Give a stay cue before moving or changing positions.
2. Move like a snail when you change positions.
3. Move the least of your body when changing position, preferably hands/arms only, not your upper body or head.
4. Always keep at least one hand on the dog (especially when you have the dog elevated) when you change positions. Even the tiniest movement counts, such as putting down the shears to get the clippers.
5. Move like lightning when there is a danger either to the dog or to you.
6. Think ahead about a few "backup plan" ways to move your hands, arms, limbs away. (e.g. don't get tangled up with the dog so much that if you had to move your arm super-fast, you'd end up hitting the dog/table/wall with your elbow.)
7. Facing the dog with the full-body means "Stop, stay there."
8. Turning away (even with your eyes or head, especially with your upper body/legs) means "let's go" to the dog. So if you need to grab some equipment, be extra slow and cautious.
9. Always give a cue for jumping off the table. Never let a dog jump off the table without the release cue and lower the table to the lowest setting. If you let the dogs jump whenever they please, they can get hurt, and dogs can learn that it is okay to jump even when they are higher up in the air.

10. Get familiar (and take notes so that you can monitor any changes) with the dog's behavioral triggers (from the owner and from the dog itself) and make a plan where and which position will possibly work best for you all.

Other People's Movements

I find it incredibly distracting if other people move around me while I groom dogs, even just for nail trims. The closer they are, the more significant impact their movement has on the dog most of the time. A still, quiet person is usually well tolerated by the dog (and me), but anything moving affects the dog's movements and our blood pressure, big time. I try to keep anything moving out of sight and hearing distance from doggies if I want them to stay still and focused on me. It's just like when you are trying to teach kids math in Disneyland. They are way too distracted by Minnie Mouse, noises, smells, and tastes to pay attention to you. The same applies to doggies: Whatever moves is like either Disneyland or Scare City, so avoiding distractions as much as possible is the fastest way to get a cooperative and still dog. Some pups are either super chill or super well-trained, or both, and a high-distraction environment is not a challenge for them. But it takes time to get there with high energy level dogs or dogs with previous traumatic experiences in such an environment.

I used to be a huge fan of Cesar Millan. After learning more about canine body language and training methods from other trainers, seeing his process challenged, I found more comfortable and respectful ways to handle behavioral issues for nail care. I have to give him one thing, though, for sure. His general guideline to calmness with the owner's presence, **"no touch, no talk, no eye contact"** works wonders in most situations. I find that's the least distracting way if the pawrent wants to stay. That helps the dog to connect with me (or the care provider) and focus on the job.

In most cases, I ask the pawrents to move out of sight and make no noise. No phone calls, no digging in their handbags, just being there quietly. It helps enormously. Some doggies will still wiggle if they figure out that their pawrents hadn't left. For those, I usually ask them to go and wait in their car. I often show them a video of their doggy being amazingly still on the table while working on them and letting them know about the doggie's triggers to learn what to practice at home. When pawrents see how their dog does for nail care, it'll be either a huge time for celebration if the doggy cooperated well, or a huge boost to work on that needs a bit of a tune-up. Just talking about behavior doesn't have the same effect as a video does.

For the anxious pups who desperately need a nail trim, we go about another route. Bringing in a familiar face will, in those cases, help them to calm down by having pawrents there as an anchor into familiarity.

Other Pet's Movements (Indoor/Outdoor)

Most doggies do pretty well alone or if their buddy is hanging around if they have one. And I mean a packmate. New pets are like Minnie Mouse in Disneyland. A distraction. Most of the time, well-meaning, but a distraction all the same. That is the #1 reason why I work by myself and only one doggy or one pack's pups at a time. That way, I can control happenings amazingly smoothly; doggies will engage with me right away, and they'll cooperate incredibly well, off-leash on the table.

> **Fun Fact**
>
> Believe it or not, something like 95 percent of my canine clients behave excellently with my cats. And that wasn't the case all the time. I have three cats. It's more like two and a half cats since Miss Luna is a five-pound poppy-seed-size rescued little black pearl we live with. She is the toughest, though. I keep dogs separate from kitties who are not kitty compatible just yet. Most of them are just fine, and it often happens that I have at least one cat with us at the spa for grooming if not on the grooming table while I am working.

Mr. Chips assisting for the spa day

So in my experience, cats, unless they are running or are a visual trigger for doggies, are okay around grooming after letting the pup sniff the cat. They can become an entertainment after proper introduction to the doggies and can actually calm dogs down. Again, if they are running and playing with each other, that means movements that can be leveraged at breaks, but not for nail trimming.

Moving Curtains, Blinds and Other Hidden "Ghosts"

If you have an A/C, it can sometimes cause a smaller heart attack for timid doggies and you simultaneously. It is especially problematic when you're trying to do very delicate work, such as nail trimming. E.g. when the A/C was off and started working automatically, the air moved the curtain. Some doggies metaphorically poop their pants just because of that. So for very timid dogs, we'll need to be extra cautious about the surroundings and possibly provide care for them on the ground to prevent accidents, such as the dog suddenly flying off of the table.

Surfaces

Shiny Surfaces

Shiny surfaces can scare doggies, too. Narrow hallways or stainless steel tables are not the BFFs of hounds. Most of them find it strange, they do not know them and do not like them, so it's a good idea to keep that in mind on your way to the groomer/vet. It never hurts to let the care provider know about your doggy's preferences or work-in-progress triggers.

> **Fun Fact**
>
> Most of the care providers will be pleased to get any info about your dog's sensitivities, so they don't have to figure them out by themselves via trial and error and experience a cardiac arrest. I sincerely hope, though, that the care provider will ask you about it upfront. That is a reassuring sign of a *caring*

> *care provider*. If they do not ask about sensitivities, behavior, etc., I would perhaps proceed with their service, but I would not leave my dog there by himself for sure. Chances are they use the "let's get this over with" method and equipment such as muzzles, grooming loops, and restraints to get done fast. That's an unfortunate recipe for traumatized dogs. Find more info about *picking a high-quality service and a caring care provider* later on in a separate chapter.

Try to think about any triggers the doggy has in advance, so you'll be able to prevent accidents from happening.

Smells

To put it into perspective, dogs have about 300 million olfactory receptors in their noses. Humans have about 6 million. The canine smell is about fifty times greater than ours.

Here is a super interesting TED Talk about the dog's smell.:

(https://www.youtube.com/watch?v=p7fXa2Occ_U)

Smell of Places

Every place has a unique smell; grooming shops, vet clinics, boarding facilities, homes, surfaces, such as a grooming table, etc.

After you've seen the video above, you'll realize how incredibly important it is to pick a place and a care provider who can keep the doggy calm and relaxed. That extends even to smells. If the doggies were anxious in that place before, they'll leave "anxious scents" after themselves, and new furry clients will pick up on it right away. They will be soon wondering what kind of torture chamber did they get to explore.

It is useful to distinguish between a doggy who is generally behaving worriedly in most places and those who are wiggle butts all the time but put on the brakes at the groomer. It is worth figuring out the triggers and working on them, even if it means finding a new care provider.

Smell of People

Every human has a different smell that dogs can identify. I am talking about our natural smell, without perfumes.

It gives dogs a sense of security if they can or are allowed to sniff you (and other pets).

In my practice, I patiently wait for my turn to get sniffed when we meet, let it be at the first time or the twentieth. I enjoy all the benefits of this—a calmer, more trusting, more cooperative dog.

I highly recommend avoiding freshly applied (better yet completely eliminating) colognes, perfumes, and fragrances on yourself at grooming time, if possible. Your doggy will feel such a huge relief, will be super happy, and will probably even reward you with calmer behavior.

Smell of Treats

When it comes to smells, we have the jackpot in our hands. Treats are best friends for most canines. We can do magic with powerful treats and can calm a wiggly pup to focus on us, big time even in scary situations. I have dedicated a separate section to treats since it is crucial to have the right type, size, smell, texture, etc. for the specific happening around. Providing the right treat for the right distraction or trigger will help you level or overturn worry with yummies so your dog will likely cooperate willingly. The right treats will help you reinforce your dog's behavior fast, on time, and or a more extended time without filling him up. Prepare to get a well-behaving pup and to get sticky! See the Emotional Comfort Measures for more details and the most irresistible recipe! :)

The Smell of Home/Excitement

Collar, leash, blanket, etc. are a great way to keep dogs comfy for nail care, mostly when done in a facility. I like to take the collar off and move it in the direction I want the dog to move right by his/her nose. The second I take the collar off I keep in close proximity to the dog to avoid a rush of excitement. It'll provide a steady joy if kept close by at all times.

Please don't say, "Do you want to go for a walk?" followed by not fulfilling what he had hoped for. That will be a significant negative score on the trust board and though it might seem minuscule, it will slowly destroy trust between the participants.

Temperature

Temperature is another factor that we can use to our advantage. Some dogs prefer hot, some like cooler weather or room temperature. I know pups who lie flat in the sun to sunbathe, even here, in Texas, summertime! I know, right? I'm from Europe, and before I moved to Austin, I was convinced I love hot weather. It turned out I had no idea what hot weather was!

With the A/C, we can play around with the grooming area's temperature or go outside if the weather "cooperates." Again, it is perfectly great to do your dog's nails outside.

Some dogs, especially elderly dogs, get so cold on the tile and prefer to lie on towels, blankets, or doggy beds.

If you have a dog who doesn't want to cooperate, spending 5-10 minutes outside together with the dog in the hot weather in the shade often helps them appreciate the cooling effects of the A/C indoors a lot more so they'll be more chill.

Other doggies who don't want to cooperate can often be "domesticated" when you do their nails while they are wet and in the tub. I find that trick very helpful and prefer that method over using a muzzle or other restraints. Again, this last trick is among the last-resort tricks before the muzzle. It works like a charm for doggies who had a traumatic experience on the grooming table about nail care, and they appreciate being in the tub for a change. Of course when a non-slip surface in the tub is provided for the wet dog yoga.

Restraint Options

This section is for those who work in an environment where they frequently meet with dogs in dire need of nail care or in other words that are severely neglected. That can happen in average households as well; you do not need to be a volunteer at the shelter to meet dogs like that. I suggest restraint specifically for those cases when the dog urgently needs nail care and is not cooperating at the moment in a way that makes the care provider trust he can do it without injury to someone. Keep in mind, any kind of restraint works like a pressure cooker. You are working with serious powers, and if you are not mindful and knowledgeable enough, you and others can get hurt easily and badly. Proceed with caution!

Touch

Touch is well tolerated for most dogs, from their owners, at least. From strangers, physical contact—even a stroke—can be translated as a trigger by dogs who are not used to strangers petting them. Care providers count as strangers, especially for the first time. Later on, they can become an appreciated human somewhere between a stranger and a doggy owner. Ideally, closer to the doggy owner status, sometimes they love us more. Or maybe it's just my biased perspective after being kissed forever by my furry clients sometimes.

We can quickly test this on a doggy when we ask the owners to pet the dog. After we get permission, we can quickly determine whether the canine is or is not interested in us. If the dog is moving the other way rather than approaching the dog showing sensitivity/anxiety signs when we try to pet him or us, we'll know that it'll be a long road to love, especially when he does not respond to treats either.

If he'll let us pet him, that is an incredibly good sign that they have at least that much trust in people. Then we can hope for a dynamic change in behavior and a smooth nail care session sooner rather than later.

If the dog is not showing any progress letting us pet him, yet he needs a nail trim, we need to find the safest and most comfortable solution to meet his need for nail care and comfort. It can involve the pawrents, coworkers, new position, and restraints as a last resort to bring relief for the dog with long nails.

Hug

Hugs are a more "personal" level. Many dogs won't be thrilled if a stranger tries to hug them without the introduction first (mine included). Care providers will often need to work on our relationship with the dog to get to this level, at least let them sniff us.

In the case of timid dogs, a hug often makes them freeze. Keep in mind that they are still not because they are thrilled to be working with us, but because they are afraid to say no. Try to use hugs as a last resort and do not use up too much patience credit with them, because these cases can become he bit me out of the blue cases. There were signs that we just did not notice or acknowledge or did not interpret them correctly or on time.

Hold

Holding doggies in the arms or on your lap is another more personal thing for them. You'll have to earn this privilege. A lot of practice, socialization, food, and other positive reinforcements and fun experiences work amazingly. The more dogs see we listen to them and respect them, the more trusting they'll become.

Restraint by Multiple Care Providers

Having multiple care providers help with the dog's hold can sometimes be the safest and most effective way to deal with extreme nail situations. Of course, as always, it's best paired with the transparency and training suggestions to the owners. Holding down the legs the dog is lying on is a great way to keep him from getting up. However, with larger dogs, one person won't be enough to do that plus keep the head away, so we need to call for backup. When working in a team, always make sure there is a "captain" who tells what gets done, when, and how. Others have a say in the planning phase, but the captain leads the work to keep the flow smooth and organized. If the dog is showing late sensitivity signs, you might want to combine this with muzzle/cone or sedation with veterinary assistance to take the edge off the experience. Can't emphasize enough, disclose the dog's behavior, and educate or refer out the pawrents to trainers.

Leashes/Grooming Loops

Leashes and grooming loops can be incredibly useful to help doggies who are in desperate need of a nail trim and indicate an unfortunate lack of training and socialization skills. Often grooming loops help us succeed with nail trimming in those challenging cases keeping everyone safe.

I used leashes incredibly rarely in the past but always went for them before I used a muzzle. Doggies often freak out when they are that restrained around their faces, so you can expect a lot more wiggling when you muzzle a dog, especially when they are not used to wearing it.

When we need to use muzzles and work alone, I recommend using grooming loops as well, since dogs can quickly remove the muzzle. It is not safe for the groomer in those cases to use muzzles only by themselves on a dog that actively fights nail trimming, muzzle, and/or the care provider.

It is incredibly essential to keep in mind that the dog can still move its head pretty far, and can pinch you big time through the muzzle, so triple check your type of muzzle and setting (size, loose/tight) before you go ahead and start the nail care. And as always, if the doggy is not in crazy pain due to long nails, the least invasive and most effective way is to let the doggy owner know what to practice at home and postpone the initial nail care to another time.

Whenever we proceed with higher-level restraints such as leashes, we'll always use our pup's patience credit way faster, which is not desired. It will pay a toll on the dog's behavior.

I do not trust collars in general, since they are often very loose on the dog's neck and can come off in a split second, especially on a dog who is actively trying to get out of the hold. I am generally suspicious of thin plastic buckles because they can break without warning. For this reason, I do not recommend using a collar instead of grooming loops.

Elizabethan Collar/Pet Cone

The E-collar/cone (not the bark or shock collars) can work as a backup plan to avoid the dog's teeth reaching your soft tissues. You want to pair this method with at least restraint or a grooming loop in severe cases because dogs are flexible. And when that is combined with determination, a bloody scene will be likely.

Harness

Harnesses are a great last resort tool to keep dogs desperately needing a nail trim still enough to perform one. They'll still be able to significantly move their heads, so it is not the safest way to go from the care provider's perspective. Harnesses can also be used for disabled doggies to give them extra support if you're not able to or do not have professional help nearby.

Nail Trimming Hammocks

To cut to the chase, I don't like nail trimming hammocks as the go-to tool to do routine nail trimming. The reason for that is people think it's the perfect solution as is. It restrains the dog without it looking like restraint since it's "so cute" and dogs either freeze or try to fight but won't succeed. So the "tool" covers the care provider's need for safety, but it totally ignores the dog's need for comfort. Remember the still vs. cooperative section? If that dog is comfy in the hammock, that's the reason why they are still and "cooperate", they should be comfy without that as well. If they are not, they were not happy there in the first place.

However, I can see this hammock being useful for cases where the dog is tiny, fights big time, and needs a nail trim urgently due to the nail situation (not general "I want my dog to get a nail trim yesterday" kind of pressure from the pawrent). Sometimes the hammock keeps dogs less stressed than an E-collar or muzzle would, so it's worth a try in similar scenarios detailed above.

Please make sure it won't be your go-to tool for dogs' sake because your dog will become a ticking time bomb, super frustrated and freaking out.

Muzzles

Muzzles are one of the last tools I go for. They are very handy though when it comes to a desperate need for nail trim and safety at the same time. Be mindful of choosing the type of muzzle you'd like to work with.

Generally speaking, dogs can get a better grip in basket/mesh style muzzles and can take it off easier. The soft, fabric muzzles all around are probably the hardest to take off for the dogs.

- **Metal wire, basket styles** will keep you safe from bites, and you can even reinforce dogs with treats if they are not too anxious or feisty for eating. Wire basket muzzles rarely fail if kept on. Beware, will you get crazy bruises if you get in the way of a dog that tries to shake it off.
- **Leather basket-style muzzles** will be more comfortable for the dog and for you as well in case you get hit with it.

- **Plastic basket styles** can work as well, but make sure you test the muzzle properly before putting it in use!
- **Tunnel-shaped muzzles** are pretty good if you pick the right size. You will be less likely to get bruises if you get hit with it, but can get pinched between the jaws and that is a nightmare to get freed from. If you pick the wrong size (too tight), it can cause breathing difficulty for the dog.
- **Mesh muzzles** tend to fail due to fabric and sewing errors, so I would definitely avoid those for large, powerful breeds.
- **Mesh in the front, the fabric around the side muzzles** that fit loosely to enable the dog to breathe and open its mouth is not my favorite to go to, because the dog still can bite us through it.
- **Short snout muzzles** can work pretty well if we can manage to keep them on. Dogs with short noses (at least in my experience) tend to be very cautious about their ability to breathe so anything that stands in the way that is not well tolerated by them.

Regardless of the type, picking the right size is crucial since if it is too large, it'll come off or even enable the dog to bite with it on, making it much harder for us to release ourselves from it. Or if the muzzle is too tight, it can cause breathing difficulties for the dog, which can be life-threatening.

When you need to use muzzles, always check the dogs' behavior and vitals. How is their breathing? How is their pulse? In case they freak out of it right at the beginning, I highly recommend stopping the procedure and referring the dog to a veterinarian, and keeping him monitored or probably sedated for nail trimming to avoid any serious complications.

As we have seen, there are many types of muzzles out there; fabric, mesh, plastic, metal, wide size varieties, and styles. From a grooming perspective, a well-sewn fabric or mesh will work best for small and medium-sized dogs. Metal or leather basket muzzles are great for larger, more powerful breeds. Plastic, mesh, loose-fitting ones are soft, but dogs might be able to bite with them on, still causing bruises or more severe injury to the care provider. Mind your choice and plan before committing to a style!

Combinations of the Tools Above

There are cases when the desperate need for nail care and safety for participants requires us to take more invasive actions to meet comfort and safety measures for all. Those are the cases when we need to use one or more of the above at the same time, like physical restraint, muzzle, and leash, or even medical restraint, like sedation or anesthesia with veterinary assistance. In those cases, we'll need professional help on-site to avoid significant injuries to the dog and care providers. One skilled professional for trimming and filing the nails, another one or two for restraining/medicating the dog will keep all participants safe.

If your dog has a history of traumatic nail care experiences and has ever been suggested to get his nails done under general anesthesia or sedation, I highly recommend asking for a professional dog groomer and a dog trainer's help instead of jumping to do it yourself.

Medical Restraints

Sedation

Some dogs get super anxious, afraid, and nervous due to previous uncomfortable or painful experiences, lack of experiences, or other mental circumstances. The only way they can be safely groomed/their nails trimmed sooner is under sedation or anesthesia. Those situations require medical staff on-site and I recommend performing ONLY at veterinary clinics to care for any complications that arise promptly.

Early training or just training at any point in the dog's life, socialization, and desensitization are super important to prevent this from happening to your dog or resolve it if it has happened already. It is extremely tough on the dog's body and emotions. If you do the math, most fluffy dogs need a haircut about every six, eight or twelve weeks. Their paw hair and nails usually need to be trimmed and filed every four to six weeks. That would be about ten sedations a year which is obviously not recommended. Often those dogs get one to two nail trims a year, so their nails will be extremely long by then, they'll be in pain, so it's a vicious cycle. That can be stopped and transformed with attention to detail and knowing what you do to desensitize your dog/client to nail care.

If you are having a hard time deciding whether your dog's issue is fueled by traumatic experiences or some medical issue, I highly recommend consulting with a **veterinary behaviorist** who sees not only the behavioral part of the situation but can detect any underlying medical causes for troubling behavior and suggest solutions.

Sedation or Anesthesia

For the most severe cases, general anesthesia can/needs to be used as a last resort solution to get the dog's nails done. Sometimes nail trim can happen when the dog receives teeth cleaning or other scheduled surgery. Dogs with severe anxiety will be at a greater risk of hurting themselves, others, and pump themselves up so much that they will need medical care to calm them down without going into shock. So getting their nails done at a vet clinic will be a proactive way to keep them comfortable and safe.

Again, prevention and desensitization are super important to keep our dogs comfortable and happy and bring them back from this desperate stage to a manageable one without medical restraint for the rest of their lives. It can take significant effort, time, and money to reach a level of comfort for all of you; however, saying this with all my heart, it is worth it and in most cases, it can be done by finding the proper care provider and approach.

Triggers - Trim, File, Both Or Postpone?

When our clients lack training, socialization, or desensitization (i.e. strays, newly rescued pups) or had an unpleasant or painful experience in the past, they are in pain and do not trust the situation yet, are scared, etc., they will react accordingly to their worry. Depending on their experience with the process we're trying to do on them and the kind of experiences they have had, they will either use early discomfort signs or late discomfort signs.

Early discomfort signs are harder to detect because they are very subtle. Late discomfort signs are straightforward to understand, but often it's too late. We talked about both, so now you have an eye to notice them and come up with the best plan that suits your dog's needs now that is aligned with your future goals to get nails done restraint-free.

Training and taking time to get dogs used to nail care are always more comfortable and faster than desensitization after a stressful experience. However, desensitization is doable!

Take your time; use breaks if necessary, be flexible.

Don't force stuff! No one says you have to get all four feet done on the same day (except when the nail situation interferes with comfort and health, but you might want more experienced staff on-site for that at the beginning).

Elevating the dogs helps them to focus on us. Use treats to reset their minds and keep their focus on you and the task.

Practice the holding tricks and angling the equipment without the dog. Focusing too much on these on a dog while you get the hang of it will bore your dog and he will wiggle more, so you will lose your patience faster. Practice without the dog as much as you can to keep them curious and entertained!

Practice the positionings and the location without doing any nail trimming or filing. Get the dog comfy around by itself, without the "exam" experience.

Don't go wild if your dog doesn't want to cooperate. It's not the military, we are not training "robo dogs". Cooperating doesn't mean someone will do what the other one wants at all times. That is a dictatorship. Cooperation is when both of us are trying to figure out what the other one needs and wants. Then we discuss and make a plan so everybody's needs are getting met.

Sensations - the Importance of a Pain-Free Experience

One of the biggest reasons dogs freak out for nail care is the sensation caused by a faulty way of angling the clipper. It affects dogs who had their quick trimmed to bleed in the past even more, but dogs who never had a nail trim react to this as well with about the same worry. When we learn how to hold the clipper so the cut will be sensation-free, dogs will react less, trust more, and we can get done sweat-free. See the chapter about the nail trimming method itself for more info on this!

Physical Comfort Measures - Practicing Positionings for Nail Care

I'd like to underline the importance of practicing nail trimming positioning before attempting to start clipping. It has two significant benefits—both you and your dog get a chance to get used to the positioning only. That will result in a smoother trimming experience because both of you know what to expect, and the "nail care dance" will be smoother and fewer toes will be squeezed. There will be a dedicated chapter for this as well, just wanted to plant the seed of preparation for a rather sooner joyful nail care session.

Table Manners for You

Another crucial part of keeping dogs still is the way you move and behave around the grooming table. If you stay calm and collected, move slowly with mindfulness, dogs will tune in on that. If you rush, make sudden movements, guess what? The dog will tune into that. They will make sudden, fast movements, too. To keep dogs still, moving slowly is vital. I use cues/requests "stay" when it comes to changing my position, and only move after you see the dog has "rogered" the info.

As a general rule, when you face dogs with full-body, they translate that as stay. If you move your head, arm, turn your torso, and take a step in any direction with any body position, they will translate it as "LET'S GO!!" and move with you or straight out jump.

If you move before the request, the dog will most likely move along with you, even if that means falling from the table. I like to practice table manners without any tools around as one of the first things to get this elevated doggy dance going. Dog gets used to the table, getting up there, he sniffs around, we turn a couple of times, do a few stays there, sit, stand, one front leg up, one hind leg up, so that we get to know each other's body language and requests. Then, I will introduce tools as the next step.

You learn to lead the dog on the table so you'll project more comfort and confidence that your dog/client can tune into.

Table Manners for the Dog

To work with dogs off-leash on the table (to reach the joyful stage), I like to let them sniff around and explore not only on the table but also in the spa. That will bring them peace of mind about the environment, they familiarize themselves with my table's parameters, how it moves up and down, etc. and they will be okay with it. Doing this goes a long way and makes you and your dog/client graduate from still to joyful cooperation.

The Care Provider's Behavior

Whether you are the care provider or looking to find one, care provider's behavior also has a significant impact on the dog's behavior. The work environment, whether he/she is compassionate, his/her previous experience, comfort, and training all play a role in the response they work up to the dog's (and your) reactions and the actions they will take as well.

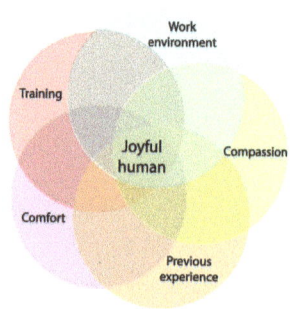

Influencers of the care provider's behavior

The more fulfilled he/she is, the more creative and flexible he/she will be.
Let's take a look at the five groups one by one and what they include!

Work Environment

A salon/vet office's setup and regulation can affect the groomer's/vet tech's comfort and room for custom approaches with dogs. Care providers that accommodate the one-on-one, low-distraction approach are doing a big favor to all pets and their humans in their care. Dogs connect easier to a calm person, especially in a low distraction environment, so that the work will be smoother and less triggering. The following elements also influence the "spirituality" of the business. Calm and caring vs. busy, rushed appointments.

Work environment factors:

- The facility's rules and regulations
- Workload per groomer/vet tech
- Salary (just to make ends meet or enough for financial stability)
- Relationship with other team members
- Relationship with boss
- Number of breaks allowed
- Setup of office (organized multi-dog, one dog at a time, etc.)
- Stress or absence of it

Compassion

Whether compassion is present or absent in the care provider, it makes or breaks the dog's experience. If the care provider is compassionate, he/she will make sure the dog will get everything he needs to be done in a less invasive way to his comfort.

- Presence or absence of compassion

Previous Experience

The care provider's previous experience with nail trimming and dog handling can set the tone for nail care.

If care providers learned to trim nails with the "sit means sit or else" method, they will likely use that very same technique. So it's great to ask the care provider when they use muzzles, will they let you know about your dog's behavior in detail, will they stop if your dog doesn't cooperate, etc.

If the care provider has been hurt before while doing nails or hurt dogs for nail care, they will be nervous, and the dog will pick up the energy. Confidence is vital to help the dog tune in to our calm and collected state of mind so he will be willing to cooperate. We need to work on ourselves to become care providers capable of creating a relaxing inner vibe for ourselves and dogs.

- With the dog in question (bite, growl, etc.)

- With owner (understanding or a past uncleared dispute)
- With the breed (uncleared past traumatic experience with a specific breed)

Comfort

Physical comfort influences how open the valve is to our compassion reservoir. If we are "preoccupied" with things such as the below, we will be less likely to take the time and be less likely to stay calm.

- Health/energy/injury
- Temperature
- Comfort (the comfort of uniform, lack of quality collaboration among colleagues)
- Confidence
- Elimination needs
- Hunger/thirst
- Years of experience
- Family affairs
- Combination of the five groups

Training

Our training and knowledge are a significant indicator of how many tricks we have up in our sleeve to care for dogs thinking outside of the box when needed. The more we know about the task at hand, dog behavior, communication skills, and compassion, the broader behavior challenges we will be able to resolve fast, without using muzzles, hammocks, etc. The more we practice, the better we react with dogs to build trust, comfort, and collaboration.

- Grooming skills (nail trimming, etc.)
- Dog training skills
- Communication skills with humans and dogs

The better we communicate a dog's behavior to their pawrents, the more likely they'll do their fair share of work at home to transform their dog's behavior sooner.

To work on our communication skills, I highly recommend the book **Connecting Across Differences - Finding common ground with anyone, anywhere, at any time** by Konnor, Killian. https://amzn.to/3APCsEB

Chapter 4

The "Thinking Outside the Box" Mindset

Why Compassionate Nail Care and Dog Grooming?

I came across the book "Compassionate Communication" by Marshall Rosenberg and it completely changed how I approach every situation in my life, including grooming dogs. I found this mindset especially helpful for nail care, because when dogs fight back for a pawdicure, their feelings and needs are not aligned, and they feel a desperate urge to show it. The more they fight, the more this simple little method will do its magic.

Most of us, professionals and hobby dog owners alike, can't translate canine communication in detail due to lack of experience in dog training and canine body language decoding. We only get surprised when they bite us one day without a sign or warning. Yet, we could not see the enormous amount of subtle warnings piling up before the reaction.

Perhaps the most significant reason why I wrote this section in such detail is that dogs were always there to comfort me in the hard times. They licked my tears off my face and made me giggle at times my heart was in pieces. I feel it is time for me to give back to them and listen with compassion and empathy when they feel hurt in their standards or they have experienced physical pain and are just reacting due to that.

Ever since I have been applying the concepts that Dr. Rosenberg developed, it has made an enormous difference in every aspect of my life, be it family relationships, work relationships, or my relationship with dogs.

- It changed the way I experience and translate happenings around me
- The way I figure out solutions to "tricky doggy" cases,
- How I experience stress, anger, danger,
- How I explain my feelings and needs, and
- How I translate other people's/dogs' reactions and their feelings and needs such that they may try to communicate with verbal or physical "attacks".

You can find many of Dr. Rosenberg's mind-blowing works online. He has many books and audiobooks (https://amzn.to/2VLO2R3), videos, and courses. There is a worldwide community of the compassionate communication enthusiasts. As a quick intro to this mindset, here is a short and wonderful little video of a TEDx Talk by Louise Evans (https://bit.ly/3hKMiQB). It is only about fifteen minutes long. (See the resources at the end of the book for more details!) I think that is the quickest and the best introduction available to this lifestyle and language.

The method's nickname is the Giraffe language. Since giraffes have the most massive heart of any land animal, they became the symbol for compassionate communication.

The compassionate way of living, experiencing, communicating, and understanding inspired me to introduce the compassionate communication experience to dog grooming, to professionals and dog grooming fans.

Nail trimming without leashes, loops, and force can be an everyday grooming routine for care providers, and pawrents as well. You are about to learn all the tools and methods to achieve an effective and joyful pawdicure for your pets and furry clients.

Pets, especially dogs, gave me so much compassion in the hard times, and they still do. I would like to return the favor and spread the word to keep dogs and care providers comfortable before, during, after, and between nail care appointments.

I introduce you to a leash, grooming loop, muzzle, harness and punishment-free grooming routine in a comfortable, gentle, compassionate way. One dog nail at a time.

What is Compassionate Dog Grooming?

Why should we take pawdicures and doggy spa days to the next level? What is beyond getting all grooming steps done? The answer is joyful collaboration. It's not only that we provide coat and nail care to our pets or clients, but it's the experience that makes it magical for all participants. The bond you build and cherish and the cooperation dogs respond to by trusting you are the gifts of this process to me.

The ease of nail trimming and filing might seem a faint cloud of hope right now, but I promise you will see transformations as you build the trust back between you and the dog you care for.

I find it makes or breaks the deal when we choose the environment we work in, the preparations, the training we put in, and in one word, the mindset we bring to the grooming or exam table. I find it much more fun when we pay attention to what goes on in the other person/species and work as a team. Even when we are not speaking the same language, it is possible to establish a connection and build trust.

I consider nail care and dog grooming compassionate when they fit the following criteria (including, but not limited to):

- The first three priorities are the dog's health, safety, and comfort
- The care provider is willing and able to provide an environment where the dog feels comfortable and free
- The care provider understands dog behavior and body language and is willing to create a plan based on the dog's comfort level, not just rush through clients based on routine care for all (Quality work over quantity!)

- Excluding the use of cages
- Excluding the use of cage dryers
- One dog (or only one household's dogs) booked for one appointment and no other clients present at the time, especially not in the grooming area/room. Arranged supervision needs to be in place for other dogs in a separate room/area.
- The low-key atmosphere, no movements around, no distractions from outside, etc. (See environment chapter).
- Refraining from the routine use of grooming loops, muzzles, or leashes.
- Suggesting behavior modification (or trainer) to the pawrents if necessary (the dog is afraid, not cooperating)
- Gentle holding techniques for dog handling
- Use positive reinforcement, classical conditioning, counterconditioning, and protective use of force (e.g. grabbing a young child's arms at the last minute, when he wants to run into the street to catch a ball and preventing them from running on the street is a form of protective use of force)
- Not using the punitive use of force on dogs "to make them behave" (grabbing the chin hair, ears, etc. and/or pulling on them "because you wiggle you deserve punishment")
- If a dog shows early, especially late discomfort signs, we listen to him, stop, or postpone the grooming step or the full grooming if necessary, and we make a plan together with the pawrent about how to desensitize the dog (Unless the dog's health is in jeopardy. Then we consider alternative methods, like muzzles, grooming loops, cones, restraint by multiple people, mild sedation, anesthesia or combined)
- Providing resources to dog owners to educate them about dog grooming positionings and the importance of exercising their dog right before the grooming/vet appointment to help the dog be calm and relaxed for the session
- Assign dogs, preferably to the same care provider at the time of groomings
- Hairless drinking water access at all times
- No routine ear hair removal. Instead, check, evaluate, and customize ear care plans, keeping the dog's needs and the owner's willingness to cooperate as priorities
- No regular anal gland expression. Owner education about symptoms, prevention, etc.
- No routine ear flushing
- No routine use of eye ointments
- No use of dematting rakes on the whole dog (opening up a few spots and matted bunches where we can get a "comfort/safety grip" between the skin and the matted area to block sensation is acceptable)
- Providing frequent pee breaks (at least once per hour)
- Providing clean water at all times
- No deshedding rake use on a longer coat (such as Pomeranian, husky, etc.). Use a particular type of long pinned, coarse brush, high-velocity blow-dryer, and thorough brushing instead to loosen up the coat

66 NAIL IT!

- Using small, i.e. the quietest hand blow-dryers possible
- Use ear protection to care provider and dog as well for blow-drying
- No use of electric nail grinders
- No use of toenail polish, soft claws, or toe grips
- Nail filing is mandatory after nail trimming
- No use of bows, rubber bands, or silicone bands, any bands preferably
- No use of bandanas
- No hair dying
- No ponytails
- No 3D haircuts (e.g. turtle shape cut in Standard Poodle's hair. Google it!)
- No use of whitening or darkening shampoos
- Excluding the use of perfumes or colognes
- Excluding the use of leave-in shampoo or leave-in conditioner
- No use of dematting sprays, solutions, etc.

What is Undesirable Dog Grooming?

It's essential to see what not to do and what to avoid, so I collected some guidelines for you to think about.

I consider dog grooming undesirable if any of the following applies:

! The opposite of the criteria mentioned above
! Pulling on the skin (dematting) for an extended period when the dog shows sensitivity signs
! Goatee grab (Grabbing the hair by the chin to keep the dog's head in one spot. See images on the right. Even if we smile or tell them to stay still, it won't make it more comfortable for the dog. They will act out of fear or to avoid the pain that comes with when they pull their head away.)

Goatee grab

- ! Hitting the quick on dog nails
- ! Not changing the clipper blades frequently enough, causing skin burn (due to metal blade parts heating up to burning hot). Skin irritation due to too short sanitary trim. That kind of sensitivity depends on the individual dog only. It's like aftershave bumps and itching. Some men get it; some don't. Keeping track of sensitive skin can help us use a longer blade and prevent itching/sensitivity
- ! Regular use of grooming loops, muzzles, harnesses instead of talking with the owner to desensitize their dogs to triggering grooming steps

The images about the goatee grab are from one of the biggest wholesale groomer suppliers out there. I would love to encourage them to educate their groomers/models about compassionate dog grooming and to please stop promoting these painful holding techniques.

I haven't seen a hairdresser grabbing a client's beard like that to keep her client's heads still. In my experience, we can quickly negotiate with or train a dog to cooperate and pick holding tricks that are compassionate, safe, and comfortable for canines and care providers.

The "Thinking Outside the Box" Mindset

Could we generate the "thinking outside the box" mindset? If so, how? Can it be applied to dog nail trimming? I was trying to answer those questions for a long time. Let me cut to the chase, it is possible.

First, to be as accurate as possible, we need to make a clear observation of what is happening, i.e. a step-by-step view of the situation. Then we need to determine how the dog is feeling. Is the dog afraid, excited, worried, or in pain? Then, based on that, we can try generating doggy needs. Which doggy needs are met or unmet in that specific situation where we would like to change their behavior? They may need to relieve themselves or they haven't had a single off-leash run in weeks, and they have so much pent-up energy they can't help but wiggle like crazy on the table. Or they are not used to having so many people around, let alone strangers standing so close to them, so they need some space. Or maybe they have arthritis and are in pain when we lift one leg. Or they have an acorn stuck between the toe pads on the opposite leg we are trying to elevate and feel the pressure of the acorn, and protest against proceeding.

Once we have a clear observation about the situation and pinpoint both the dog's and our feelings and needs, we can develop strategies to fulfill all of those needs. Now, this is a fantastic little feedback loop here. Why? Because once we have met a few of the dog's needs in front of us, they will be more trusting and will almost instantly become more cooperative.

To develop fast working strategies, we also need some basic knowledge about dog behavior and canine needs from a health perspective. We can get close enough to the dogs' hearts so they feel comfortable and cooperate willingly.

Giraffe Language in Action

When I am trimming dog nails, I want to make sure that I am working WITH the dog in question, not DOING stuff TO him. (The same applies to my human clients, and anyone for that matter.)

Here is the difference. When I can behave in a way or alter the environment, choose tools, etc. so the dog feels comfortable, the dog will sense that I care about his needs. He will feel respected and will be much more likely to cooperate and usually do so for much longer.

When we are rushing to get through grooming the dog, using force and restraints on him, and still proceed regardless of discomfort signs, the dog will be exponentially more anxious and a lot less cooperative. He'll either fight us or be so terrified he will freeze. His trust in us and the process gets broken or eliminated and he will do everything in his power to avoid this experience.

Just think about when you suspect someone is demanding something from you. Will you cooperate? Most of the time, we want autonomy, the freedom to choose, and we'll probably do the opposite of what they have asked us to do. Or we'll do it, but out of an energy within us that makes all of us pay for it dearly.

I remember a very embarrassing but also an educational story from my childhood that perfectly illustrates why it is not beneficial to push others to do things they don't want to. On a hot summer afternoon my tipsy dad demanded from us (my sister and I, we were about ten-to-twelve-year-olds) to collect the soft plums from the ground and put them in his barrels for fermentation for his moonshine. We were really not thrilled about it, not only because of the yucky plums but also because we did not enjoy being around him when he was drunk. On top of everything, we were on our way to meet friends, and collecting the plums made us late. Dad left us doing the job and went to meet with someone. We were super annoyed but did not have the guts to not do it, so we did the job with some extra work. We collected a good amount of dog poop as well in the barrels. We promptly stirred the contents as he ordered us and went on with our business. That year, every time someone was drinking from that moonshine, I was giggling with my sister about our dirty little secret.

Was our move considerate? No. Was my dad's demand considerate? No. We all acted out of a place when we were in so much pain, that we did not have enough "giraffe juice" in us to consider the other people's needs. We all paid for it. It would have been less annoying for us if he let us collect the plums the next day. It would have been more considerate if we did not put dog poop in the fermentation, given we knew dad hates even dog hair around food, let alone poop in it.

When we are in pain and can't express our feelings and needs, we will do these tragic things and end up even sadder and experience more emotional discomfort and distance from the other person.

If only my dad had the power to request rather than demand! If only we had the compassion to see his pain, and deal with being late and the aftermath of the moonshine with more empathy. All three of us were in so much pain about the past and the present that none of us had these powers to think compassionately or negotiate respectfully which resulted in a grudge and delicious poopshine.

Doggies are wired the same way. They can bear things for a while; show some discomfort signs along the way, then they'll blow up when they've had enough. And surprise! The dog "mauled someone out of the blue".

When we emphasize and accommodate dogs so they feel comfortable, they will trust us. The experience for all of us will become gradually and exponentially more joyful and fun. When we invest time and patience to build trust, we'll save time, because training and building trust from ground zero are much faster than desensitization and building trust back from the lost faith. Building trust up again after we lost it takes less time than forcing the dog to get stuff done and turning lost trust into holding a grudge. Months or even years later, when you realize just how much further your trust got destroyed and how much more intense your dog's reactions are, you'd do anything and everything to be able to go back in time to today and start the desensitization now.

A symbiotic relationship with our furry clients/friends/family members and their pawrents will result in a forever grateful and loyal relationship. And those great experiences will result in unforgettable memories and reviews so your business will grow organically.

> *"I no longer remember what you did, but I will never forget how I felt in your care."*
> ~ Speaking Giraffe,
> Speaking Jackal Languages

Speaking Giraffe, Speaking Jackal Languages

The Giraffe language was designed and has spread all around the world by Dr. Marshall Rosenberg, Ph.D. He came up with the giraffe and jackal symbols for this "way of life" to describe how we express ourselves and hear others. He has an abundance of practical giraffe tools to communicate in a way that creates a joyful environment within and around us. We can use the method on humans and other species with a little bit of modification. In the following sections, we will get to know the four steps of the Giraffe language for dogs, and we will translate jackal expressions to giraffe.

The 4 Steps of "Thinking Outside the Box" in Dog Nail Trimming

Whenever we translate life happenings to the Giraffe language, we change our perspective on the situation. It does not mean we are justifying the action, and we agree, approve, or despise. We just include every participant's feelings and needs to see the full picture.

In a nutshell, there are two ways we can express ourselves: the giraffe way and the jackal way. When we speak the jackal language, I predict it will be tremendously much harder to deal with a situation so that all parties feel satisfied at the end. Jackals think in a domination "doing to" mindset, while giraffes think and talk to keep both parties as equal members of the conversation. Jackals show characteristics of being selfish or selfless. Giraffes are self-full, making sure to find strategies that take care of others and themselves at the same time.

So a dog's need for a nail trim and the care provider's safety is equally important. Or a dog's need for playtime is just as essential as the care provider's need for efficiency or food (lunch break on time). Let's take a look at how we could generate a translation from jackal to giraffe!

There are four steps in the Giraffe language and how I use them in practice with dogs:

1. Observation
2. Feelings
3. Needs
4. Request (in case of doggies, since we can't talk with them with actual words, we'll be trying out strategies mostly and see whether they work by the dog's body language as a response.)

We'll go through the steps so you can translate canine behavior into feelings and needs. And when it comes to strategies, we can think outside the box to fulfill those needs. It will be magic in action! First, let's look at how most people are thinking and how it affects nail trimming outcomes.

Thinking in a Way that Disconnects us

We have been taught to think in a way that focuses on strategies, who is right, punishments, rewards (*Book suggestion: Alfie Kohn: Punished by Rewards*), blaming, shaming. We get angry, we think depressed, and we judge others and ourselves. All this mindset creates a flow of energy in us that resonates with dogs and generates anxiety within them. Depending on their past experiences, they will either fight or flight. They can tell something is not right energy-wise, and they'll try to get as far away from that (us) as they can. Either by biting us so we'll run or biting us so they can run.

So to be able to make the first giraffe step in the giraffe dance, the clear observation, we will learn to eliminate this "jackal" type of thinking. Below is a four-item list that covers these dead-end streets in communication.

Thoughts that Block Connection and Communication

1. **Diagnosing or judging**
   Bad dog! Why can't you stay still like an average dog?
2. **Denying responsibility**
   Whose fault is it? I can't cut your nails because you won't stay still!
3. **Deserve-type thinking**
   Punishments, rewards. Bad dog! *Slap-slap!* You deserve no treats.
4. **Demanding**
   I want you to do this, no matter what, or else!

When we are thinking in these terms, we think about our needs only or we have an enemy image in mind. Either of those blocks the connection we are trying to build between the participants. So whenever we find ourselves thinking that way, we'll need to translate that to giraffe observation

Observation

The first step is observation in the giraffe dance. A clear observation is when we describe what is happening, step-by-step with PLATO (after Dian Killian.) PLATO means we include **P**eople, **L**ocation, **A**ction, **T**ime, **O**bject. (Who? Where? What? When? With what?).

> ### Example
>
> The jackal example we'll translate to giraffe is this:
> *That vicious little monster attacked me when I was trying to trim his nails.*
>
> In giraffe, we could say: *When I approached Toby with the clippers in my hand, he came forward and snapped at my hand.*
>
> Now, that's a clear observation, without judgments or demands. We are taking responsibility for our actions, and we are not punishing anyone.

Notice your feelings while reading the jackal sentence and notice what is going on in you when you read the giraffe sentence. For me, it was like this when I started learning the Giraffe language. Reading the jackal sentence, I was ready to punish. I felt uncomfortable, scared and wanted to show who the boss is around here. My way or the highway! And when I read the giraffe translation, I started to open up what might be going on in the dog and how we could do things differently to keep the dog comfy enough so he won't see the need to use his teeth.

After making clear observations, I started to see the dog's feelings and needs easier, and my mind soon opened up to strategies "outside the box" to remedies that not only get the nail trim done but also keep the dog comfortable.

Feelings

First, let's make sure we are thinking about the same as Giraffe-speakers when it comes to feelings and needs—they distinguish between feelings when needs are met and feelings when needs are unmet.

I would like to invite you to take a look at the previous list of words that are blocking connections. Often, we mistakenly use those words as feelings. Like I feel betrayed or I feel cheated or attacked. Surprisingly, giraffes do not consider anger, depression, guilt, shame, blame, regret, and remorse as feelings. They think about them as THOUGHTS that they translate into real feelings. To make it easier for you, I have a cute little cheat sheet to figure out your and your dog's feelings when needs are met and unmet. (You can get the pdf version you can print and laminate to make it treat and tear-resistant.) We are so used to saying, "I'm good" or "I'm okay" or "Not so good" that we miss out on using the beauty of the English language to describe what is going on within us exactly.

Keep in mind; feelings change all the time, so keep an eye out for new ones popping up!

> ### Example
>
> Read back to yourself the jackal and giraffe sentences from the previous step. Imagine it's you there with the dog. Notice your energy level in the two scenarios. My guess would be you got angry, deeper maybe felt disappointed, that you were just trying to help the dog, but the methods you've tried did not provide the results you had hoped for. Or if you are a care provider, you might have felt/are feeling angry at the ignorant owner for not having their pet socialized to such a situation. With this kind of thinking, we tend to drift away from thinking about the real needs and solutions for them. We wander away to punishment, to jackal land to give what they "deserve" or just move past it so the sensations will hopefully subside rather sooner.

Now in the giraffe land, we have a radically different state of mind. My guess would be as Giraffe-speaking persons; we might feel worried, shaky, cautious, frustrated, alarmed, annoyed, or irritated. Or all at once and more! Feel free to explore the list below to find out how you would have felt in a situation like this! And try to come up with the ones that apply to you and try to guess how the doggy might feel!

When we are working with dogs, everything is about energy. They can read us incredibly well. They can tell when something is off, and it'll show in their behavior. Once we learn how to keep calm and collected by developing our complex feelings and needs, we will control our energy that will result in cooperative dogs around us. With this new method, we can break habits that have led us away from being connected to life within us and in others. We can now build new habits that help us stay connected to our inner peace and inner peace and joy in others. (Get the printable feelings, needs lists here: http://www.wholesomegroomingacademy.com/page-nail-it)

Check your feelings and needs vocabulary! Visit shorturl.at/emxA8 to see human needs on the Center for Nonviolent Communication website! https://www.cnvc.org

Doggy Feelings List - When Doggy Needs are Met

Calm	Curious	Trusting
Relaxed	Mellow	Ecstatic
Secure	Sensitive	Surprised
Comfortable	Joyful	Astonished
Confident	Proud	Amazed
Energetic	Hopeful	Expectant
Alert	Thankful	Appreciative

Doggy Feelings List - When Doggy Needs are not Met

Longing	Lonely	Cautious
Suspicious	Hesitant	Paralyzed
Jealous	Disappointed	Confused
Shocked	Puzzled	Tired
Shaky	Exhausted	Cold
Hot	In pain	Dizzy
Numb	Bored	Dull
Moody	Disinterested	Gloomy
Mournful	Apathetic	Anxious
Frustrated	Overwhelmed	Worried
Alarmed	Startled	On edge
Afraid	Shy	Scared
Fearful	Sad	Irritated
Tense	Short-tempered	Hot-tempered
Uneasy	Annoyed	Frantic
Rambunctious	Upset	

Did you notice that there are more feelings for when needs are not met? It's because to survive, dogs (and humans) have needed to be aware of a lot more that could potentially go wrong and do harm to them. Animals developed an apparent sense of alertness for safety reasons.

Physical Sensations List

To make the situation more intricate, feelings can manifest in physical sensations and symptoms. Our bodies can also become overwhelmed, which will make it trickier to stay in giraffe land. To get the whole picture and possibilities, we need to be aware of the physical sensations our bodies or our dogs' bodies might experience. Adding these physical sensations to the equation will help you find the needs behind the behavior and develop a strategy that fulfills those needs in the fastest and most effective way.

Hot	Feverish	Cold
In pain	Rapid heartbeat	Shaky
Achy	Thirsty	Bloated
Hungry	Fatigued	Ticklish
Crampy	Sore	Tired
Itchy	Dry	Wet
Pressure	Knotted	Numb
Sensitive	Bruised	Tight
Dull	Dense	Frozen
Shortness of breath	Tender	Tight
Nauseous	Shaky	Trembling
Throbbing	Pounding	Shivery
Wobbly	Dizzy	Twitchy
Bubbly	Tingly	Electric
Burning	Horny	

Doggy Needs

Let's look at the third step—the needs. The great thing is, all doggy needs are universal, so all dogs have the same needs. Everyone has multiple needs in them at all times. If we take a more in-depth look, we can identify them and figure out which one is the most vivid within. The strongest one is the priority, but all the others matter. Collect as many as possible. Our task is to fulfill those needs so that everyone benefits, without having to compromise. You may wonder how that is at all possible. Well, with the four steps, we can meet everybody's needs! Let's take a closer look at the needs. (Visit Wholesome Grooming Academy (https://bit.ly/3B7ZgzP) for a printable, pdf format to download Doggy Needs.)

Check your feelings and needs vocabulary! Visit shorturl.at/emxA8 to see human needs on the Center for Nonviolent Communication website! https://www.cnvc.org

CONNECTION

Acceptance	Affection	Appreciation
Belonging	Closeness	Communication
Community	Companionship	Compassion
Consideration	Consistency	Cooperation
Empathy	Inclusion	Intimacy
Love	Mutuality	Nurturing
Reciprocity	Respect/Self-respect	Safety
Security	Shared reality	Stability
Support	To know and be known To see and be seen	To understand and be understood
Trust	Warmth	

AUTONOMY

Choice	Dignity	Freedom
Independence	Space	Spontaneity

HONESTY

| Authenticity | Integrity | Presence |

PEACE

Beauty	Communion	Ease
Equality	Harmony	Inspiration
Order		

MEANING

Awareness	Celebration	Challenge
Clarity	Competence	Consciousness
Contribution	Creativity	Discovery
Effectiveness	Efficiency	Growth
Integration	Learning	Mourning
Movement	Participation	Purpose
Self-expression	Stimulation	Understanding

PLAY

| Joy | Humor | Adventure |

PHYSICAL WELLBEING

Air	Food	Movement/Exercise
Rest/Sleep	Sexual expression	Water
Shelter	Touch	Safety *(protection from life-threatening situations)*

Example

With this mindset, we can concentrate on our needs and the dog's needs, and we won't be drowned in anger (and depression, guilt, shame, blame, regret, and remorse) and thinking about ways to punish. We will notice that we need safety and effectiveness. We will also be aware of how the dog might feel. Having many feelings handy from both parties, we can pinpoint all of our needs in the situation.

What could your needs in the sample situation be?

What could the dog's needs be?

Check the list and develop two piles of needs (doggy needs and your needs) to find a great strategy that meets them all!

My suggestion for doggy needs would be: need to pee/poop, space, trust, safety, fun, harmony, peace, understanding, respect, consideration.

As a care provider, my guess for my needs would be safety, effectiveness, joy, understanding, cooperation, and closeness (to get the nails short enough).

Strategy to Satisfy Doggy Needs

Now that we have our clear observation, feelings, and needs, we can develop strategies that meet all participants' needs. With humans, we can talk to figure out which methods work best for everyone. With dogs, it's more like trial and error. To determine whether one strategy works or not for dogs, we need to make a list of possible scenarios (when you get the hang of it, you can do it in your mind; no paper list necessary) and give the items on the list a try.

Examples

Knowing the dog reacted by trying to bite us when we were trying to get closer to him for the nail trim, we have a few options to deal with the situation.

It can be that the dog had stressful experiences on the table previously (stool sample, blood is drawn, nails trimmed to bleeding, etc.) where you are trying to do the nail trimming. In this case, the dog is more likely to react to the location or the tool. If you put the dog on the ground with some belly rubs or change rooms and the clipper to nail file, the dog will feel more comfortable and will more likely cooperate.

Another possibility is he got a painful nail care experience in the past, and he is trying everything he can to keep it from happening again. He gets triggered more by touching the feet. From your own experience, you know that you will do anything and everything to prevent an emotionally painful experience (let alone a physically painful one) from happening again, especially when you see the red flags closing upon you. We need to be very mindful about how precise our work is on dogs to avoid further injury and we need to work on their thoughts about us touching the paws before attempting a nail trim.

For cases when the nails are super long, curled back, or grown in, we need to use the protective use of force to help dogs get some relief from the pain. We will talk about those cases later when we put together an action plan for such a situation.

It can be that the dog is not used to being touched and is trying to prevent a future occurrence. Trimming nails without touching dogs is impossible, so we need to develop strategies that help the dog be comfortable with being held, petted, nails touched, and trimmed.

> Perhaps he had a traumatic experience with someone in the past, and you remind him of that person, so he is reacting to that. If you were to reach out to a staff member of the opposite sex, for example, that sometimes solves the problem in a second.

These are just a few examples of what we can do to get the dog comfortable so that he will cooperate.

I am positive that the giraffe mindset is as necessary as the nail trimming method part of this book, where you learn the error-free way to perform trimming dog nails.

I hope you are excited and interested in speaking Giraffe with dogs and humans and you give a try to the techniques shared here on your dog nail trimming journey!

Chapter 5

Training Dog Minds

How can we get dogs to become comfortable when petted by pawrents, family members, by strangers, when on the table, in the car, lying on their sides, being observed in specific spots, when touched between toes, on armpits, ears, lips, privates, paw/toe pads? It is a constant struggle for pawrents, trainers, and care providers to ensure that these different experiences to the nail trimming session will keep the doggy within their comfort zone. It's even more challenging when those steps are happening back to back, like riding in the car to the groomer, being petted by strangers, new environment, new smells, close-up observation, the sensation of nail trimming, etc.

This book's goal is to help you perform nail trimming while always keeping in mind that the environment, the equipment, the method with which you use the equipment, etc. are crucial to having a calm dog.

In this section, I'll introduce a few methods that you can use for preparation and desensitization so that your doggy can enjoy the pawdicure to the fullest right from the beginning.

For doggies, who had a "ruff start" and missed the preparations for some reason, got hurt while trimming nails, or were straight up traumatized, this section is going to be the life-saving first step of the nail trimming journey. We will discuss not only training but desensitization as well.

Dogs behave "good" when they have the experience, training, and exposure to things we would like them to be comfortable with or around. Dogs are not born with this superpower, but need training and supervised exposure to new situations. We can track and modify behavior based on how they react to triggers such as sounds, sensations, noises, smells, etc. to keep dogs comfortable and cooperative for nail trims. Often they experience a ton of things before they'd get to the pawdicure session itself. I find it incredibly crucial for pawrents and care providers to understand that dogs can be "pre-triggered" before the appointment, so it might not only be the nail trimming situation but many previously "skipped lessons" as well. Let's take a look at how a doggy behaves (ideally) when he gets prepared extensively before arriving at a vet office or a grooming salon.

- Doggy is comfortable in the car
- Doggy is comfortable in a new environment (groomer, veterinary office, etc.)
- Doggy is comfortable with a new person approaching
- Doggy is comfortable with a new person touching him from the tip of the nose to the tip of the tail
- Doggy is relaxing on the grooming/exam table

- Doggy is comfortable in different positions on the grooming/exam table
- Doggy is comfortable around louder equipment (shears, clippers, blow-dryer)
- Doggy is comfortable in the tub
- Doggy is comfortable on ramps, stairs or shiny, slippery surfaces

The training mentioned above and desensitization tricks are separate topics themselves. We will learn more about training and desensitization in the tutorial videos since the written format is not the most effective to explain subtle dog behaviors. We will also see how to modify the dog's reactions and how to time your responses, like when to get the treat out, how, etc. (See the Resources page at the very end of the book for more information on the tutorials!)

Whenever it comes to nail trimming, it is essential to determine how comfortable the dog is at the time of start/arrival, meanwhile, and after to be able to make a custom care/desensitization plan.

Let's take a look at some training methods I find instrumental not only in the short-run (fast behavior modification) but in the long-run (comfortable dog not just meanwhile the nail care but also later on on the upcoming sessions) as well.

Bark Jargon - Important Phrases in Dog Training

Operant Conditioning (OC)

Operant conditioning is a type of learning where consequences modify behavior. You change dog behavior by planning which consequence applies for each behavior, and you do it with precise timing and consequently. Keep in mind, the environment around us comes with some consequences of its own.

In operant conditioning, there are four kinds of consequences. There are two major groups. We can either add something to the situation or take something away. (+ -) The effect this has on future behavior can either increase or decrease it, resulting in the total elimination of behaviors.

In operant conditioning, what is getting linked is the behavior and that what follows the behavior, which then has the power to influence the likelihood of that behavior happening the next time.

Wrapping it up: dogs notice that performing that behavior leads to a consequence they like or want to avoid, and they make a decision to engage in that behavior again or not.

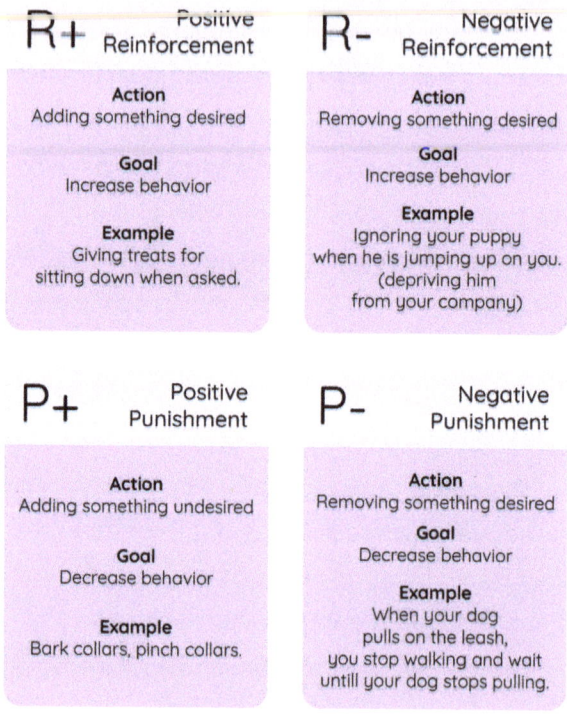

Operant conditioning
1. Positive reinforcement
2. Negative reinforcement
3. Positive punishment
4. Negative punishment

Operant conditioning may teach the dog to cooperate in the short-run out of hope for treats, toys, etc. or act out of fear and avoidance of punishment, but it has its limits to achieve actual enjoyment and excitement for an old trigger. It has the "doing to" not the "working with" mindset built into it. Phrasing it in another way: "sit means sit no matter what" does not consider the dog's point of view, like unknown injury, discomfort due to hot/cold ground, pent up energy due to lack of exercise, etc. could build fear in dogs and both you and dog will pay the price in the quality of the connection between you two.

Let's look at different approaches for changing the dog's emotions that bring comfort and cooperation in the short-run and in the long-run!

Classical Conditioning (CC)

It is a type of learning (first described by Ivan Pavlov) in which a stimulus elicits a response. In classical conditioning, two events are getting linked as they happen, regardless of what the learner is doing. Dogs trained with this method learn to associate a tool or sound with a biological need (food). Associations can happen between any two elements in the environment that are noticed/experienced by the learner, in our case, the dog. This method is one great way to help dogs learn how to be just as excited when seeing the nail clippers as when seeing a bag of treats, their dinner ready, or their leash.

For an association to happen, the dog has to notice the two events *and* notice their relationship. Just because two things happened near each other in time doesn't mean that they will be associated. The more noticeable each event is (or, the more prominent the trainer makes it with timing), the more chance of an association, and the faster it happens. The more you know about your dog, the better you will present the two events for a faster association.

Counterconditioning (Cc)

We replace an undesirable or maladaptive response with a more desirable response with a stimulus, utilizing customized conditioning steps.

Example: Dogs who previously were shaking or hiding when you grabbed the nail clipper start to drool (ready for food), wiggle, maybe even do the zoomies when they see the nail clipper due to Counter Conditioning.

The Basics of Counterconditioning

- **Before Cc:** The dog reacts to the trigger (doorbell) fearfully with barks, growls, attacks, etc.
- **During Cc :** You set off the trigger (ring the doorbell) and give the dog a high-value treat, playtime, etc. (same type consistently for the time of learning) every single time one to two seconds after hearing/seeing the trigger. You repeat the steps at random intervals and many times.
- **After Cc:** Hearing/seeing the triggers, the dog is not sensitive anymore but excited about the upcoming "reward."

Desensitization (DS)

It's a technique very often paired with counterconditioning. We keep the **dog below the threshold (relaxed and alert) and exposed to fears in an increasing hierarchy of intensity to diminish the fearful response over time**. We keep the scary thing at a **comfortable distance and at a low enough intensity** that the **dog can stay relaxed** during the entire training session. Over multiple sessions, the frightening thing/situation can move closer or be more intense, **resulting in a comfortable and cooperative canine**.

I used to run long distances, and I like to describe the process with a metaphor very close to my heart: CCDS is a marathon, not a sprint. My persistence helps me provide the patience for dogs who need time to get comfy around nail care. We conserve patience, and won't use up all of it right at the beginning, because we won't have enough for the rest of the distance.

Prioritizing Triggers for Desensitization (DS)

When doing DS, we need to be aware of the **importance of the intensity of the triggers**. For example, it brings a different level of fear in dogs when they see the clipper, vs. when they feel the cut's pressure on their nails, let alone the pain when hitting the quick.

To determine which steps we need to take and in what order and speed, we need to do the following steps from the dog's perspective :

1. Make clear observations! (What does your dog do when you do X? Use PLATO! (see chapter 4, clear observation!)
2. List the dog's triggers! (equipment, sound, smell, motion, your movements, etc.)
3. List the dog's feelings!
4. List the dog's needs!

To determine which steps we need to take and in what order and speed, we also need to see the situation from your (the care provider's) perspective :

1. Make clear observations! (What do you do when your dog does X? Use PLATO!)
2. List your triggers! (dog behavior, equipment, sound, smell, motion, etc.)
3. List your feelings! (How do you feel about trimming X doggy's nails?)
4. List your needs! (What are your needs when it comes to trimming X doggy's nails?)
5. Break up the process into smaller sections based on how you prioritize your and the dog's triggers by strength!
6. Based on your dog's lists and yours, think about strategies to help fulfill both of those needs!
7. Start to work on them separately in smaller sections!

Let's see a few examples of what can trigger dogs! We'll list them in a 1-10 scale format. One is a milder trigger, 10 is the biggest trigger, which brings out the highest discomfort signs.

1. Environment (visual distractions -movements, certain smells, sounds, etc.)
2. Touching the paws (no clippers around)
3. Seeing the clippers
4. Going toward the dog when they see the clippers
5. Lifting the feet while having the clippers around—not in hand
6. Touching the leg with the clipper around
7. Touching the nail with the clipper around
8. Raising the feet with the clipper around
9. Lifting the feet while touching the nail with the clipper—not cutting yet
10. Raising the feet while touching the nail with the clipper while holding the nail with fingers (conditioning to the nail trimming and filing positions)
11. Lifting the feet while touching the nail with the clipper while doing a small snip off of the nail

We need to practice these triggers separately, put the lessons together, and have the dog pass the desensitization training and be comfortable around nails.

Case Study

Let's say you are working on your dog to be comfy with you touching the paws. After a few repetitions, your dog says, "I'm not ready for that" by pulling away his feet. If you acknowledge the dog signaling his need for space and comfort by touching the leg higher up (or other body parts) where the dog was comfortable before, the experience will build trust in your dog. He will feel respected and heard and will start to trust you again or for the first time ever. Depending on the dog's past experiences and connection with the care provider, signs of trust can show within a few tries to several sessions. Keep in mind, the more trauma the dog had in the past, the longer it takes to work through it. If you take your time and practice, you will build a rock-solid foundation for nail care. Just like breaking up a cracked foundation of a house and replacing it with a new one, it takes time, but it can be done!

Try not to give in to the urge to "let's just do this for a little longer"! Going at the dog's pace might seem to take forever, but it's guaranteed to be faster than a detour due to losing trust again by pushing your speed on a dog that is not ready for that pace yet.

Adjusting your action plan (listening to your dog's body language) will tell your dog, "Buddy, I got your message. We will stay within your comfort zone. I understand it took time to get you to hate nail trimming so much. I am willing to take the time to do better for you and will respect your comfort (keeping in mind your threshold), and you will enjoy nail trimmings, I promise."

By breaking the steps up based on your dog's reactions and comfort level this way, you will build a solid trust between you two and will be able to work faster with the rest of the steps most of the time.

The process is very similar to paying back credit card debt. The more money you pay back over the monthly payment due, the faster you will be able to pay it off since the APR will be less. Yeah, often, that means taking on extra hours at work or side gigs, but you can make it happen!

Remember, if you just kept going with the "let's get over with this" flow as before, you would give everything in your possession to be at the place where you are today. The best time to start to work on the least amount of triggers is right now!

Hand in Hand - Operant Conditioning and Classical Conditioning

Operant conditioning and classical conditioning are separate models; yet they are inseparable as experiences. Every time you are applying operant conditioning, you will be getting classical conditioning along for the ride. Why? Because chances are the learner is actively noticing what things go together all the time. Every time you are applying classical conditioning, your dog is also behaving in some manner and might be noticing the consequences that follow the actions he is taking. While these forces are happening all the time, whether we intentionally harness them or not, the more we understand them, the more effectively we can create behavior change in our furry or less furry learners.

Reinforcer (R) - Dog Love Languages

All canine needs (see needs list) can be the inspiration of reinforcers that we use to connect and communicate that what the dog did we find desired (beneficial or cool). By using reinforcers, we let the doggy know that we would like to see it more often. Try to list your dog's favorite reinforcers, which you can apply to get him to connect the dots between two actions. Treats or toys are the ones most people go with.

Conditioned Emotional Response (CER)

It is a learned emotional reaction or response to a specific stimulus. It can vary by culture and by situation whether a response is considered a desired or not desired one. Feel free to refer to positive and negative ones based on what is beneficial or ideal/not ideal for your household, your situation, and your needs. Keep in mind these might change over time.

Examples for Not Desired Conditioned Emotional Response (-CER)

- ! Chewing on a leash
- ! Barking uncontrollably at others while walking on a leash.
- ! When you have a toddler around your wiggly Labrador and she knocks over the baby by going wild and excited for walkies (seeing you grab the leash)

Desired CER (+CER)

- A dog that sees a leash as a hint for an upcoming walk and does the zoomie (vs. hiding due to getting hit with the leash by the previous owner in the past.)

- a household dog at a war zone which goes and hides when he hears the screeching sounds of attack (we want them to protect themselves)
- working military dogs who are trained to bear through the sounds of bombing and gunshots and keep working with the handlers (we want them to protect military and civil personnel)
- a service dog that ignores people and focuses on the job.
- a family dog that engages with new people around.

You can create a CER for just about anything. In reality, we always are. Most dogs have a strong CER to their leashes, to getting in a car, or to see you grabbing your doggy walk clothes and shoes. My dog gets excited when I open the cabinet door where I keep the blow-dryer for human hair. He knows it's "fetch time" when I am drying my hair. (I kick the ball, and he fetches it while he keeps one in his mouth just in case, ready for the apocalypse.) We have been playing this game since he was eight weeks old, he joyfully got used to the dryer's sound and sensation. Win-win.

My cats go wild to the sound of opening the can of juicy cat food. It helped one of my murder mittens owners to climb down from a treetop once. They act very disappointedly when I open up a can of beans or coconut cream. (Very similar sound.)

Our pets -just as we do- make all sorts of predictions at all times and have feelings related to those predictions. As trainers, you can and should apply this "paw power" purposefully and with respect. (I feel sad when I see people teasing dogs by pretending they threw the ball when in reality, they didn't. That is a great way to ruin trust "in a fun way". Your dog will lose faith in you and will wish you knew better.) Predictions happen whether you are teasing purposefully or not.

Watch out for habits and your dog's behavior, because sometimes even they condition us to do things for them! Toki, my "maligator", (Belgian Shepherd - Malinois, [Mal-*uh*-n-**wah**] French, for "don't get one!" ;-) learned to ring the doorbell for pee breaks very early on. Like around two and a half months old. And he also realized that I would fly to the door when he rings the bell (timing is critical, so I dropped everything to make the connection between two actions -doorbell and pee break- happen). He not only noticed it but also connected a few more dots. He started to do it to invite me for fun runs in the backyard. He is a smart guy, sometimes smarter than me.

Progress

Depending on what kind of experience your dog gets exposed to regularly for getting his nails to the proper length, your dog's connection with the topic and his behavior will either improve fast, improve slower, or will not change. It can even get worse each time in cases when we go over the dog's threshold, especially when hitting the quick. So a precise training method, as well as an accurate nail trimming technique, are critical for a speedy recovery, aka counterconditioning and desensitization. (CCDS).

If your groomer or vet does not use CCDS or restrains your dog for trimming nails (while you are still doing CCDS at home), your dog's emotions and behavior will change a lot slower or will not change at all for the better.

Note that there can be cases that require care providers to use muzzles, restraints or even sedation, for safety reasons for all. If a dog is severely neglected (ingrown nail, pain in other body parts, for example, arthritis) and shows late discomfort signs, we need to emphasize not only the dog's need for nail trimming but the care provider's safety as well. Just a friendly reminder to be self-full, not selfish (I will muzzle all dogs no matter what) or self-less. (I know this doggy, he bit my colleague, the last time, let's give it a go without a muzzle and hope for the best.)

I would like to encourage the pawrents and care providers to discuss possible options for the dog and develop action plans that pawrents, professionals, and dogs alike are comfortable with. We will talk about action plans in detail later on.

To make progress, you need to eliminate methods that are not CCDS based on your dog's experiences and stay under the threshold at all times unless nail care is medically necessary. Finding a care provider who is willing to take the time -care providers should charge for extra time accordingly- is a great way to go. Another way is to speed up your training process and learn to do the paw care yourself. If dogs feel safe and listened to, the CCDS progress will be much faster. So the sooner you can reclaim trust in your dog, the quicker you will see improvement and reach your goal of a happily cooperating dog.

Dogs with traumatic experiences can get triggered faster and more intensely, resulting in a more significant training setback. Once the dog learns to trust, the process will be much faster. Unfortunately, and fortunately, I know more than one dog who suffered a lifetime of getting their quick hit by their previous groomer/vet/vet tech/owner. However, I am glad to know them and help them ever since they contacted me, so at least the future is bright as can be from our meetup and after.

When dogs show sensitivity signs, their fear is just as real as a person's reaction to seeing a spider when they have arachnophobia. My mom is like that. She sees an insect, and she runs knees up high and screams. I can stay calm for "spider bros" and other insects, even grab the creatures by the hand (as long as I know they are not poisonous) or scoop them up with something and evacuate them from the house without an elevated heart rate.

When dogs freak out for nail trims or "just" get stiff, their fear is just as real as the person who fear of spiders seeing one. If you imagine how deeply terrified one must feel when seeing, let alone putting a spider on their bare skin, you can probably better empathize with dogs who are frightened of nail trimming. They might be reliving or imagining scary scenarios and scare themselves even further. Because it is the most frightening thing imaginable to them, they often do anything and everything in their power to make it stop.

Summing it up, the fear is genuine to your dog, whether we realize it or not. It is critical to understand the importance of taking the time and going as fast or slow as your dog can between the steps. Sometimes even the babiest of baby steps are needed. If you can change your goal to listen to your dog (instead of listening to the urge within you to make progress), the trust will restore over time. If you push your dog faster than he can handle and go at or over the threshold, you will lose trust again, and you are likely to be back at square one if not further back. So the fastest way to get to the destination is the pace your dog can handle willingly.

Chapter 6

Nail Care Tools

About Nail Care Equipment in General

Choosing the right type of equipment will depend on your and your dog's comfort level. I will be detailing a few of my favorites and some that I do not recommend and reasons why. If your dog has an intense fear of clippers, you can start fresh and use a doggy nail file. People use Dremels as alternatives as well; I do not recommend them.

With the method I am detailing later, we will not put pressure on the nails while clipping. Dogs respond incredibly fast to the absolute pain-and-pressure-free experience. Based on my method, I prefer using nail clippers and hand nail files, and I avoid Dremels. Even for dogs who get triggered by the nail clipper, I like to desensitize them for it, since usually, it takes less time than to desensitize them for the Dremel. Plus I trust and like nail clippers way more than Dremels.

Having the proper size clippers and all other necessities handy will help you proceed with the doggy pawdicure safely, comfortably, and effectively.

The shape, size, and positioning of the nail will determine which nail care equipment will work best for your canine-human pawdicure team. e.g. If your dog has a wider nail base and thin nail tips on all nails, you'll probably be good with an XS clipper size (or a kitty nail clipper) and a nail file, no need for multiple clipper sizes.

Sometimes our pups have different nail sizes, so one type or size of clipper won't do the job, especially when the nail has curled back and is super close to the skin on small doggies. Those are the cases when we call for our human pedicure equipment for help. Those tools, however, require advanced skills and lots of experience.

I highly recommend that you trim your dog's nails with safety equipment for yourself. Good quality protection glasses will protect your eyes from tiny clippings and will enable you to finish the nail care without a detour to an ophthalmologist.

Get the pdf with the linked tool list here:

http://www.wholesomegroomingacademy.com/page-nail-it

Nail Care Equipment in Details

In this section, I will talk about the equipment we can use to observe nails and to make them shorter. We will discuss the pros and cons of each to help you decide which will work best for you and your dog.

Macro Lens for Smartphone

You may be surprised that the first piece of equipment I am suggesting is a lens. I highly recommend getting one since observing where we will work and what we will need to deal with are critical elements to all participants' comfort, confidence, and safety.

Note: New phones, such as the iPhone 13 Pro Max, are capable of a zoom that will be enough for you, so if you have a phone like that or similar, you do not need the macro lens. For the most detailed looks, though, you'll want to get it.

So as the first "stuff" to get, I suggest a 10x-20x zoom lens for your smartphone. And if your phone has HD resolution, even better. If not, you can ask a friend to borrow his or use this task as one more reason to get one. :)

On the right, you see the 20x lens, and to the right of that is the 10x lens. It was surprising for me that the 20x lens is WAY smaller than the 10x lens. Its petite size comes in handy since you'll need to put these super close to claws to get it to focus and snap a sharp close-up image.

Being able to use a lens like this is pretty much your ticket to a safe nail trim. Once you master keeping your pup still for this type of snapshot, you are all good to go for a nail trim in most cases.

Macro lenses

Feel free to play around with taking images from the side, top, paw pad side of the nail, zoom in, and get familiar with your dog's nails and his layers!

Round-Tip "Pre-Haircut" Shears (Scissors)

Round-tip shears work amazingly well. My favorite brand is Con-Air Pro, six-inch long shear. They cut the hair efficiently and have round tips so you can't poke a dog unless you are really trying. The blades are not super sharp, like haircut shears, so even if you accidentally pinch the skin, you have to try pretty hard to cut the dog with them.

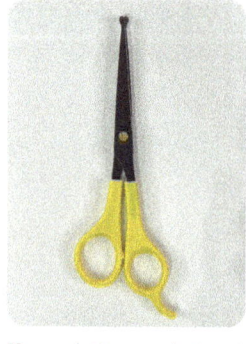 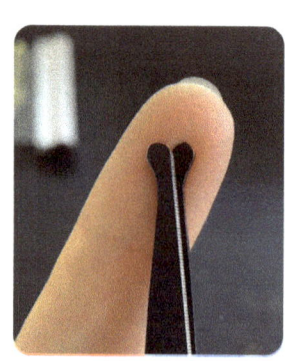

Round-tip pre-haircut shear | Heart-shaped tip for enhanced safety

I use these shears for:

- paw hair trim (paw pad boomerangs, tow mohawks, toenail socks, shaping the paws up)
- eye area trim
- ear area trim
- lip line trim
- muzzle/beard area trim
- sanitary trim for dogs with sensitive skin
- full body pre-haircut (especially on dirty or matted dogs)

Nail Clippers

There are 3 Major Types of Nail Clippers

1. Scissor style clippers
2. Miller forge or plier style clippers
3. Guillotine style clippers
    - Quickfinder nail clippers (guillotine-style)

Scissor Style Clippers

Scissor-style clippers work amazingly well for puppies, small and, in some cases (thin nail tip type), even for medium dogs. I use the scissor-style clippers made for cats/small dogs on toy/miniature or medium-sized dogs. My favorite brand is Boots and Barkley and Up and Up for this nail clipper type, and I got mine at Target.

Beware, the nail file part of the set does not work at all. I repurpose that part for craft projects and though I don't use it on dog nails ever, it is still worth purchasing since this is the tiniest, very sturdy, lightweight, and a most compact nail clipper with finger rest that I have come across. It is very handy because it fits most places when I have limited room between the nail and the toe pad even on the tiniest dogs.

Scissor style nail clipper with finger rest

Breeds I suggest use This Clipper are:

- Puppies of any breed
- Pomeranian
- Chihuahua
- Toy and Miniature poodles

- Maltese
- Shih-Tzu
- smaller terriers, like cairn terrier
- Schnoodle
- Morkie
- Pug
- Brussels griffon,
- Any crossbreeds of the above
- Any breed with the thin nail tip type, as long as the nail's tip can fit into the opening of the clipper

Plier Style Clippers

The plier style (also called Miller Forge style) works great on medium/large dog nail sizes, such as standard poodle, doodles, Old English sheepdog (bobtail), Malinois, German shepherd, the larger size of pit bulls, Staffordshire terriers, great Pyrenees, Saint Bernard, etc.

It enables you to get a better grip and deliver a more powerful clip on thicker nail tissue.

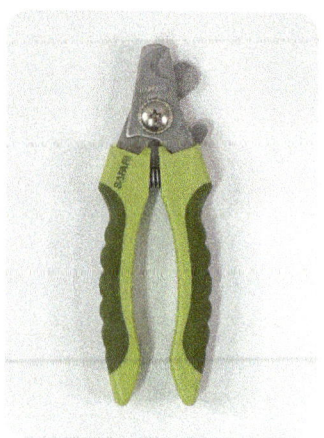

Plier style nail clipper

My favorite brand is Safari, and you can get it on amazon.com. I am talking about the medium size clipper here for the dogs mentioned above. The large size is gigantic, and you have to have a massive dog with huge, thick nails to need those. I have used my large Safari nail clipper only about five times at most on Malamutes and Saint Bernards that had very neglected nails in my career.

Some of you may have questions about why I recommend small-size clippers for large dogs. I love the medium size for larger dogs because the method I use is built on the trick of cutting only tiny pieces off of the corners of the nail. That way, you do not need a large opening between the tips or the clipper's blades, since we are not slicing the nails like when we are cutting wire, but we are sculpturing it like when we are eating a whole apple.

To use the plier-style nail clippers safely, believe it or not, we need to remove the so-called safety flap. See the video on how to do it in the course! You can log in here:

http://www.wholesomegroomingacademy.com/page-nail-it

Note: Once you remove the safety tongue, there will be open space between the blades to see what you are doing. See the holding techniques chapter and the course's videos for more info on why removing it is critical and how it aids visibility and safety at the same time.

Guillotine Clippers and Quickfinder Clippers

From a positioning and comfort perspective, this style is not an ideal tool for nail trimming.

The angle we need for cutting the nail **blocks our vision** so we can't use it safely since we can't see what we are doing.

It has a large metal part upfront, and it **will fit mostly only medium to large dogs**. It's too large for small or petite dogs.

Guillotine style clipper

Guillotine style clipper

To put the least pressure on the dog's nails, we need to cut from the nail's thinnest edge, no other angles are doable in comfort. There are two sharp edges on a scissor or a miller forge style clipper, so you have multiple options to play around with the angling. In the guillotine style, only the moving cutting edge is sharpened; the metal piece upfront is blunt, so it limits your ability to angle it around as needed to keep the pressure off of the dog's nails.

If we want to keep the pressure off the nails, the only way this style works is by angling the handle closer to the dog's leg, where there is no room to hold it that way. With other angles, the dog will feel the pressure due to the blunt edge putting pressure on the nail, so the dog will wiggle away.

Human Fingernail or Toenail Clippers

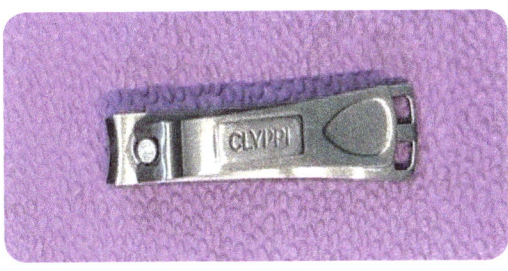

Flat, human nail clipper

Plier style, human nail clipper

Human nail clipper (Clippy) can be used to trim super tricky, "curled back" tiny nails on tiny dogs.

And the thinner, pointed, miller forge style to deal with the same tricky cases on large dogs or small dogs with very thick nails.

On the left, you see the Clippy brand, a flat human nail clipper. This flat nail clipper is great for small size dogs and puppies. It is also great for cases when the regular cat nail clipper won't fit, and you need to trim the nails without space for working the clipper in between the skin and the nail's inner curve. It is small and fits well in minimal space around the nail. The opening is not too wide, so it works on narrow spaces and dogs with small nails.

However, we need to be mindful when we use this because it doesn't have a rounded tip. If it gets too close to the dog's skin and you clip it, it will cut the skin open right away with ease. We need a very calm, still dog, and a steady hand of a very skilled care provider when we are using this type of nail clipper to play it safe.

On the right, you see the miller forge style human nail clipper with the pointy tip. It works great for cases where space is minimal, yet the dog has thicker nails. Again, a safety notice is necessary since it has a pointy tip. You need to be very cautious about positioning it because, just like Clippys, the clipper style will cut the skin like butter if you misalign it, and it hits the skin.

Both clippers require maximum precision and a very calm dog to proceed safely. These clippers are for cases when the nail's inner curve is very close to the skin, and there is no room for the plier-style clippers in there. See the right image below. Those are the cases these clippers are useful.

When the nail is thicker and I have a limited space to trim the dog nails, so the skin is very close, I

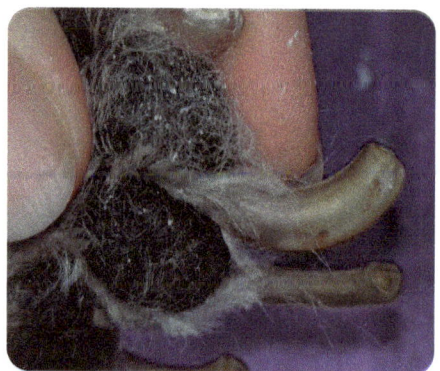
Straighter nail - wide inner curve

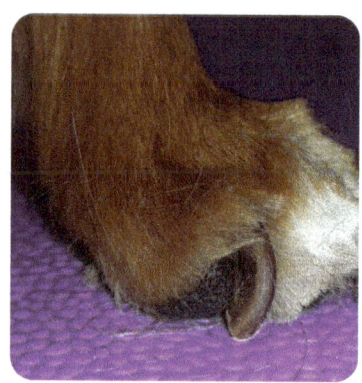
Curled nail - narrow inner curve

prefer to cut only halfway in the nail thickness. So I am not encircling the whole nail, but halfway only. I make a cut, and that half pops off, so I can use less pressure on the nail yet stay safe around the sensitive parts, like the skin.

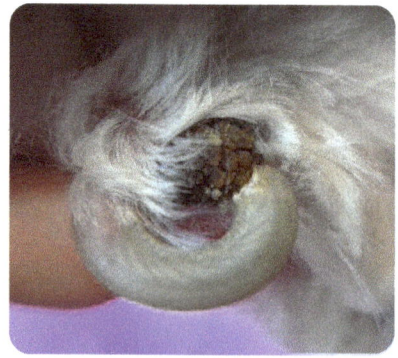
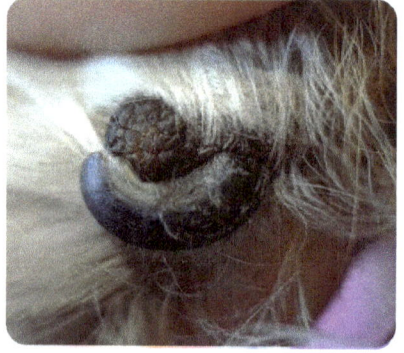
Curled nails - with room (left) and with no room (right) to trim nails between the pad and the inner curvature of the nail

On the left image above, you see a lighter-colored nail that is straighter, so the inner curve is farther away from the paw pad. The toenail itself is long, but it will be relatively easy to trim since there is a lot of room between the inner curve of the nail and the paw pad.

You see a brownish-colored toenail that has curled back and is super close to the skin on the right image above. In that case, I'd use the larger, pointy tip nail clipper (black handle) to succeed without putting a lot of pressure on the pads and nail (miller forge style clippers) and making the dog nervous and worried because of the pressure around the nail that we'll cut him.

You see the light-colored dewclaw, curled back on the left side above, with the tip very close to the skin. However, it is the more straightforward case of these two since there is plenty of room between the dewclaw's inner curve and the skin.

On the right side, that is one of the trickiest cases to deal with because there is no room between the dewclaw's inner curve and the skin. (Again, the color of the nail has nothing to do with the trickiness of the cut. See the nail care myths section above.)

How to Tell What Type of Nail Clipper my Dog Needs

Generally speaking, the scissor-type is for the toy or small-sized dogs (with thin nails), and the plier style is for medium or large dogs (with medium or large size nails).

We need to observe how far or close the nail is from the skin (toe pad).

When the nail is curled back and is super close to the skin, you will need the proper size **nail clipper made for humans** to cut the nail with good access to the horny tissue.

If you can fit the clipper between the nail and the skin (toe pad), then the **regular dog nail clipper types** (scissor or plier depending on the size) will work great.

We'll talk about how to use them in specific cases later in this chapter and you can watch them in action in the Nail it! course.

How to Choose the Nail Clipper Size

Depending on what you are facing, you probably will be good to go with a small Safari clipper for medium to large breeds and a little cat nail clipper, scissor-style for small dogs and puppies. For severe cases, when the nail curls super close to the skin, you will need to use the flat nail clipper designed for humans.

As a general guideline, here are the nail clippers (sorted by size) paired with some typical breeds I use them on.

Scissor Style Puppy/Cat Nail Clipper (Comes Only in Small Size) for Toy - Miniature Size Dogs (and Cats)

- Puppies, adolescents of all breeds

- Chihuahua
- Pomeranian
- Pug
- Brussels griffon
- Toy or miniature poodle
- Miniature schnauzer
- Shih-Tzu
- Schnoodle
- Morkie
- Yorkshire terrier
- Silky terrier
- Cairn terrier
- Their crossbreeds
- Doodles with taco nail type
- etc.

Plier Style, Safari Small - Medium-size nail clipper

- Standard poodle
- Doodle
- Saint Bernard (medium size dog)
- German shepherd
- Belgian shepherd (Malinois)
- Staffordshire terriers
- Bernese mountain dog
- Great Pyrenees
- Husky
- Their crossbreeds
- etc.

Plier Style, Safari Medium - Large Size Nail Clipper

- Large size Saint Bernard
- Large size great Pyrenees
- Malamute
- Great Dane
- Their crossbreeds
- etc.

Nail Care Tools   95

Custom Measurements

The nail clipper's proper size **depends on the nail thickness by the nail's tip and around the "proper nail length" area,** which we will learn about next. (Shoot a few pictures of your dog's nails.)

So first, let's see how wide they are throughout the length of the nail. (See the nail width section for more info.)

The nail diameter at the line of the proper length (regardless of whether we will reach that goal with one nail care appointment or not) **is our best indicator** to decide which size fits our dogs' nails.

Check what your dog's largest nail diameter is at the proper length with a ruler or a caliper, or just eyeball it and give one size a try. (See the proper length in the next chapter!)

Hand Nail File

Nail filing is super important. We detailed what can happen to dog nails with rough edges. The most comfortable nail file from a dog's perspective is the hand nail file from Safari. I find it very comfy and effective.

Parameters of a Handy and Effective Nail File:

- Surface: preferable metal, about #150 grit
- Shape: U shaped so that the nail won't slide off of the surface
- Length: 80 mm for the nail file and the same for the handle
- Width: 13-15 mm
- Thickness: 1 mm
- Weight: the lighter, the better, unless you want to combine nail filing with weight lifting
- Handle: ergonomic, comfortable handle, preferably short, so you have more wiggle room around the dog angling it
- Fineness/grit: #150 grit
- Safety: rounded tip
- Material: metal nail file, plastic or wooden handle

Safari Large Nail File

It works fast, has a curve so it won't slide off the dog's nail like a flat emery board or regular doggy nail file and has a very comfortable handle. It is sturdy, easy to clean, and quiet, so both dogs and care providers love it since the dog will stand still and won't wiggle for the doggy pawdicure.

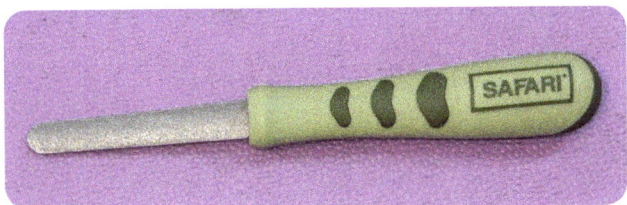

Safari™ Dog nail file

You can use this on toy, small, medium, and large dogs as well.

Emery Board

Emery boards can be a backup plan. The smaller, thinner, the better, and the more room you have. The travel size is good, or cut it with a shear that you don't mind getting blunt. It will slide off the dog's nails, making the nail care session a bit longer and less comfortable but it can work if nothing else is around or you need results on the budget.

Old/New Emery Board + Sandpaper

A working emery board covered in sandpaper is the DIY tool version for the emery board. Use a piece of sandpaper (#150 grit) and wrap the emery board in it. The thinner and smaller the emery board you use, the better, as more space is best for nail care.

Using an emery board will help keep the heat away from the paw pad.

If you want to keep your dog the most comfortable and save time, you can go with the Safari nail file we mentioned. You might go with the emery board/sandpaper combo if you need resolution on the budget.

Nail Grinders or Dremels

See the top ten nail care myths for details at the beginning of the book. These are not suggested tools

Headlamp

Headlamps are fantastic since you have the flexibility to move around; you are not tied to light fixtures on the ceiling or walls. You can be mobile and go with the dog wherever he feels comfortable. You can do nail care even on the couch. I suggest a bright one, with a couple hundred lumens at least to see everything very well. Try not to make eye contact with the dogs when you use headlamps; it's not comfy for them to look into the bright light. Use treats, ear/butt rubs, and your voice for reinforcement instead.

Another essential feature is to be able to rotate the light up/down. Super important: your neck will be glad if you pick a lamp that has this feature.

Brush

Some pups arrive at the nail care appointment with muddy nails. In those cases, the first step is a foot soak and a good brushing on the nails to clean them so we'll see the layers well. A soft nail brush or a toothbrush works great. Try to **get a soft brush** and do not press down too hard, as the nail bed's skin is pretty sensitive, just like on our hands and feet.

Treats - Toys

See the dedicated sections for more information.

Knee Pads/Gardening Pads/Towels/Pillows

Knee pads are very comfortable for a more extended nail trim session on the ground where you have to favor an elderly or disabled dog and move around or kneel/sit comfortably.

Elderly pups often have a hard time standing for a long time even on four feet, not to mention nail care on three feet. So I work around them and knee pads are beneficial.

Towels are an excellent replacement for knee pads, and you can use them under the doggy if you are working on a skinny or elderly canine. It works great under your butt, too, if you are working on the cold tile.

Pillows work great for butt support for care providers and you don't have to worry about unfolding towels as you change positions.

Grooming Loops, Muzzles, Hammocks

I prefer desensitizing/training doggies to get used to nail care instead of using leashes or muzzles. However, sometimes the dog's nails are in such bad condition that even though the dog is not cooperating, the benefits of relief from painful nails outweigh the possible discomfort of being restrained.

For those hopefully rare occasions when the doggy won't cooperate but desperately needs a doggy pedicure, or cooperates at the beginning but the nails have grown closer to the skin so the dog might react for nail trimming, we have a few options to work with.

Grooming Loops
The least restrained option is a grooming loop hooked to a groomer's arm. Most dogs are okay with that, since it keeps them pretty mobile, yet it protects the care provider.

There can be situations when the doggy is badly traumatized (won't even let us touch him at all), he may need a second helper around the waist.

Muzzles
For doggies who can't stand for that long (paw hair trim, nail trimming, and filing) and they are reactive, we can use a muzzle and the coworker's help.

Using muzzles alone on a reactive dog is not safe, so use a coworker or a grooming loop as an additional safety measures as well!

Grooming Loops and Muzzles
We can combine the two for cases where the dog is snapping at the tool or at us, to prevent injury.

Cones to Keep the Head Away

Cones can be very beneficial to keep the head of a reactive dog away from us if the dog desperately needs his nails done. Having a variety of sizes handy or the one that fits the dog will make it a safe way to proceed in dire cases. You can use the cone in combination with a coworker's help (holding the dog) or in combination with grooming loops and/or muzzles.

Using cones alone on a reactive dog is not safe, so use a coworker or a grooming loop as additional safety measures as well!

Styptic Powder or Groomers' Super Glue

See the First Aid section for more information.

These measures are a backup plan, but they'll just expire on you untouched by this technique you are learning about.

Nail Care Equipment Care

- Alcohol or Disinfectant Spray/Liquid (clipper disinfectant will do)
  Spray down before and after each dog. Let it dry.

- Oiling (clipper oil will do)
  Use one drop on each side by the fastener in the middle. Wiggle the arms a bit and wipe off any access oil. Do it before you put your clipper away for the day.

Shear, Nail Clipper Care

The same disinfectant spray and oil will work what you use for clippers on both. Clean the shears and clippers before, and after each use. Towel dry them and oil them before putting them away to keep them sharp and last long for you. Before use, wipe away any leftover oil. Keep them in a pouch so the humidity won't get to them.

Nail File Care

Use the disinfectant spray before and after each use; there is no need to oil the nail file. Keep it in a pouch so humidity and rust won't get to it.

Links to Recommended Equipment

To download a pdf about the most up-to-date nail care tools with clickable links to buy them, go to http://www.wholesomegroomingacademy.com/page-nail-it and download the list!

List of Equipment to Avoid

- Low quality, old, dull, or rusty nail clippers. We do not want rusty things anywhere around nail trimming due to Tetanus bacteria.
- Guillotine-type nail clipper, including the "Quickfinder" style.
- Plier style nail clippers with the stopper blocking the view (you can't see what you are doing. Injury is guaranteed. Get the stopper/tongue off or move it out of the way)
- Low-quality nail files with grit that do not file the nail smoothly.
- Nail grinders (also called Dremel)
    - Standard electric nail grinders
    - Rechargeable (cordless) nail grinders
    - Heavy-duty nail grinders
    - Nail grinders with the safety cap

Chapter 7
Canine Anatomy in a Nutshell

A well-built canine given enough exercise is likely to take care of and wear down his nails naturally. A lot depends on the legs' positioning, how the dog is walking, running, etc.

We are going to explore the topic without exhausting all malformations or deformations.

Nowadays many breeds' bodies are covered with a long coat, so it's trickier to observe their structure. Combining that with how groomers are trained to hide malformations with a "correcting haircut", it is harder to spot abnormalities that can cause trouble for dogs wearing down nails than ever.

Many breeds have some characteristics, making it incredibly hard for them to keep their nails the proper length. Others will wear down their nails to a raw stage on some nails due to their feet/legs' shape, weight, etc.

The Positioning of the Front Legs

Based on the positioning of the front legs, some dogs might need less or more assistance for wearing off their nails. Let's take a look at the front legs to familiarize ourselves with body shapes and leg positionings.

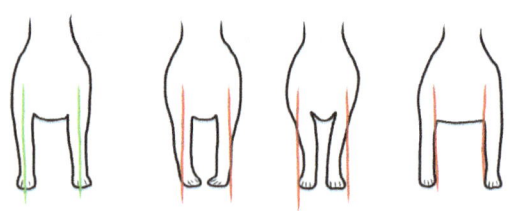

Positioning of the front legs
1. Standard, straight front
2. Pigeon-toed front
3. Narrow front
4. Wide front

On the first drawing, we see the **standard, straight front** (green lines). Dogs who are built similarly will more likely be able to wear off their nails as long as they get enough fun runs. Walking a few miles a day on a leash will not do the trick in most cases, even for the best-shaped canines.

The **pigeon-toed front** is visible on the second dog drawing from the left. Dogs with this type of front legs will probably need help with nails, even when exposed to enough exercise. They will be more likely to develop pain in their feet, pawrents might notice the dogs licking their feet, discolored hair around feet following the frequent licking, etc. When structural pain develops, the dog will be less likely to move around due to pain, and even more frequent nail trimming is necessary. Dogs with pigeon toes more often than not need assistance with nail care.

The narrow front on the third drawing shows a narrow stand on the front legs. Dogs with narrow front stand also need assistance with their nails.

The wide front on the fourth drawing shows how it looks when dogs have a wider gap between the front legs when standing. They are more likely to wear off all four toenails by themselves when exposed to enough exercise. Though they are at higher risk for joint pain due to more workload on the upper leg/shoulder area.

Shape of the Front Legs

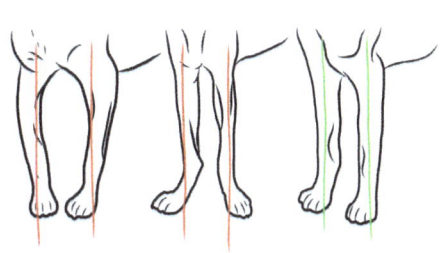

Shape of the front legs
1. O-shaped legs
2. X-shaped legs
3. Straight legs

Compared to each other, the legs' positioning tells a lot about the nail quality before looking at the nails. We can also get some extra information about possible joint pain and resistance for lifting legs, feet, etc. by knowing more about the shape of the front legs. The first image shows a dog with **O-shaped legs**. The middle doggy has **X-shaped legs**. The one on the right has **straight legs**. Dogs who have O or X-shaped legs will have a more challenging time filing their nails and will be more likely to experience joint pain in their lower leg and feet later on. They can have one longer or shorter leg, which causes extra pressure, work, and discomfort in the body. Dogs with O and X-shaped legs will be more likely to frequently adjust or change their position when you are doing the nail trimming while they are standing on three feet.

When you are working on dogs with O or X-shaped legs, lift the legs slower and keep an eye out for the adjustment hop before doing the first clipping. To avoid injury, give the dog a second to adjust and wait with the cutting and filing to keep them comfortable and prevent injury.

Shape of the Feet

The shape of the feet also significantly influences whether the dog needs or is less likely to need help with his nails. It also affects whether the dog will develop pain around the paw. On the two left foot drawings, you see the **cat foot shape**. The foot is tightly shaped and rounded. Dogs with this foot type will be less likely to develop pain around their feet, be more likely to have a better balance, and stay more active in their golden years.

On the right side, you see the **hare foot shape**. The foot is loosely built, spreads out, is more expansive, and the toes are farther apart. The shape of the foot is more oval, and the toes stretch out farther toward

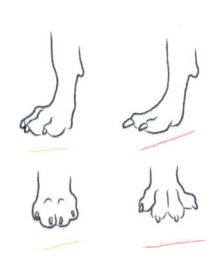

Shape of the feet
1. Cat foot shape (left two)
2. Hare foot shape (right two)

the toenails. If you compare the green and red lines, you see the difference in length and width between the two foot types. Dogs with a hare foot structure will have a more challenging time filing their nails, but they can wear them off in some cases.

They will likely need different sizes of doggy shoes for the feet shaped this way, so keep in mind to order the appropriate sizes.

Hind Legs

Shape of the hind legs
1. Normal stand
2. Narrow stand
3. X-shaped stand
4. O-shaped stand

The hind legs' shape also affects how effective dogs will be wearing off their nails while running and walking around.

Generally speaking, often dogs need less assistance for the hind nails than for the front ones since they wear them off easier with more weight on the back parts when getting up, jumping, etc.

In the first image, you see the doggy hindquarters with a **normal stand**. Legs are parallel and horizontal. Dogs built this way will have the most leisurely time wearing their nails most effectively while living their everyday doggy lifestyle.

On the second doggy rear-end drawing, you see the **narrow stand**. Dogs with this build will most likely be able to wear off their nails themselves. However, just like narrow front legs, they will be more likely to develop pain and discomfort higher up on their legs and hips later down the road.

On the third woofer booty drawing, you see an **X-shaped stand**. We probably will need to provide some assistance with their toenails. Joint pain and uneven wearing on bones are likely over the years.

On the fourth canine rump drawing, you see the **O-shaped stand**. Dogs who stand this way will likely be able to file their two inner nails but will need help with the outer two. Depending on the foot shape and positioning, they might need assistance with nail trimming on all fours.

Hind Legs While Moving

The way the canine moves and positions the legs is also crucial in how well the dog himself will wear off the nails.

In the first drawing, you see a dog who is keeping his **legs normal and parallel**. It is easy for the dog to wear all four toenails off naturally on each foot.

On the second drawing, you see the **legs worn close together**, inwards while walking/running. The two outer nails will probably be shorter on the canine in these situations.

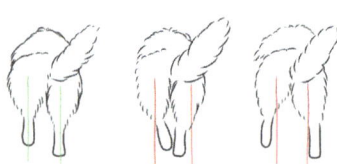

Hind legs while moving
1. Normal, parallel legs
2. Legs worn close together
3. Widespread

In the third drawing, the doggy is walking/running in a **widespread** of the hind legs. They might be able to file the nails themselves.

Dog Nail Anatomy

Nail Types By Location on the Leg

Toenails

Most dogs are born with four toenails on each foot, and they are located on the front of each paw unless the dog had a genetic malformation or an injury. So an average four-legged dog has sixteen toenails.

They are usually very mildly curved, but if they are left to grow longer, they can twist sideways or curl back up to 360 degrees by the nail base and cause a lot of pain for the dog if they grow into the skin.

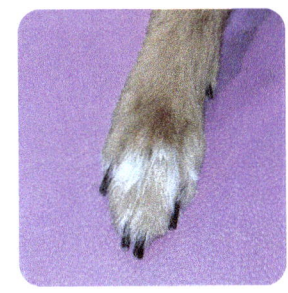
Toenails

Dewclaws

Dewclaws are located on the inner side of the legs, a bit higher than the toenails are. Most dogs are born with one dewclaw on each front foot. Dewclaws can be firmly or loosely attached. They provide the most benefit when they are firmly attached.

Dewclaws are beneficial, and there are excellent reasons to keep them. Dewclaws help dogs get out of icy water or steep, slippery, rocky surfaces more efficiently, and help them work faster while digging. Many doggies hold toys and food better between their paws while eating/playing on the ground.

When the dewclaw is loosely attached and the nail is taken care of properly, given they are not that beneficial, in my opinion, it is still not enough that would justify going as extreme as removing it. Usually, they are well covered with fur and are not in the way for everyday activities.

However, if you take a look at doggy feet in the US, you often only see four toes and no dewclaws. It's because of an unfortunate procedure of getting the dewclaws removed. The mutilation (let's call it what it is) is done around the time of birth most often without pain management to achieve a "cleaner look" and/or to avoid getting caught in things as a "well-intended precaution". It is a popular "procedure" in the U.S., unfortunately. Wonder no more why so many dogs are protective about their paws! They might not have been able to fight against the removal of dewclaws as newborns, but the pain and discomfort remain and they will tell all about it in their own way.

> **Fun Fact**
>
> Dogs can have one dewclaw on each foot but can even have double or triple dewclaws on one foot. The front dewclaws are firmly and closely attached to the bone and muscles in most cases; however, sometimes, they can be attached loosely.

> Most of the time, the loose attachment is on the hind legs. If we are talking about a second dewclaw on the same leg, that is usually also attached like a flap of skin with a smaller dew claw hanging at the end.

It is important to note that dewclaws, regardless of the type and number of attachments present, are not dead appendages. They are fully alive parts of the dog with blood vessels and nerve endings, and they need mindful attention when it comes to nail care.

For some breeds, the front dewclaws touch the ground when the dog is running, which helps to gain traction, so they wear down naturally when the dog is exposed to outdoor exercise regularly in a large backyard or on an appropriately sized field, or enough doggy gardening by digging holes if that's their thing.

If they do not touch the ground or the dog is not running or digging "enough" to wear them down, the doggy needs regular nail care appointments for the dewclaws.

Dewclaws tend to curl back and, if not taken care of, grow into the skin, which is extremely painful for the dog, as you can imagine. The great news is that it is super easy to figure out when your dog needs a doggy pawdicure session. We'll get into greater detail on this in the upcoming chapters.

> ### Fun Fact
> Some dog breeds even require double dewclaws as a standard for the breed, like great Pyrenees or the Norwegian Lundehund. Yep, there are polydactyl dogs as well, not just kitties.

"Other breeds with rear dewclaws are:
- Portuguese sheepdog (single or double)
- Icelandic sheepdog (double preferred)
- Cão Fila de São Miguel (single)
- Saint Bernard
- Estrela mountain dog (single or double)
- East Siberian Laika
- Anatolian shepherd dog (double)
- Beauceron (double; they should be close to the foot to provide a larger weight-bearing surface)
- Catalonian sheepdog (double and joined together)
- Briard (double; close to the ground)

"**The polydactyl champ is the Norwegian Lundehund,** which has at least six toes on each foot. These dogs climbed craggy rocks searching for puffin birds, using their extra toes to help keep a good grip. Unlike other breeds whose extra toes are almost exclusively limited to the rear feet, they occur on all four feet in the Lundehund and appear to be caused by different genes. The Norwegian Lundehund should have at least six toes and eight pads on the front paws, and five toes should rest on the ground. The rear feet should have at least six toes, four of which should rest on the ground. The toes even have extra joints, said to aid in its climbing dexterity. The Lundehund has at least six toes on each foot to help with climbing rocks. According to ZorroIII/Wikimedia Commons, the Lundehund has at least six toes on each foot to climb rocks. The Lundehund is a rare breed, so rare it has little genetic diversity. Not only does it have enough toes to run out of little piggies going to market, but it's also the most limber dog in existence, able to spread its front *legs to the side like a fisherman expounding on the one that got away, and to touch its head to its back like a teenage gymnast. Nobody knows if these traits could be genetically related. The Lundehund remains one of the most mysterious and threatened of breeds." From Petcha.com http://www.petcha.com/which-dog-breeds-have-the-most-toes/*

Rear Dewclaws and Second or Loose Dewclaws

Some rear dewclaws are firmly attached to the skin and muscles, even on the hind legs. They look and feel just like the front dewclaws.

Most often, though, the rear dewclaws are loosely attached to the skin and leg. In those cases, it is much easier to get to see the "opening of the nail" because you can move the dewclaw around. You can quickly just get a hold of the dewclaw and gently twist it to the desired angle without causing any pain to the dog or having to lift the leg up at all. See the images for guidelines.

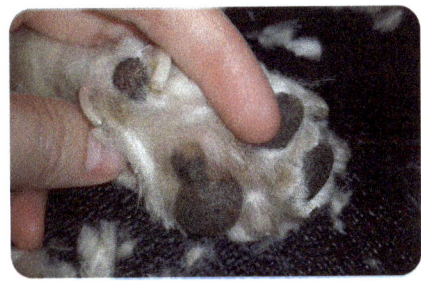
Double dewclaw on the rear foot

Declawing - say no to unnecessary and painful amputation!

Say no to mutilation! You have the power to stop this madness! You, as a dog owner, can put your foot down and can request the breeder to not remove the dewclaws from your puppy.

You, as a veterinary technician or a veterinarian, can educate the owners and can say no to owners or breeders requesting removing the dewclaws.

Take the dog's side and help them avoid a traumatic and painful experience right after birth!

The Structure of the Nail

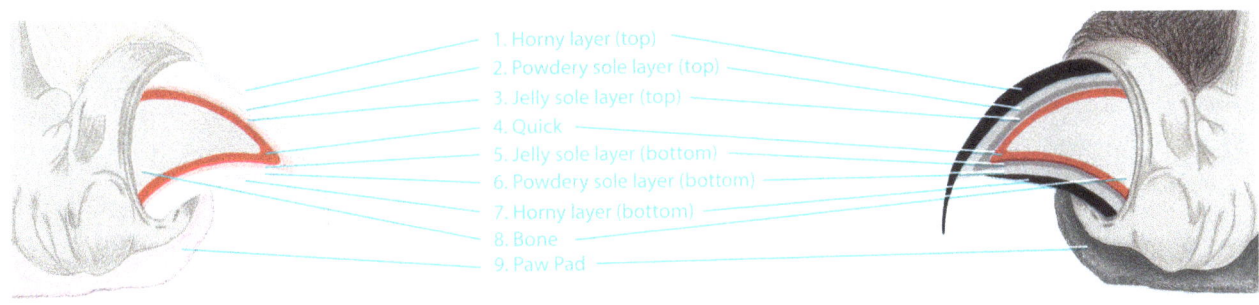

1. Horny layer (top)
2. Powdery sole layer (top)
3. Jelly sole layer (top)
4. Quick
5. Jelly sole layer (bottom)
6. Powdery sole layer (bottom)
7. Horny layer (bottom)
8. Bone
9. Paw Pad

Layers of the Taco nail type - drawing

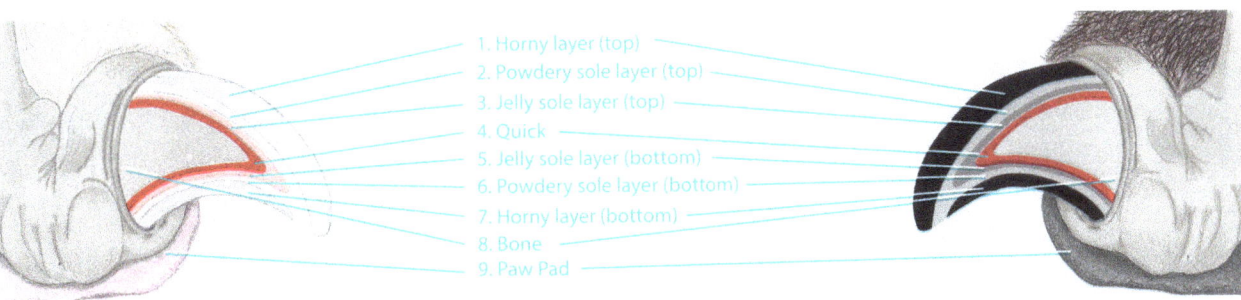

1. Horny layer (top)
2. Powdery sole layer (top)
3. Jelly sole layer (top)
4. Quick
5. Jelly sole layer (bottom)
6. Powdery sole layer (bottom)
7. Horny layer (bottom)
8. Bone
9. Paw Pad

Layers of the Hot dog nail type - drawing

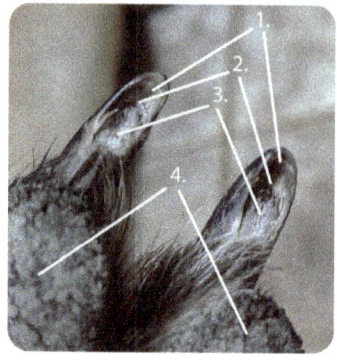 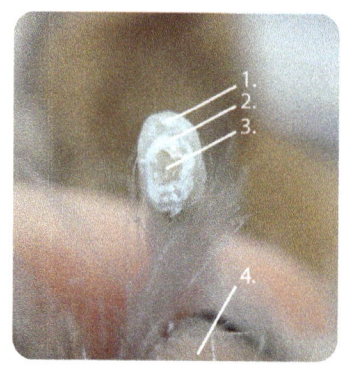 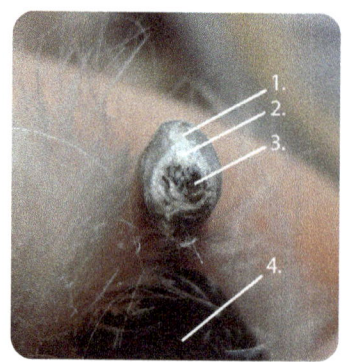

Nail layers in real life - paw pad view

Taco nail type (left)
1. Horny tissue
2. Stop sign (soft tissue meets horny tissue)
3. Soft tissue
4. Toe pads

Hot dog nail type (middle and right)
1. Horny tissue
2. Powdery sole layer (soft tissue)
3. Stop sign, Jelly sole layer (soft tissue)
4. Toe pads

About the Nail Structure in General

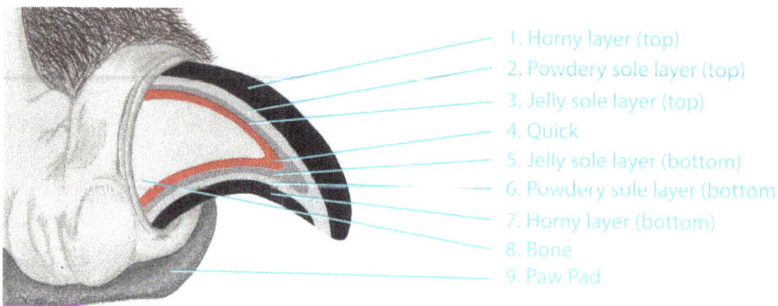

1. Horny layer (top)
2. Powdery sole layer (top)
3. Jelly sole layer (top)
4. Quick
5. Jelly sole layer (bottom)
6. Powdery sole layer (bottom)
7. Horny layer (bottom)
8. Bone
9. Paw Pad

Hot dog nail type - drawing, side view

It is not just practicing nail trimming that keeps us safe but also the matter of a solid understanding of nail structure, positioning the dog, the equipment, and ourselves, and many other circumstances happening all at once.

This section is probably the most crucial part: the nail structure itself. We will cover topics such as the skin, bone, quick and sole layers, and all their characteristics so that you'll be able to successfully analyze your dog's nails at home to prepare for the pedicure and to make it happen without sweating and bleeding.

Let's start with the skin and bone; then we'll go from the nails' outer side, the horny tissue toward the inner side, the layers of the soft tissues. This way you'll see the most familiar parts first—horny tissue, and as we dig deeper, just as we will at the time of the nail care, you will get to see the other layers of the nail and explore where to stop the process without bleeding.

Skin

The skin (epidermis) is the outer layer, covering the dog's full body. It looks like a sleeve, where the nail is embedded, just like your gloves into the sleeve of your jacket when you're off skiing. It is full of blood vessels, nerve endings, and is pretty thin and sensitive at this part of the body. We will need to be very mindful and gentle with our shears around here.

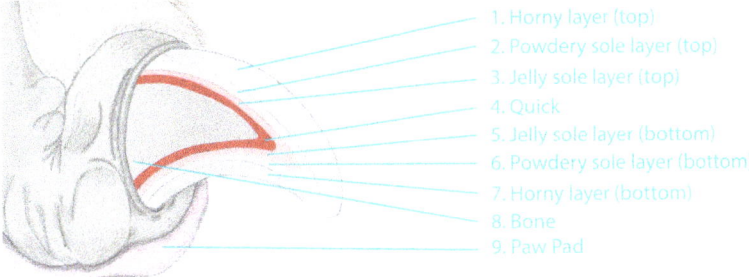

1. Horny layer (top)
2. Powdery sole layer (top)
3. Jelly sole layer (top)
4. Quick
5. Jelly sole layer (bottom)
6. Powdery sole layer (bottom)
7. Horny layer (bottom)
8. Bone
9. Paw Pad

Hot dog nail type - drawing, side view

Bone

Hopefully, you'll never see this layer in real life, only in drawings. This layer is also pretty rich in blood vessels and gives the shape and attaches the nail to the rest of the body with a solid foundation. It is the most inner layer. It has blood vessels and nerves.

Horny tissue

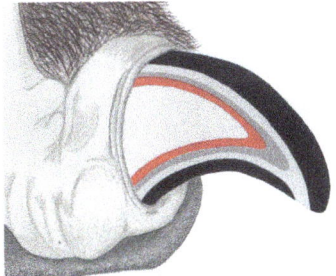

Hot dog nail type, black layers are the horny tissue

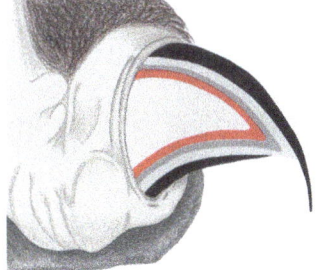

Taco nail type, black layers are the horny tissue

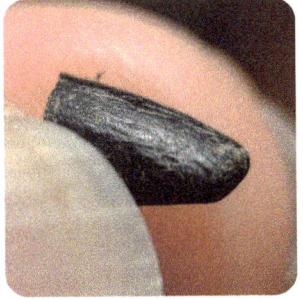

Tip cutling of the taco nail type, top/side view

Tip cutling of the taco nail type, bottom view

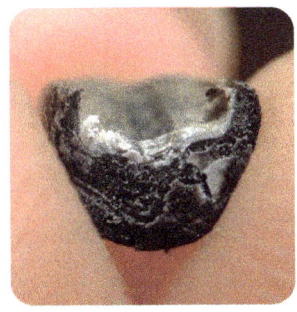

Tip cutling of the taco nail type, cut line view

Description of the Horny Layer
The epidermis of the skin has been modified in this area into a hard, protective, horny layer, which is the wall of the nail. This horny tissue does not have any nerve endings nor blood supply. The horny layer is the layer which we'll work on the most when we are cutting or filing dog nails.

Texture of the Horny Layer
Firm, Shiny.

Color of the Horny Layer
Since I don't think I will ever get to collect all the nail color shades and nail patterns, I would like to show you a few here to give you an idea. If you get hungry for more than that, I'd be glad to invite you over to my nail image gallery so you can see the incredible diversity of nail colors. Just email me at betty@WholesomeGroomingAcademy.com and I'll send you a link.

Color of the horny layer:

- Clear
- White
- Brown
- Black
- Gray
- Multi-Color
  - Striped
  - Dotted
  - Spotty
  - Smokey
- Variations of the above

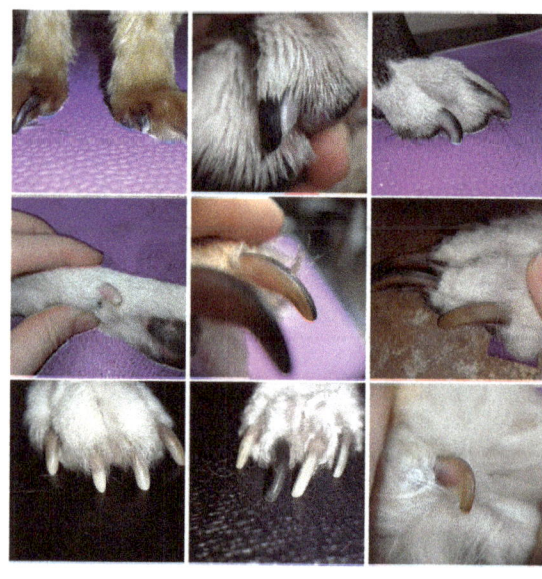
Nail color variations

You may ask okay, but how am I going to be able to tell what applies to my dog's nail color(s) and how can I still stay safe while cutting his nails since there is such a significant diversion here in color?

Well, the great news is that with the guidelines and rules we'll talk about in a few pages, you will be able to figure out how to stay safe.

There are many colors of the horny nail tissue, and there are only two soft sole tissue colors. That is the topic we'll dig deeper into in the next part to get the answer to your question. So read on!

Unique zebra nails

Location of the Horny Layer
The horny nail tissue is the most outer layer of the nail. You can see it from the sides, from the top, and from the bottom as well. It encircles the soft tissues. See the nail tip types section for more relating images about the shapes of the horny tissue.

Shape of the Horny Layer
Circle, oval, or horseshoe-shaped depending on the nail type and the part of the nail we are analyzing.

Dog's Sensations When We are Working on the Horny Layer
Since this layer is the hardest part of the toenail which we'll deal with, it is vital to keep it in mind that if we squeeze this layer with clippers, it'll cause a squeezing sensation on the soft tissue layers underneath. That sensation will make dogs react to nail trimming big time.

That is why it is super important to cut only the tiny edges off of the nails, very thin layers (less than 1 mm in thickness) one by one, to keep the pressure minimal or nonexistent on the softer parts. Once we do this highly effective prevention, we'll deal with a comfortable, and much calmer dog, who trusts us and the process, and stays still throughout the pawdicure session because it is sensation free.

When we cut off bigger chunks at once, and I mean bigger pieces over 1 mm thick "slices", we put a lot of pressure on the sensitive parts. The pressure will tell the dogs that we're not aware of the sensitive parts, so they'll do everything they possibly can think about to avoid us cutting off to much. Knowing this I think it's easy to see the light at the end of the tunnel and understand how effective we are going to be at changing the dogs' behavior for nail care. And this was only the tip of the iceberg.... I mean dog nail!

Sole

Definition of the Sole
The sole (after Dr. Jeff Vidt) is a layer of the epidermis and is very similar to the horny nail tissue, the nail's wall. It does not have any nerve endings or blood supply.

The sole layer has two sublayers: the "Powdery" and the "Jelly" Layers.

The powdery sole layer is the light gray, the Jelly sole layer is the dark gray layer on the drawing on the right. See the color details in the color of the sole layers section in more detail.

The soft sole's outermost layer that is in direct contact with the environment is usually a bit darker than it is on the inner side. (See the images below with the orange backgrounds for comparison. You can see all this with your bare eyes in real life with average vision.)

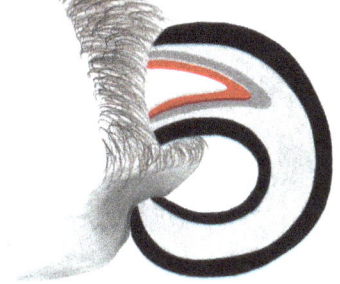

Sole layer – gray layers
Dark gray – Jelly sole
Light gray – powdery sole

Powdery (Dry) Sole Layer

Description of the Powdery (Dry Sole) Layer
The powdery layer is possibly the "old", leftover Jelly (soft) sole tissue. This old Jelly (soft) tissue dries up and becomes very powdery.

It is still protecting the live part of the nail, but since it is powdery, it helps the dog wear off his nails easier.

On some dogs, where the quick does not grow down in the nail, it gets especially powdery when it becomes way too long, e.g. after several months of no exercise or nail trimming. When we are doing the nails of a dog in this case, even though the nail could be super long, so is this powdery layer, so we can cut the nail back to the proper length easily.

Powdery (Dry) sole layer by the cut (white, powdery nestled in the inner curve of the black, horseshoe shaped horny tissue)

Texture of the Powdery (Dry Sole) Layer
Powdery, dry or layered like a croissant.

Color of the Powdery (Dry Sole) Layer
The powdery layer's color is mostly white, light gray, or pale yellow on all nail colors unless it is absent. Expect a lighter color than the Jelly layer.

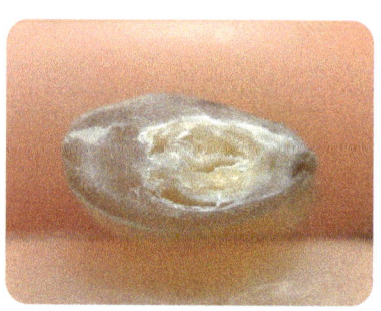

Powdery (Dry) sole (looks like a croissant in the middle) encircled by the light colored, horseshoe shaped horny tissue

Shape of the Powdery (Dry Sole) Layer
Circle or horseshoe, depending on the shape of the nail.

Depth/Thickness of the Powdery (Dry Sole) Layer
It can vary from being absent, taking up a few millimeters to stretching out over a centimeter-long part of the nail.

Location of the Powdery (Dry Sole) Layer
Right below the horny layer.

Sometimes it is so thin; it is barely visible. Sometimes it does not develop at all; it is absent. That usually happens for the taco nail type. (See nail types below!)

Dog's Sensations When We Work on the Powdery (Dry Sole) Layer
No nerve endings are present here, and since it is soft, the dog should not have any reactions. Keep in mind to cut tiny edges off, not "full circle slices", so we won't put pressure on the horny surface, creating pressure on the soft layers, resulting in a reactive dog.

I feel for these dogs who are labeled as biters or mean or high maintenance dogs. They are only trying to let us know that they are in discomfort or pain, and they want us to stop what we are doing. The more pain they are in physically or mentally, the more late discomfort signs they will use, to make us get their memo.

Sole Layer Comparison

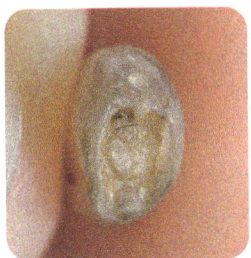

The tip of worn, but untrimmed toenail

Same nail after a clipper cut

Take a look at the nail tips above! On the left, you see a worn, but untrimmed, unfiled nail tip. Notice the top is naturally worn down shorter than the rest. See the slightly gray areas on the outer sides indicating it's a worn down nail, not a filed one? Filed nails of this color have whiter nail powder left after filing, plus the surface looks more artificially scratched than worn off smoothly like here.

The top right image shows the same nail after a cut. The powdery layer looks very layered here (not typical) that resembles a croissant. If you scratch it with your fingernails, it'll fall apart into little powder easily.

The collage to the right shows a collage of the three nail layers you'll meet by the nail tips while trimming or filing nails, horny tissue, powdery layer, and the Jelly layer.

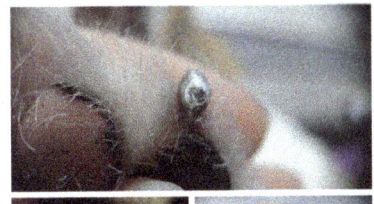
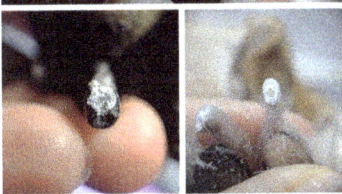

Layers of toenails

Jelly (Soft Sole) Layer

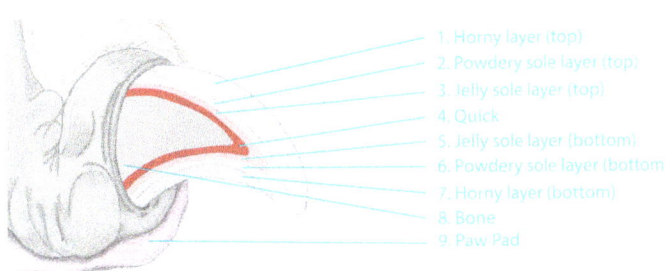

1. Horny layer (top)
2. Powdery sole layer (top)
3. Jelly sole layer (top)
4. Quick
5. Jelly sole layer (bottom)
6. Powdery sole layer (bottom)
7. Horny layer (bottom)
8. Bone
9. Paw Pad

Jelly layer - pink

Definition of the Jelly (Soft Sole) Layer

The Jelly or soft layer of the sole is the closest layer to the quick. It does not have any nerve endings, nor a blood supply. However, since it is pretty close to the quick, dogs often show early discomfort signs since they can feel us working around the quick layer that has nerve endings. The bull's eye in the middle third of the nail is our stop sign when taking a look at the nail from the tip (bottom side).

Texture of the Jelly (Soft Sole) Layer

Soft and shiny, similar to Jelly.

Color of the Jelly (Soft Sole) Layer

In a nutshell: **the Jelly layer's color is mostly pink or creamy on light-colored nails and primarily dark gray or black on dark-colored nails. But can be either one on nails with multiple colors or color patterns.** Keep in mind that these layers are the closest layers to the quick, and they are a lot softer than the horny nail tissue. So even in the case of them being similar in color, there is no way that you can mix them up if you compare their structures along with their colors as well.

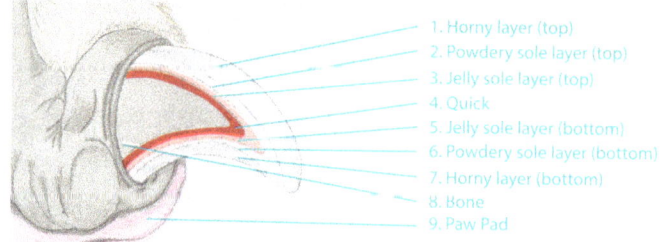

Jelly layer on light color nails - pink layer

Differentiating between the Jelly and powdery layers is the most important task to stay safe. Once you get the hang of figuring this out, you'll be confident in finding this stop sign super easily. This differentiation is the biggest step toward a predictably safe and joyful nail care experience.

The next section will detail the color characteristics of the "stop sign", the Jelly (soft sole) tissue.

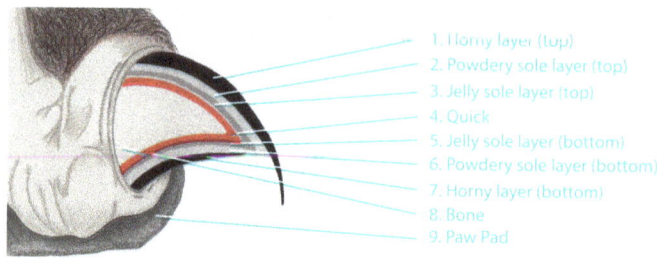

Jelly layer on dark color nails - dark gray layer

There are only two primary colors of the soft sole tissue: black and pink. Most of the time, the black dot appears on dogs with darker nail colors and the pink one on lighter nail-colored dogs.

In about 70-80 percent of the cases, it is either darker horny nail tissue with a black spot (soft tissue) in the middle or a lighter color horny nail tissue with a pink dot (soft tissue) in the middle.

In about 20-30 percent of the cases, the dog we are working on has multiple nail colors or has inherited the opposite color for the "soft sole tissue", than their horny tissue would suggest. Usually, it shows as a striped or smokey horny nail tissue with two to three different colors involved.

In conclusion, even when the white/black color is dominant, the inner soft sole can still be the opposite color.

Knowing the textures can help you distinguish between the layers, and tell when to stop cutting and start filing.

Color Palettes of the Jelly (Soft Sole) Layer

Light Colored Nails

See the top left image.
- White
- Cream
- Smokey
- Gray
- Light pink

Dark Colored Nails

See the images on the right.
- Smokey
- Gray
- White
- Cream
- Black

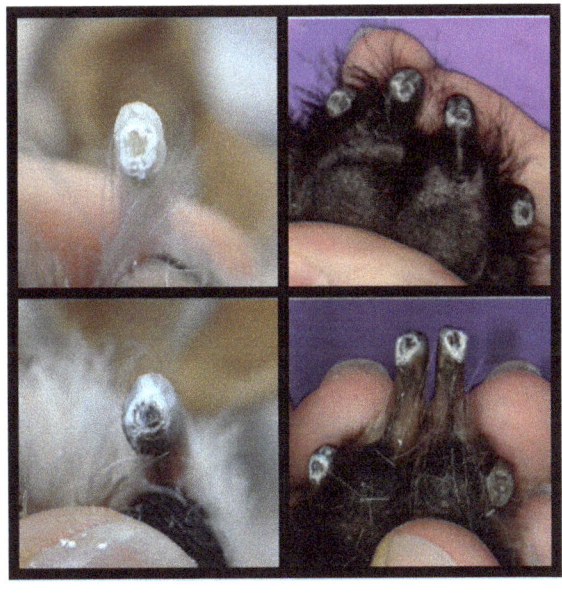

Color palette of the Jelly layer

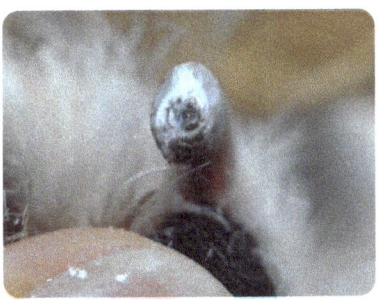

Color of Jelly layer on a mixed color nail - tip view (Dark gray)

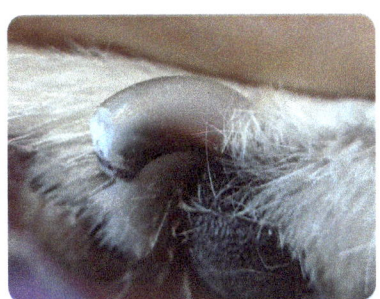

Color of Jelly layer on a mixed color nail - side view (Dark gray and pink)

Mixed Colored Nails

See the bottom left image to the right. When the nail has a stripe with different nail color on the side or is smokey with a different nail color, then

- Any variations of the colors above can be present in the Jelly sole layer.

How come that dogs can have a darker spot (Jelly layer) in the middle of the nail, close to the quick when they have lighter colored nails and no stripes on the outer surface?

It's because dogs can inherit different pigments from their parents. I don't know the exact genetics of it, but if one of the dog's parents had black nails, and one had white or clear nails, the dog can inherit the color of the horny nail

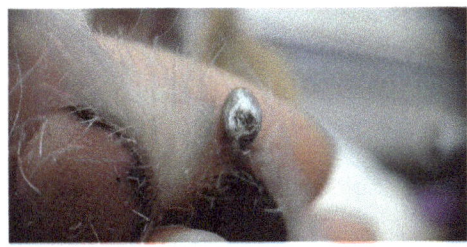
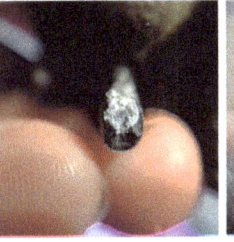
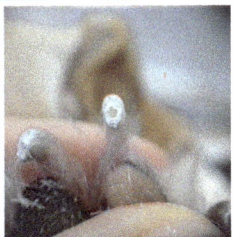

Comparison of Jelly layer colors by nail color
Top: mixed color nail
Left: dark colored nail
Right: light-colored nail

tissue from one parent and the softer, Jelly sole layer's pigments from another parent. That's how I suppose the genetics works based on the dog nail color variations I've seen in my practice.

Shape of the Jelly (Soft Sole) Layer

Dot or oval, depending on the nail's shape when we imagine getting a slice out of it.

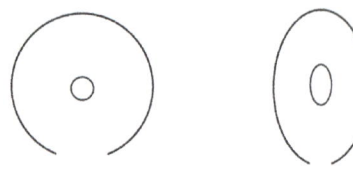

Shape variations of the Jelly layer

It should be a tiny dot-like spot, like a 1-1.5 mm diameter dot on small-medium dogs, and more like a 1.5-2 mm spot on medium-large dogs.

If you go further to expose like 2-3 mms of the tip, the dog will likely show at least early discomfort signs. You may even see some blood leaking from the quick at this point, like a drop or two.

This Jelly layer is a fairly thin layer that I haven't seen becoming thicker than a millimeter. So when you reach this layer, the quick is right on the other side of the dot, no more than 1 mm below the surface.

Going tiny by tiny is critical to approach this dot precisely and to avoid full-blown bleeding of the nail.

Location of the Jelly (Soft Sole) Layer

Encircled by the powdery (dry) layer.

Depth/Thickness of the Jelly (Soft Sole) Layer

Usually no more than 1 mm. Right on the other side awaits the quick to be left alone.

Dog's Sensations When We Work on the Jelly (Soft Sole) Layer

The Jelly sole is the spot where I like to stop the nail trimming procedure. We are getting close to the quick, and even when we are cutting the edges of the horny surface only, there will be an itty-bitty pressure on the quick, so dogs feel that we are right there by the sensitive part. Experienced dogs (who are comfortable and not afraid) will show minor early discomfort signs at this point, like a tiny-tiny movement of the feet; I do not suggest going any further than this.

Quick (Corium)

Definition of the Quick

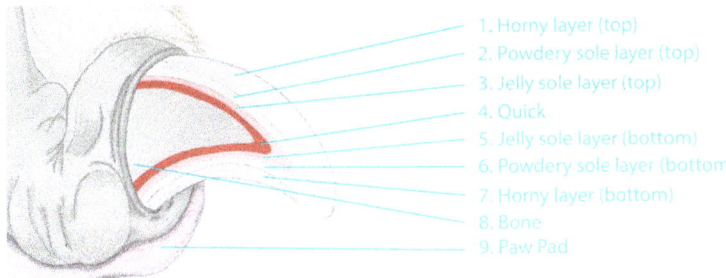

Quick - red layer

See the red layer in the image above! The quick part of the nail is the dermis or subcutaneous tissue of the nail. It is also called the corium. This layer has a rich blood vessel and nerve supply, which explains the pain and bleeding that occurs when care providers cut/file/grind into this layer with nail clippers, nail files, or nail grinders.

> **Fun Fact**
>
> Often people say that we "need to find the tip of the quick" to stay safe, but once we are already there, it's too late, as the nail will already be bleeding by then.
>
> There is another layer right after the quick (Jelly or soft sole), which we will need to locate to stay safe and comfortable, without bleeding instead of the popular but faulty phrase "tip of the quick."

Texture of the Quick

It is soft and bleeds when you hit it, so you can't see much, other than blood. The deeper you cut in, the more bleeding will occur, and the harder it is to stop the bleeding.

Color of the Quick

Red, bleeding occurs when you hit it, so you cannot see much other than blood when you cut in it.

Shape of the Quick

The very "tip" of it is a dot or an oval-shape when approached from the tip of the nail. Generally speaking, it encircles the toenail and provides nutrition for the nail.

Location of the Quick

The quick encircles the bone and is encircled by the powdery and/or soft sole layers.

Dog's Sensations When We Hit the Quick

It is excruciating. Bleeding occurs, and unpleasant memories are born.

Remember, how does it feel when your nail turns backward, or something pokes under it? Super irritating, right? Even when it's not bleeding, it hurts like crazy for days. You might get goosebumps just by thinking about the memory of such a situation. Now imagine when dogs get their nails trimmed so short, they bleed for minutes, and blood gets everywhere. I am detailing it to eliminate the myth that bleeding dog nails do not hurt. They do, dogs are just better at not showing it since it is a survival instinct to not show illness or pain.

Nail Types by the Visibility of the Sole

As we learned initially, we get the most useful information about nails when we take a look at the nails from the paw pad side. Otherwise, the horny layer is in the way and blocks our ability to see the layers regardless of the nail color.

To get this revealing view, we can either flex the foot back or we can have the dog on his back and take a look at the nails from the paw pad side. We can use either of these options to take a look-see at the nails and determine what type of nail our dog has.

There are **two nail types**, and I have named them **hot dog** and **taco** to make learning fun and easy. I got inspired by some scientists having the guts to name the genetic mutation I have "MTHFR gene mutation". After that, I wanted to bring some laughs into dog nail anatomy.

Let's take a closer look so we can tell them apart!

Dogs can have either or both nail types on their paws. Having one nail type on one nail (let it be toenail or dewclaw) does not mean the dog has the same nail type on the others or on all fours. Nail color is not a factor determining the nail type; at least, I have not seen any correlation.

Taco Nail Type - Visible Jelly Sole

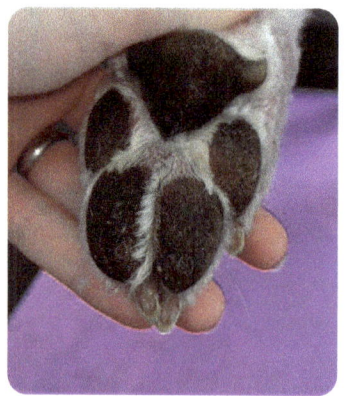

Taco nail type - visible Jelly sole

In the case of the taco nail type, the horny tissue partially encircles the soft tissue and exposes the soft tissue on the paw pad side as a result.

All **the "stuffing"** (Jelly layer of the sole) **is visible** on the paw pad side of the taco, where the two ends are visible. Now you see how this nail type resembles the shape of a taco.

This nail type exposes the softer tissues on the bottom and makes the nail a tad more vulnerable to injury. Most dogs with this nail type can keep their nails the proper length by themselves, since the horny tissue is not that thick, making it significantly easier for them to wear them off while they are running, playing fetch, or doing other doggy activities that a dog gets to do.

Hot Dog Nail Type - Hidden Jelly Sole

In the hot dog nail type, the horny nail tissue encircles the nail all around, throughout the full length of the nail, meaning, the nail is covered with shiny, horny tissue all around. The soft tissue can be seen only at the very tip of the nail, resembling a hot dog. Hence the name, hot dog nail type.

You can see the hot dog (the soft layers) only at the very end because it is hidden under the horny layer (just like a hot dog is hiding in the bun). You can see only a fine line, where the two ends of the "bun" (horny nail tissue) meet and fuse. Sometimes there is a very thin gap between the two edges along or at parts of the nail. See the image on the left! Sometimes this gap can be 1-2 mm wide, depending on the dog's size and the size of their nail. At the tip, it is covered, protected by the dryer, powdery layer of the sole.

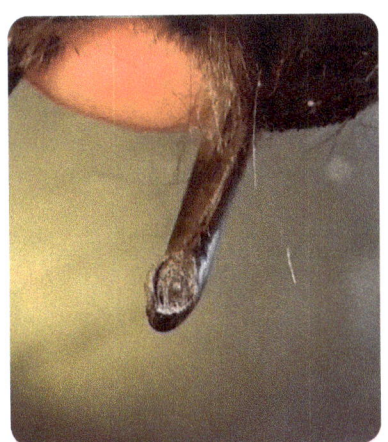
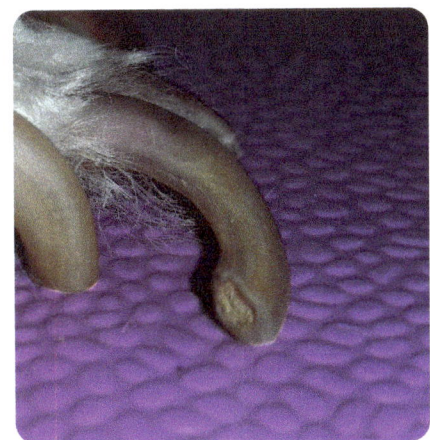

Hot dog nail type, hidden Jelly sole

I believe people refer to this hot dog nail type when they say black nails are very tricky to trim.

As we discussed before, the nail color has nothing to do with nail care safety, and by now, you can see the exact reasons why understanding and determining the nail type is the essential first step in nail care.

Nail Tip Types

Familiarizing ourselves with nail tip types will help us figure out what size nail clipper we'll need, how we can start the nail clipping itself, how to angle the clipper to avoid squeezing the edges, which side to trim first, second and third, etc. Let's take a look!

Thin Tip

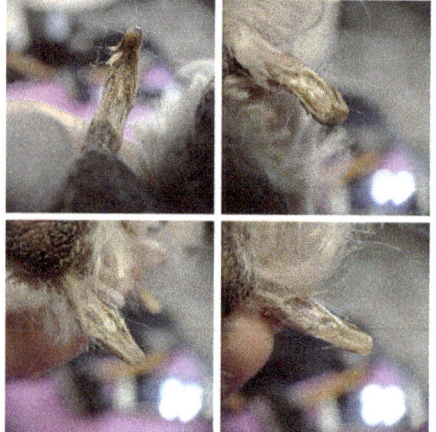

Thin nail tips

The thin tip type develops when a dog has taco nails and physically can't move enough or doesn't have the chance/space to do so.

In this case, the nail's tip, the horny surface (only), gets very long. From the side, it **looks like a cat's claw**. This nail tip type is pretty typical for puppies or elderly dogs with taco nail type.

Puppies have this thin nail tip type in the first few months of their lives since they do not move that much since they need more sleep than adult doggies do and they are fairly lightweight, so their body weight is not helping with filing. After a few months, when adequate exercise is provided, this thin nail tip usually gets worn down by the dog enough to make it safer for them to move around, to everyone's appreciation, since puppy nails are super sharp with the thin tip. Until then, they'll need some help from us to avoid scratches and split toenails.

This thin tip is pretty dangerous since the edges usually get rough and get caught up in carpet (injury: the toenail/dewclaw breaks off) or dog hair (**toenail socks** develop. See future chapter on this), causing a lot of discomfort for the dogs, especially when they break their nails off fully or partially.

After a proper nail trim and filing, **adult dogs** who have this nail type can quickly get their nails to the appropriate length by themselves with an adequate amount of exercise. If the **canine** is an **elderly** or a **young** puppy with this nail type, he will often need **more frequent nail care appointments** to keep the nails the desired length.

Pointy Tip

The pointy tip can occur when the dog has either a taco or hot dog nail type, or when the nail shape is oval, and the dog is moving less than usual.

About two-thirds of the horny nail tissue is thicker; that part touches the ground, so dogs with this nail type need to move more to get their nails filed to the proper length by only activity.

If the dog is not active, the nail eventually grows longer and develops to a thicker type of nail tip, which is even harder to wear off for the dog. It is an evil circle. Even two to three weeks of rest (injury, surgery, activity-deprived boarding, etc.)

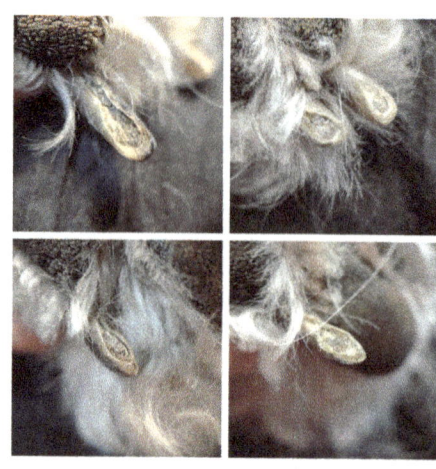

Pointy nail tip

can result in pointy nail tips and lead to longer nails for the dog to deal with. In those situations, a nail trim is recommended to help the dog catch up with nail care by activity from that point on.

Rounded Tip

Dogs who have hot dog nail types frequently develop rounded nail tips. It happens when the shape of the dog's nail is wider by the base and gets thinner toward the nail's tip.

Dogs with this nail type need to move even more than the first two nail types mentioned above to keep their nails the proper length.

Rounded nail tip

Rectangular Tip

A rectangular nail tip occurs when a dog's nail width is pretty much the same by the nail base as it is by the tip of the nail.

When doggies with this nail tip type file their nails while moving around, they end up filing a horizontal line by the tip of the nail. Hence the name "rectangular."

When this nail type gets longer, I like to file the edge by the paw pad and the edge by the opposite end of the tip so that they will need to work on less horny tissue to make that quick to recede without causing bleeding and excessive pain.

Rectangular nail tip

Nail Thickness (Width)

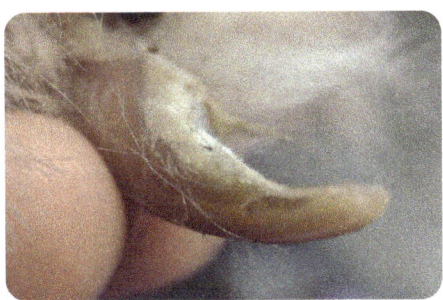
Thin nail

Thick nail

When we refer to nail thickness, we compare the nail thickness by the nail base, in the middle, and by the nail's tip.

I like to distinguish between the two common extremes to see the two ends of the scale so that it is easier to figure out where your dog is on the nail thickness spectrum. It is not a contest; it just helps us figure out how to do (angle) the nails' cuts and what size of nail clippers we need to get.

One end of the spectrum is when the nail base is thicker than the tip of the nail. The other end is when the nail has the same thickness throughout its length: the same length by the base, in the middle, and at the tip. See images on the right!

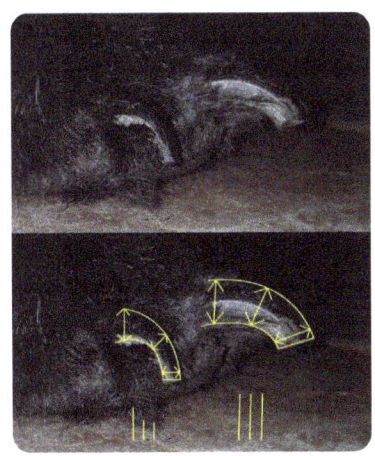
Comparison of nail thickness

Nail Length

We are talking about optimal nail and dewclaw length when the canine can use his toenails and dewclaws and can move comfortably (without any pain or pressure) and can use his feet and nails with the least chance of injury.

The dog has the best chance of achieving this when all of the following criteria are met:

Optimal Toenail Length
1. The dog's nails do not touch the ground when the dog stands in a natural position on a horizontal floor on all four legs with proportional weight on each leg
2. A too-long nail in the front does not lift the toe pads
3. The lower, inner curve of the nails is not touching the toe pads
4. The tip of the toenails are not touching, nor have grown into the toe pads.

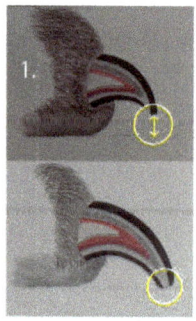 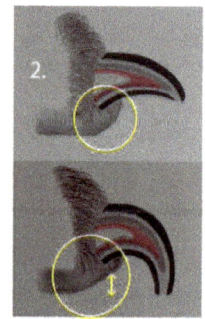 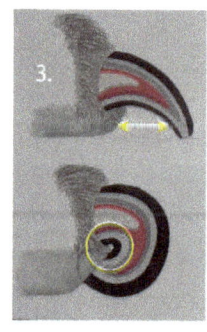 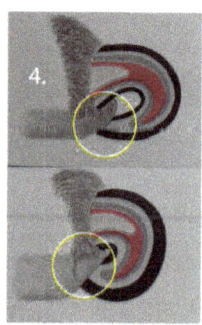

1. Tip of the nail position relative to the ground while standing on all fours.
2. Paw pad relative to the ground while standing on all fours.
3. Inner curve of the nail relative to the paw pad.
4. Tip of the nail relative to the paw pad.

Too Long Toenail
Check the nail length image for more details. On the right, you can see the nails are about 1.5" or 4 cm longer than they should be. Horrible conditions for the poor dog. This is dog neglect in action.

Photo credit: r/lbrown538 from Reddit.

Extremely long toenails

Optimal Dewclaw Length
1. The lower, inner curve of the dewclaw is not touching the toe pads
2. The tip of the dewclaw is not touching, nor has grown into the skin, is not curled back
3. Let's say the base of the dewclaw, where it attaches to the leg (yellow arrow), is 12 o'clock (white plus sign)

4. The tip of the dewclaw is between 1-5 o'clock. When the tip is between 5-6 o'clock it needs nail trimming but is not super dangerous. When the tip is over 6' clock or more, it is risky for getting caught in stuff, so the dog needs immediate dewclaw trimming and filing

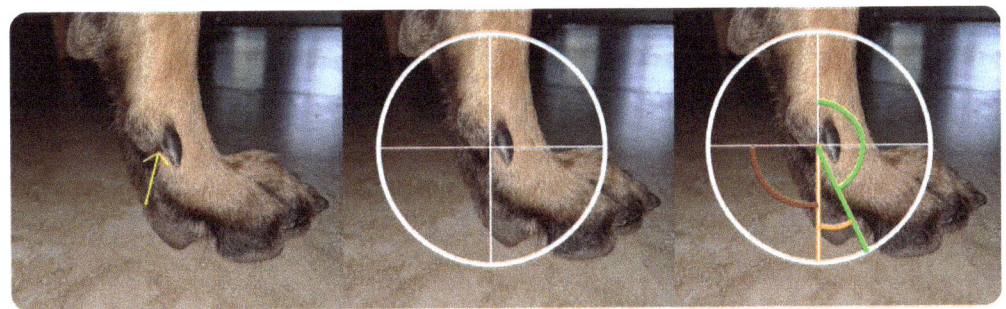

1. Tip of the nail position relative to the ground while standing on all fours.
2. Inner curve of the nail relative to the paw pad.
3. Tip of the nail relative to the paw pad.

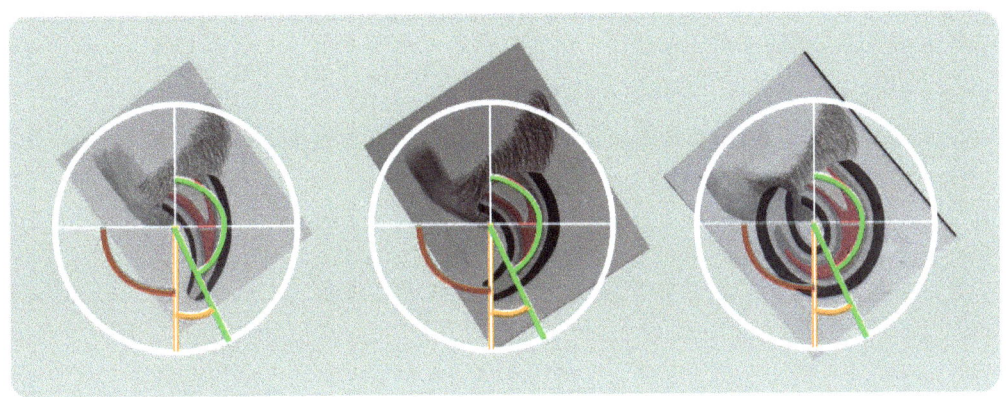

1. Optimal (green)
2. Needs trimming (orange)
3. Injury prone, urgent trimming needed (red)

Too Long Dewclaw (Curling Back To The Skin)

You can see the nail curled back into the skin; the outer curve is pressing against the skin, making it red and irritated. It is hard to notice from this angle, but the dewclaw's tip curled up like a spring, so the tip is not growing into the nail, but curling up near it toward the pads.

This situation is very uncomfortable for a reason: it is pressing against the skin on the left side. And it is dangerous because it can get stuck in stuff like hair, carpet, etc., and can tear the nail off partially or fully. Since this is a dewclaw, the dog is not putting constant pressure on the curled back nail with a quarter of his weight. Yet it still needs a serious trim as soon as possible.

Too long dewclaw - curled back

How to Tell Whether my Dog Needs a Pawdicure Session

Based on the above description, **dogs need a pawdicure session when ANY of the following applies**. It can apply to one nail only, or multiple nails, or all nails.

- The toenail touches the ground when the dog is standing naturally (not yet lifting the toe pad) 4 feet on horizontal ground
- The toenail touches the ground and lifts the toe pad
- The lower curve of the toenail or dewclaw touches or pushes against the nail
- The tip of the toenail or dewclaw touches or pushes against the skin. Or the tip of the toenail or the dewclaw has grown into the skin of the toe pad or dewclaw pad
- The dewclaw grew longer than a half-circle measured from the base of the dewclaw
- Can I see the paw pads when I take a look at the paws from the bottom side? It's important to get a good grip on the floor (especially for pups, elderly dogs, dogs with hip/muscle problems)
- Presence of toe mohawks
- Presence of paw pad boomerangs
- Presence of bushy paw hair covering the pads
- Presence of chewing gum, paint, popcorn, cereal, plant parts, rocks, sticker burrs, mud, tape, any other foreign objects in the hair around the feet or around the paw pads.

Nail Malformations (Genetic)

We talk about malformations when the formation/change had happened genetically before the canine was born.

Toenail Located Higher on the Feet

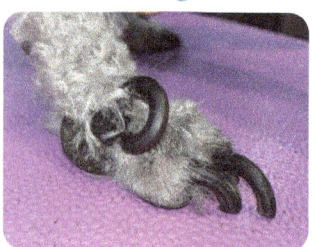
Toenail located higher than the other three - outer side view

Toenail located higher than the other three - frontal view

Toenail located higher than the other three - outer side view

Stanley's (poodle mix) toes on the outer sides are located higher on the front feet, as you see in the images above. At first glance, it might look like a dewclaw, but if you take a closer look and see how the two legs are positioned, you notice it is the outer toenail. Since the nails are not touching the ground, the dog is unable to wear them off. They need to be trimmed and filed to prevent them from curling back and growing in the skin.

Missing Toes and Toe Pads

This Yorkie client of mine, Messi (a rescue from Peru), surprised me with a not everyday view on his feet.

He is missing toes and toenails on some of his paws. In this image, you see one paw pad and only two toe pads instead of the usual four. He doesn't have any toenails on this paw.

He moves so fast in general; you can't even notice anything unusual just by looking at him while he is walking or running around. He seems to be adopted very well to the situation.

Missing pads and toes

Curly dewclaw

I am not absolutely sure whether this is a genetic thing, a result of a dewclaw removal going south, or something else entirely, but I am pretty mesmerized by the spiral of this dewclaw. Cute, isn't it?

Photo credit: u/bexecuter from Reddit.

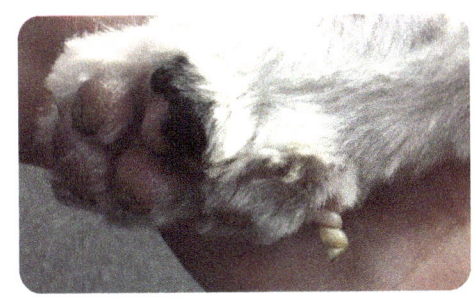

Nail Deformations (Injury, Force)

Injury Before Nail Care

Sometimes we get mild hints to investigate a little for injuries, like limping, licking, blood, mats, etc. Sometimes there are no apparent signs on the dog that something is going on and we do not notice anything unusual until we are inches away from the situation.

This red-brown crusty patch on the image to the right was my hint. Nothing was visible on the site before lifting the hair, no limping shown or other physical signs.

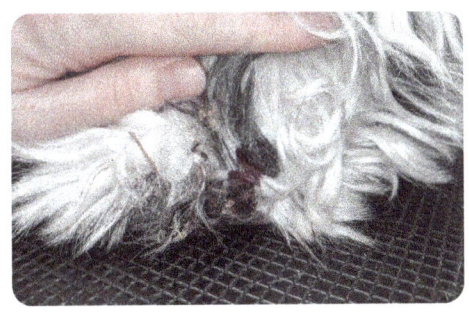
Nail injury at the time of discovery

The paw hair covered up the bloody surroundings. After spending several minutes trimming hair off, soaking the area in hydrogen peroxide to get the dry blood to loosen up enough so I could trim the hair around, I found a broken toenail. (See below!)

I could not believe how high-energy level dogs can hide any signs of pain for this injury.

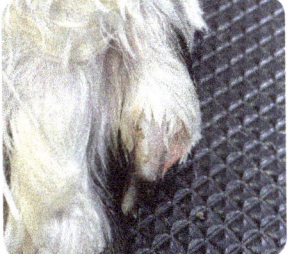
Nail injury after trimming hair and cleaning the area - top view

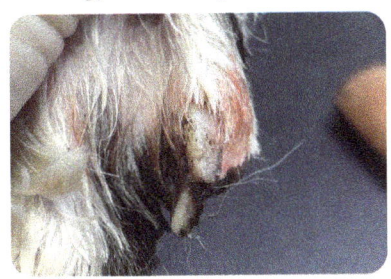
Nail injury after trimming hair and cleaning the area - top view, close up

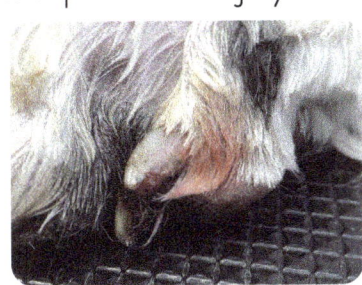
Nail injury after trimming hair and cleaning the area - side view, close up

Toenail Injury

Partially or Completely Broken Toenail

On the first image below, you see how the second from the left toe broke off halfway. It scratches, leaves marks, and even though half of it broke, the leftover is still too long.

You see that the soft tissue got exposed on the second image below, but it is still relatively well covered by the horny tissue. Recovery will be reasonably fast and relatively low discomfort.

In the third image, you see a smaller portion of the nail broke off. It got the nail short enough, so it is not touching the ground anymore, but it is still sharp and can scratch sensitive doggy areas and humans, so it needs follow-up care.

This poor girl got her nails breaking off fairly often. (See three images below.) The time I managed to take close-ups about it was one of the most severe ones. The "winner" injury got her toenail amputated. You can see the place of the missing toenail on the last image.

Partially broken toenail (second nail from the right)

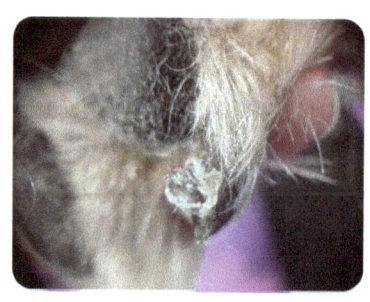
Partially broken toenail, paw pad - side view

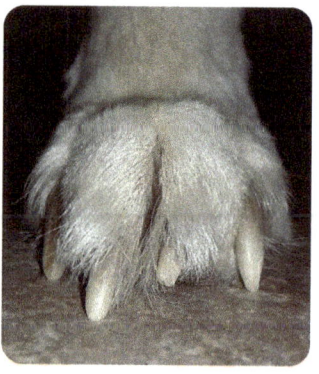
Partially broken toenail (second nail from the right)

And, the first images of this section which you already saw, but now we'll talk about the case in detail. This poor girl got her toenail halfway broken off. It broke in a way that it is still a relatively lucky case. The horny tissue covers most of the leftover nail. She has raw parts on it, but it will be much faster for her to regrow tissue there. She had a loose part pressing against the other toe when the doggy was standing, which needed to be trimmed off by a vet to help her stay comfy and let it heal faster.

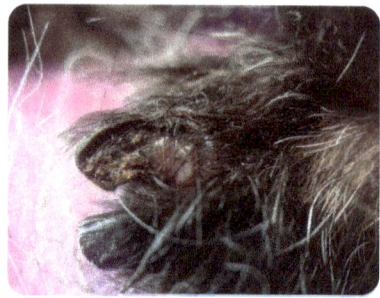
Nail broken off lengthwise up to the nail bed - side view

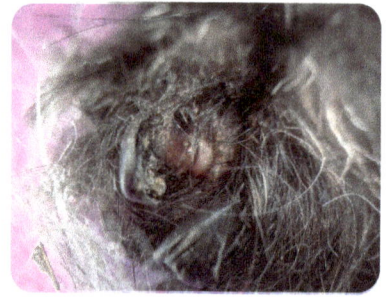
Nail broken off lengthwise up to the nail bed - front view

Amputated toenail due to injury

Layer Separation

The horny tissue of the toenail lengthwise is separated from the soft tissue. Hard to tell what caused it. Might be an injury, and the nail grew back differently, or vitamin deficiency or genetics. It needs a veterinarian to figure it out. (See images below!)

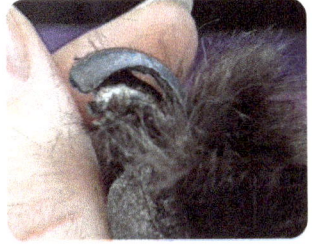
Layer separation

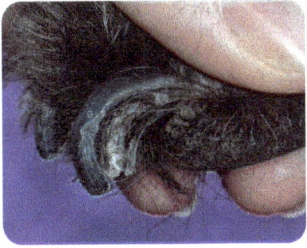
Layer separation

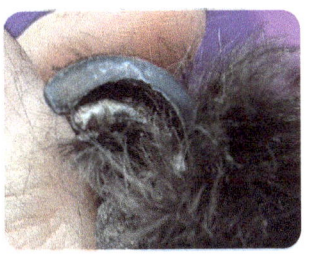
Layer separation

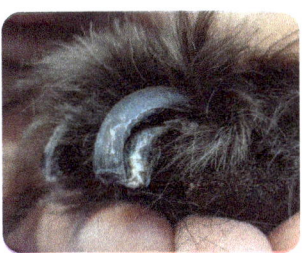
Layer separation

Toenail growth

I've met with two dogs throughout my career who had this unusual growth on one of their nails. To make it weird enough, both had it on the left, hind leg, on the most outer nail. That softer brownish tissue looks like a small comb of a chicken can be popped off or filed off the nail. It has no nerve endings, no blood vessels, and it grew back after every removal on both dogs. The nail underneath looks normal.

Toenail growth

Dewclaw Injury

Partially or Completely Broken Dew Claw, Growing Back Smaller.

This doggy broke a full dewclaw off by the skin. And this is how it grew back after the injury. It stayed this way, never got the thickness back as it was before. I trim it when doing the other nails to make sure the dog won't get it caught in anything.

On the previous page is a sample of a partially broken dewclaw. To the right, you see a dewclaw growing almost into one circle. Thankfully, it grew near the base of the dewclaw, not into it.

If you take a closer look, about half the nail length consists of only the nail's inner side; the outer half broke off.

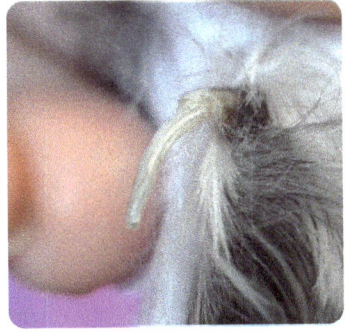
Nail regrowth after dewclaw injury

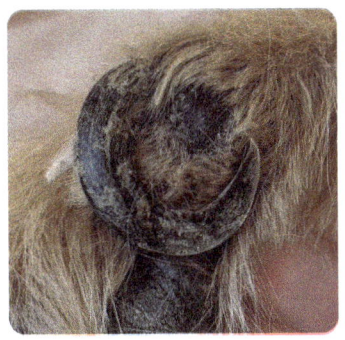
Dewclaw injury - half of the nail fell off the side

Severely Worn Off Nail Tip

In some cases, especially with bulldogs and pugs (large body surfaces with fairly short legs compared to their body), they wear their nails off to extremes by themselves. See the images below.

You can't see the powdery surface, and there is a very fine line of soft sole only, protecting the soft tissue.

Severely worn off nail - frontal view

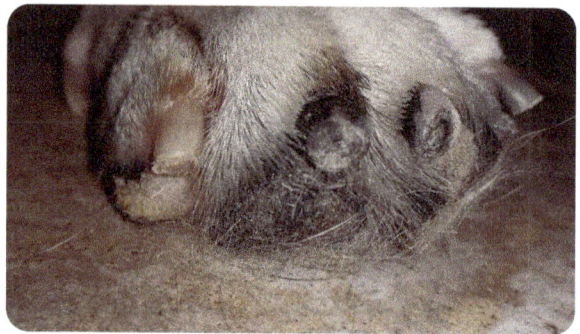
Severely worn off nail - frontal view

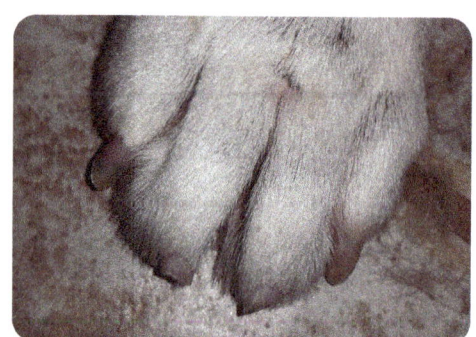
Severely worn off nail - top view

Chapter 8

Positioning Options for Nail Care

Positioning 101 for Canine Pawdicure

When we decide how to position the dog, we need to keep three things as a priority to aid cooperation from all participants.

1. Comfort and safety for the dog
2. Safe holding position for the toenails and dewclaws for visibility, trimming, and filing
3. Safety and comfort for the care provider

Keep in mind that dogs do not have to stay in the same position throughout nail care. Neither do you! So we can ask/let them move around and we can work around and choose the positions they prefer for nail care. Just like with kids, it's easier for all if the grownups offer a few options to complete the task and let the kid/dog pick the one they like. This will help the dogs to feel involved and bring them comfort that they are listened to.

We'll talk about locations and objects first, where to do the nail trim, as well as ways to position the doggy on different surfaces, heights, etc. so you can mix and match locations with positioning as your doggy and you like it best.

Feel free to visit http://www.WholesomeGroomingAcademy.com/page-nail-it to check out the videos about positions in the Nail it! course!

Top Tip

For the easiest and fastest CCDS, try out different combinations of positionings and locations (such as different rooms, outside, elevation, etc.) and stick with the one your dog likes most for the CCDS. Once your dog is comfortable with that location for a full nail trim, you can add another layer to it by doing it in different areas. Like, if you want to graduate from doing nails on the ground/couch to doing pawdicures on the table to save your back.

Location Ideas for Nail Care

Trimming Nails on the Table

For the majority of canine clients I work with, I go with using the table for the following reasons:

Pros:

- Most dogs are fine with it and they find enough excitement through the window and on the table so they will be less likely to try to move around
- It is easier to keep them close by with body language even if they try to move compared to the ground
- Our back, neck, and shoulders will be pleased to cooperate with us without pain when our back is straight

> **Top Tip**
>
> No need to lift large doggies! You can have a cue word for jumping up, staying there, even turning around, and jumping down. This will be a tremendous help so it is totally worth it to dedicate some time to teach it.

Note:
Be mindful about training a cue word for jumping up or a very specific body language so there won't be misunderstandings. We want to avoid the doggy jumping up or down (even without the table around just in the air) without us wanting them to when they see certain body language.

For example, I have a few doggy clients who have been accidentally or willingly taught to jump up in the air on their terms when anyone is reaching down to them. The doggies will jump before I can make sure I position myself and get a secure hold on them. That is especially an issue for elderly dogs, who can use up their energy by one or two jumps or can straight up hurt themselves by the sudden, unsupported movement.

In my opinion, it is much safer for the dog and your back if there is a clear verbal cue for the dog to jump up or down, instead of a body language, like reaching down to them. When we want them to help us lift, we position ourselves and the dog the way we feel it's the safest for both of us, we get a good hold of the dog on the front and back and say the cue. The dog will then assist with a jump when we are prepared, and injury will be less likely to happen for anyone.

Summary
Training dogs for a cue to jump instead of body language will be very beneficial and energy-conserving when dogs get older and have less energy. It is also helpful for adult dogs in general from a safety perspective as well.

Cons:

- Dogs and we need a bit of pre-training before nail trim time on the table. Dogs need to be comfortable being on a higher spot to ensure it'll be a smooth pawdicure session. Care providers need to be aware of their body language to be able to keep the dog on the table. See the table manners section!
- There is a slight chance (even with the proper table manners from you) that the dog will still try jumping off (until he adjusts to the location fully and stays still), and you need to be prepared to prevent it latest at mid-jump. Adjusting table height will be a great aid for going high enough so the dog won't get triggered by the ground or the height and you will not be too worried about him falling down from a higher setting.
- Puppies are not aware of heights that much, and there is a good chance that they will try to fly off the table at some point if introduced too fast to the table. So we need to spend more time on training and need to be on higher alert when working on a puppy on the table until they get the hang of it.

Note

Keeping the table's surface not slippery will help your dog/your client stay comfortable and cooperate willingly. In vet clinics, I am thrilled to see non-slip mats on the cold, yet-easy-to-clean exam tables to aid the dog's comfort level.

Grooming tables most often have the non-slip top built-in.

Pawrents can purchase non-slip grooming mats in different sizes from wholesale companies for groomers, like Ryan's Pet Supply (store.ryanspet.com) to put on the coffee table, washing machine, countertop. An on-the-budget option is a yoga mat.

Trimming Nails on the Ground

It may sound like science fiction, but most dogs are a lot calmer when elevated from the ground for nail care or getting groomed, rather than when we are doing the nails on the floor. (Elderly dogs and dogs with disabilities or who are afraid of heights are the exception. More on this later!)

The floor is where they are used to playing fetch, wrestling with us, playing tug of war, running around, and wiggling away from us. So it is generally a helpful step to focus attention on the grooming step on an elevated surface. The height creates a barrier for the dog and focuses attention on other fun things to explore on the table. (Treats, toys, looking out through a window, etc.)

You can train your dog to be still on the ground as well, just keep in mind it might take a tad longer. Removing toys out of sight on the ground helps a lot to keep doggies engaged to stay around us and focus on the task at hand.

Pros:

- It is the best position for large, elderly dogs or dogs with fewer socialization skills, high energy level pups, dogs who are not socialized to heights, etc.
- You can trim your puppy's nails while they are resting after a good run or while they are in a deep sleep (IMPORTANT!! You have to be a nail trimming Jedi and NOT make ANY mistakes to keep your puppy comfortable.)
- So, unless you are super experienced, don't attempt to cut nails on a sleeping dog! It is very traumatic to wake up to a bleeding and painful nail care scene from a horror movie where you are the victim. I'm exaggerating so this step will only be performed by students with much experience to perform the nail trim

Cons:

- Dogs are more likely to run around on the ground, and it is harder to get them focused since they are so used to the playtime there, without much practice to stay still (They can be trained to remain relatively motionless on the ground, too.)
- Bending over a lot will more likely take a toll on our backs and your patience

Top Tip

You've probably seen the viral videos of people trimming their dog's nails while their dog is licking peanut butter off of their wrapped up foreheads. I wanted to dedicate a section to detail the dangers of this and how it sets up every participant for failure and injury on many levels.

First Issue

We talked about how dangerous it is when you take a look at the dog's nails from the "aerial view" from the top of the nail. We can't see the soft layers, because they are hiding under the not transparent at all or partially transparent horny layer, and we are gambling with dog nails.

We want to know what parts we are working on at all times, 100 percent, "bet your life on it" precisely and this view is not the one we can accomplish that.

The Second Issue comes hand in hand with the first one.

Given it's a hit or miss mission due to the aerial view and holding technique, (I guarantee people will hit the quick rather sooner than later with this method), people are presenting nothing less but their own face with tongue contact already established by the dog. Guess what dogs bite when they are in pain or discomfort? Whatever is the closest to reach. In this case, people's faces.

I think we all can agree, that though for the untrained eye this wrap and lick distraction "method" might look cute and "genius" but when we take a closer look at it, it is nothing short of a commercial for plastic surgery clinics and a label factory to generate "aggressive" dogs.

There are plenty of safer and better ways to keep dogs still and all participants safe laid out in this book.

Trimming Nails While the Dog is Held on the Lap

A one-person solution is when the doggy is comfortable in your lap on his back parallel with your thighs. You can get a very close view of the nails. See the images below!

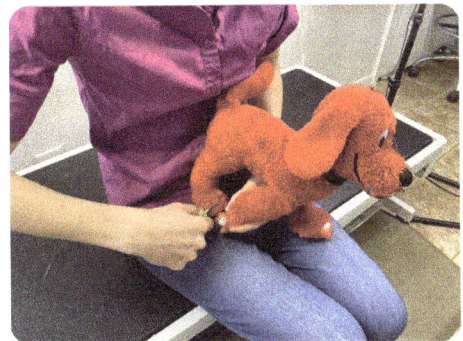
Dog on the lap - Version 1

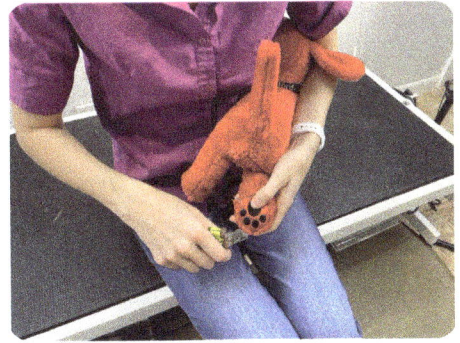
Dog on the lap - Version 2

This can be a go-to method for dogs who like close human contact in abundance. Triple check the body language to make sure the dog is still because of comfort, not because of fear! Great for small dogs. You can roll up a towel to put between your thighs and fold one to go on the top of it so you'll provide a flat surface for the dog to balance on.

Alternatively, it can be done with large dogs who are belly rubs enthusiasts when you do it on the ground. Spread your legs and they lie on the ground parallel with your legs, in-between if they are large, on the thighs if they are medium and you can handle their weight. Again, the legs are there to bring additional comfort and closeness not for squeezing a dog to stay there! See the image to the right!

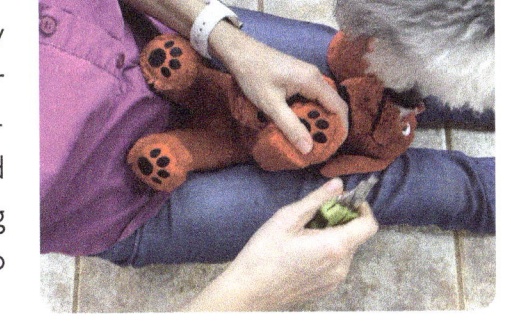
Dog on the lap - Version 3

Trimming Nails While the Dog is Held in the Arms

The two-person solution for small dogs/puppies could be when the dog is held in the arms for nail trim or file. One person holds the dog, while the other one is doing the nails. See the images below!

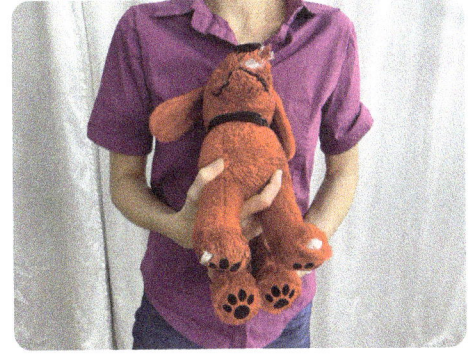
Dog in the arms - Version 1

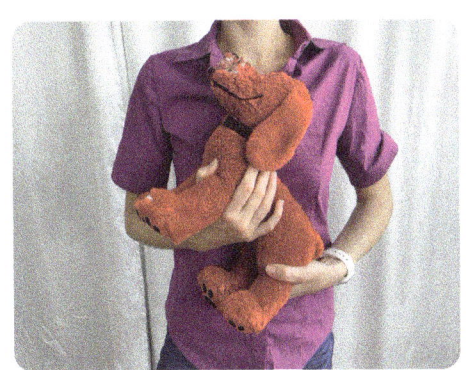
Dog in the arms - Version 2

Note

It can be physically demanding to hold a doggy for a more extended period in this position. Even a small puppy becomes heavy to hold after a few minutes.

For puppies who are fine with a new person, a team of two new care providers can make the nail care happen.

For puppies who are still learning to be independent and need their familiar human presence, a well-known person holding them can aid their comfort and bring them enough peace to cooperate.

Most dogs like solid ground under their feet, so they feel like there is an effective option to run if needed. Woofers with bad previous experiences might not be comfy enough for nail trimming when we use this method. Honoring their need for safety and an escape route will likely turn their behavior around and keep them comfortable and still enough to make the nail trim happen.

Keep in Mind!

Late sensitivity signs are pretty much impossible to control in this position and even a small adult dog can cause significant injury when biting from a "let me go or else" state of mind. In this position either the helper or the care provider can get bit easily, most likely on the face or hands since those are "presented for the dog".

I recommend this position for absolutely comfortable dogs or dogs showing gentle early discomfort size with caution only!

It is pretty hard on the care provider's back and knees to bend or kneel, too, to reach the dog's feet while in the arm/lap while the helper stands or sits. One more motivation to work on the dog's comfort level to stay still for us on the table!

> ### Top Tip
> If you want to do your groomer and vet tech a BIG favor and you want him to hang around for a more extended period pain-free, then play groomer with your pup at home and train him to be okay on the table for pawdicures.

Pros:

- Doggies with fewer socialization skills can benefit from this position
- As well as doggies with a disability. I've had amputee dogs preferring this position over belly support on the ground or the table
- Puppies might be more willing to stay still in their pawrents' arms in a new environment. Emphasizing it is a hold, not a restraint! Just because we physically can hold a dog/puppy down, we don't force nail trims

Cons:

- Adult dogs often wiggle more in the arms, especially if they are not used to being handled this way. They feel more restrained by the position and get overwhelmed by the "too much" human contact on a larger surface of their bodies

Let's take a look at the canine positions and how we can get the safest and most comfortable hold on the feet and nails in each position!

Positioning

In this section, Paco, the Sheepadoodle, and Clifford, The Big Red Dog will be my volunteers for demonstrating nail care positions.

Standing

Standing on the Table

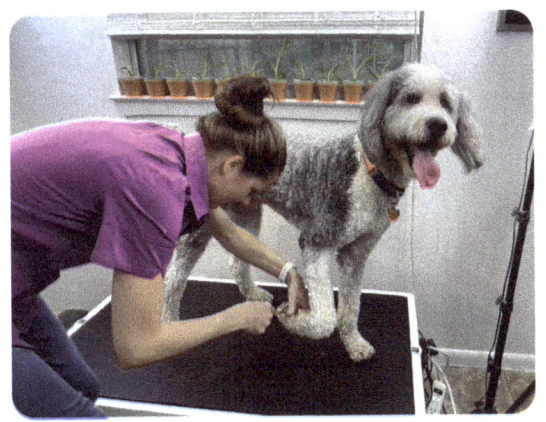
Standing on the table - trimming the front nails

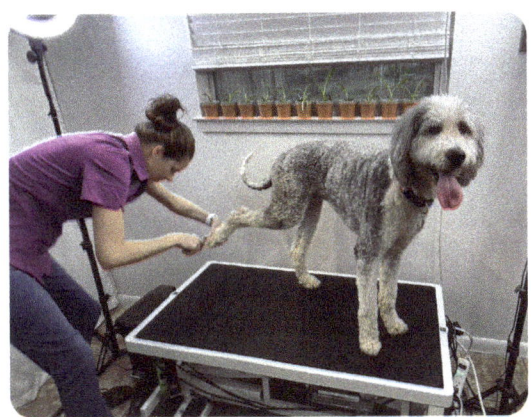
Standing on the table - trimming the hind nails

It may sound like science fiction, but most dogs stay stiller and are a lot less likely to run or wiggle when elevated from the ground for nail care, grooming, or examination. When we are doing the grooming steps/examination on the floor, the higher energy level ones will switch to play mode and run to find a toy. And when the experience is guided to the tabletop, dogs tend to find entertainment there. Like looking out on the window or goblin up the treats there they find or get. Dogs in these situations are staying still because they are comfortable, not because they are scared of being up high.

Generally speaking, the ground is what dogs use for wrestling, playing tug of war, running around, and wiggling away. The grooming/exam table is a pretty handy tool to establish fun and focus at the grooming salon or vet office, even at home, especially when the care provider has the treats and toys and has all the butt rubs handy to reinforce desired behavior and redirect attention.

Grooming with a straightest possible back is the easiest on the care provider's body (and nerves), even short-term. The more pain or discomfort, the more it hijacks our pleasurable feelings, and our patience and tolerance will suffer. Think about your mood and reactions when your belly aches. Significantly different than when you walk out of the massage salon after a ninety-minute treatment, the best length, right? Based on this, I highly recommend training and socializing dogs to be comfortable on the grooming table to make the examination/grooming/nail care the safest and fastest for all participants.

Note on the above two images:
Notice how I aided the dog's comfort and safety in the presence of a photographer? We adjusted to the situation. With Paco, I can go as high as I want when it's the two of us. Given a photographer joined us for the spa day, and Paco was very interested in him—hence the cute images of Paco facing the camera—I felt safest to bring the table to lower in case Paco decided to go for an ear rub and tried to get off the table. It did not happen, just wanted you to know even with an experienced dog, we sometimes need to adjust the prep work to the level of new distractions.

Good to keep in mind, that there is no such thing as a 100 percent "perfectly trained" dog (nor human). There can be situations where the dog gets triggered enough to not stay even though they were still in the past hundred sessions. Training a dog is not something that can be stamped as "done". We need to adjust the environment to the current state of mind of the dog, us, and the distractions. Like in the photographer's case, or when a dog is not well-exercised before a spa day. Or when I have cramps at work, I won't make the table go up as high as when I am running on full capacity and awareness. Adjusting is key to keeping everyone safe.

Feel free to customize the positioning to your and your dog's comfort level on the spa day, in that hour, in that minute. In the now.

Going back a step you all cleared two months ago is not defeat. Going lower with the table is not a failure. It is mindfulness and flexibility to be a fantastic and safe experience for all.

It might seem "handy" or a quick fix to restrain puppies or small dogs with our hands, or tools, and the idea might bring hope for a fast process in the short run.

However, I'd like to spare a "large emotional and financial expense" for the lesson, later on, that comes with this method. Whatever happens to dogs (and humans) that they did not sign up for or straight up asked you to stop, will come back and bite you in the tush rather sooner.

For one, they'll grow big in the case of a larger breed, and with more power at hand, it'll be more and more physically demanding and tricky to "keep them still" with restraint.

It's very beneficial for the future to stop when dogs get triggered and develop strategies to learn to help them be at least okay with the stimulus. I do not only want my furry clients to cooperate, but I want them to cooperate willingly.

That will build trust and a positive mindset for all, not the "let's get over with it" kind. Thinking ahead and getting your puppy used to the tools and positions for nail care will go a long way. It will not only come in handy for nail care but will be a building block of a rock-solid bond and trust between you two that radiates beyond the grooming table.

Standing on the Ground

I do make some exceptions to doing nails on the table. I groom dogs on the ground if they are elderly, are not socialized to the grooming table, or are super high energy level dogs or puppies. In those cases, they are not really aware of where they are, neither realize the depth below and just try flying off of the table at the weirdest moments with the speed of light. Their signals are harder to pick up on since high energy level dogs are either ON full speed (most of the time) or OFF when they are asleep. Their sudden and incredibly fast movements can be a challenge to our reaction time, especially when we just met the first time, and we are not used to working with them just yet. So in those cases, until the doggy gets trained to be on the table or you learn to pick up the behavior signals before "flying", the safest is to tire them out before the grooming appointment. Additionally, doing the nail trims on the ground for the first few times until both participants are comfortable and understand each other's behavior and body language better is a great way to keep heart rates in the normal range.

Sitting

Sitting on the Table

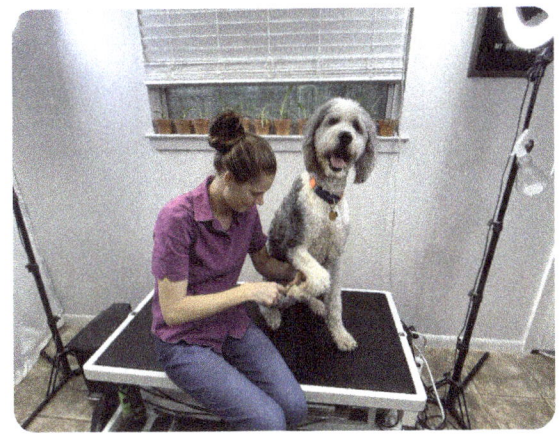
Sitting on the table - front nail trim - Version 1

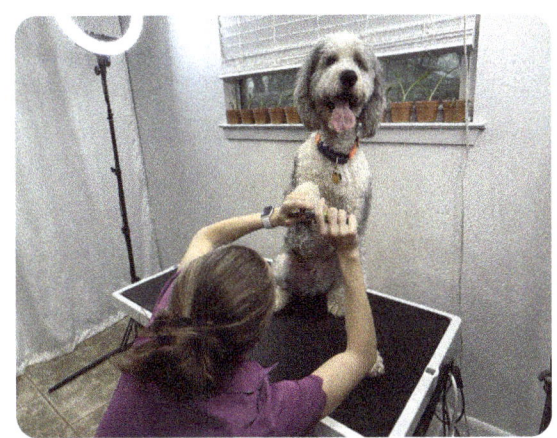
Sitting on the table - front nail trim - Version 2

Sitting is a great position for beginners or the elderly. We have more time to react if the puppy decides to explore (they need time to lift their butt), and elderly dogs feel more secure in this position, rather than balancing on three, often pretty weak legs. It is especially useful for trimming the front nails on a medium or large dog who is having a hard time balancing or is physically challenged.

In this position, we cannot comfortably get to the hind nails, though sometimes I go with this position if the doggy won't tolerate others, but this one. It can be done with many adjustments on our part and a little bit of tolerance on the dog's part since it feels funny when you lift his hind feet a bit (toward their belly) while he is sitting.

If we are working on a small dog with short legs, we probably won't be able to make this position work for us, not even on the front nails, since there won't be enough room for us to see the paw pad side of the nails let alone use the equipment there.

Sitting on the Ground

If the dog is sitting on the ground, it is even more challenging for the care provider to get to the nails' underside. (You can move the table up so you can get a better view, but not the ground, and we can't go lower either.) You more likely have to be flat, facing down on the ground.

Usually, when a dog is more comfortable on the floor, you can convince him to either stand or lie on his side, so it'll be a lot easier and faster for you all, even if you have to invest some time getting him comfy enough around you to lie down.

Lying on the Side or Back

Lying on the Side or the Back on the Table

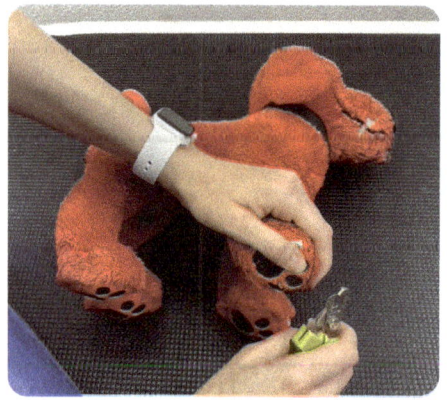
Lying on the side on the table

Some doggies are not comfy in this position with a stranger. The super submissive dogs will get into this position almost right away (not meaning that you are protected from getting bitten at all). Submissive dogs can be triggered easily, and when they get into a fight or flight mode, chances are they will dare to snap or bite to protect themselves. A large table also provides comfort for dogs when lying on it, especially if it is backed to a wall or two, so the doggy won't feel like she'll roll off easily as opposed to when we keep the table as an island in the middle of the room.

It is pretty comfortable to do the nails in this position from the groomer's perspective since you can set the table higher, which means less bending is necessary on your part.

This position is useful for cases we chose to do restrain. Getting ahold of the two legs closer to the ground (the legs on the side which the dog is lying on) will make the dog unable to get up, so you can get a more steady hold resulting in a more still dog. Someone still needs to support the head, though, possibly along with cone and/muzzles as a backup plan.

Lying on the Side or the Back on the Ground

I go with the ground for dogs who love belly rubs and are not so comfy lying on their side on the table. It works great, especially in cases when the dog is food motivated. Having some frozen treats handy (in a Kong toy, etc.) can cut the nail care time in half with a doggy who is food motivated, even when they have tons of energy and they don't really want to stop moving for a second.

Keep in mind the question, WHY is the dog moving so much and try to find a solution to satisfy the underlying need. Carefully weigh and prioritize his need for comfort vs. how important it is to do the nails ASAP, etc.

In cases where the importance of getting a nail trim done outweighs the consequences of restraint, we need to do/ask the pawrents to do CCDS at home to neutralize the effects of going over the threshold for the sake of the health of the dog.

For extreme cases, consider medical restraint, for the sake of the dog and for the sake of future experiences.

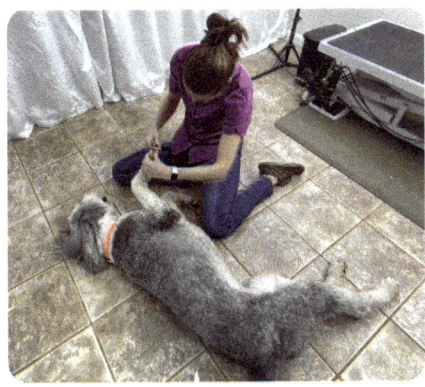
Laying on the sides on the ground

I have a vivid memory of when they took out my tonsils as a kid. I heard every crack and cut, bluntly felt it in my throat along with the three sets of nurse hands that took for strapping me in the chair and holding me still. It was not fun. Good thing nail trimming is not painful at all but has a few "weird" sensations if the dog is just getting used to it. Making nail care fun for dogs is much easier than enjoying tonsils getting removed.

Being/Sitting on Someone's Lap

Being/Sitting on Someone's Lap on a Chair

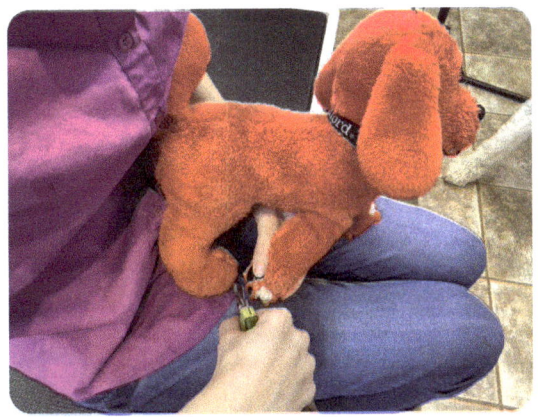
Holding the front paw for trimming and filing on in the lap

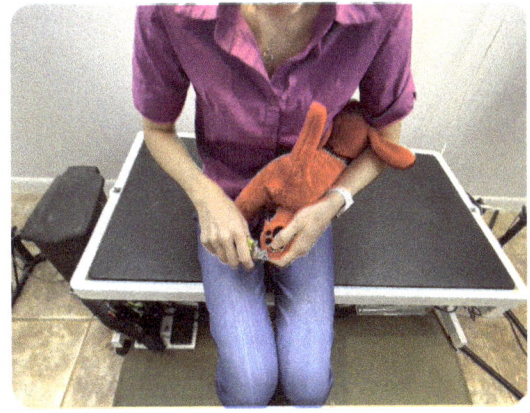
Holding the hind paw for trimming and filing on in the lap

In my opinion, being on someone's lap is best saved as a "backup plan" position to be able to finish nail care in a few specific cases only. It is tremendously hard on the care provider's back and knees, so it's definitely not my everyday go-to method.

For doggies who reacted previously with a growl, snap, bite, etc., I highly recommend *not* using this position or not by itself as a solution, since there is a much bigger human surface presented the dog to launch at. If the dog feels insecure and wants to get out of the situation with a snap or bite, the chances of an injury are a lot higher.

Dog legs can slide off your thighs easily, and it is relatively hard to keep them steady for nail trims in this position. So use it with caution.

Being/Sitting/Lying on Someone's Lap on the Ground

It works excellent for rubbing and massage enthusiastic doggies. For doggies with many triggers and those who react faster, I would not recommend this position, since there is a much bigger human surface present, so there is a bigger chance of getting bitten.

If the dog prefers to be closer to its pawrents, you can get him the most still (and provide the best access to care providers) in the owner's lap if you keep the dog's head toward your belly and the dog's feet facing yours.

If you are the one who is trimming your dog's nails, and you want to go with this position (given your doggy is short enough to reach all four legs, your dog's head should be closer to your feet and his butt closer to your belly. That provides a better view for you, the care provider, and for the dog as well since he can see your face.

Keep in mind that you do not need to use any restraint to do the nails in any of these positions on a comfortable dog. Ideally, that is desired. If your dog/client wiggles out of the position or does not even want to try it out, both mean they are not comfortable there, and we need to investigate why. (Instead of instantly reaching for muzzles or asking for help to hold down by a family member or colleague.)

Positioning the Special Needs Canine

Dogs with special needs can also enjoy nail trimming; we just need to make sure we provide the environment and method to make them the most comfortable considering their special needs.

Depending on the reason of disability (genetics/trauma/illness) we can provide customized comfort. As long as we try to see the world with their eyes compassionately, we will be able to figure out their feelings and needs and develop strategies that will keep them comfortable, and the job can get done with the dog's active/passive assistance. (Lifting a leg or staying still willingly.)

Missing Limbs

Dogs can adapt very well to significant life changes, yet they will like you a lot more if you keep in mind they have a few special needs to work around. Depending on the size, I like to keep the large dogs on the ground so they'll feel more secure there and will be more willing to cooperate. Skipping the walking/hopping up on even the lowest table is appreciated by most as well. Small dogs can be lying on the ground, in the arms, on laps, etc. They feel more comfortable if they are in a position that provides them the ability to leave if they can. So having them lie on the side that they can get up on their own works better.

Most dogs lie down much more quickly if they are on the ground. However, some doggies, especially those with a fairly new amputation or lack of trust in us or their frustration and worry about their inability to get up themselves, will probably passionately want to avoid the lying down position. We can respect that and create support by using doggy slings held by a human (not a groomer's arm) to support their front or back for the time of the nail care. I emphasized human support because a person can go with the dogs if they need to walk around a bit and take a break. Reacting instantly to that need will build trust very fast as opposed to using an immobile metal thing that we need to unhook the dog from that will delay the reinforcement of the dog feeling respected and it will build trust significantly slower if at all in a frustrated dog. Every split second counts when it comes to trust-building.

Dogs' willingness to lie down also depends on which side we're trying to make them lie on and which side they have the entirely or partially missing limb(s). How slippery or cushy the surface is also a big part of the dog's comfort level and willingness to cooperate. How much trust we built up in the past or how much time we are willing to put into it right now also influences the outcome. Dogs pick up on our energy before we even register we are frustrated or in a hurry, so try to stay as calm and confident as possible.

Docked Tail

Doggies are not like kangaroos to use their tail as an additional limb to "stand" on sometimes, but their tail is a significant feature when it comes to balancing. When it's been docked, the doggy and the nail trimming procedure will benefit from a tad more special attention. They might need belly strokes or just a bit more time to balance on three legs than other doggies do. Dogs might also be more cautious around their butt because of the discomfort they lived through the docking procedure and the recovery after removing their tail.

I do wish and work hard to make people realize that docking tails and cropping ears are mutilations. It is a big deal for dogs, and it has an impact throughout their life. I hope for a world where all breeders and veterinarians realize its effects and stop asking for and doing these procedures, along with the routine dewclaw removals. I also hope for pawrents to stand up for keeping their dog's body intact passionately and vote with their money and buy dogs with intact ears and tail. Mother Nature makes ears, tails, and nails for a reason. Most of the time, dogs do not need any interventions if the doggy lives an active doggy lifestyle. There are other ways to prevent ear infections, tail injury, etc. than mutilation. Additionally, as a quick but important detour, we need to rethink the "standard looks" for breeds, graduate from medieval thinking and consider the dog's experience when it comes to mutilating dogs for specific looks.

Visual Impairment

Dogs who have reduced vision to some degree or those who can't see at all need special attention to keep them safe, comfortable, and cooperative. If they can hear, greeting the dog verbally and letting them sniff your hand before actually touching them will go a long way in building trust. I found that often they do better in the arms of the pawrent or at least with their presence.

If, for example, the vision loss came with age, and they know and love their groomer or vet, they will be comfortable and cooperative with the care provider. When we introduce a visually impaired dog to a new care provider, we'll need to take some extra time with helping the dog get to know the environment, the care provider, etc. Check the dog's comfort level and tailor your steps based on where they are at today's visit.

Dogs who are visually impaired generally do not like to be turned much, let it be horizontally or vertically. They need their mental map intact and spinning and turning can make them lose track of their location related to the entrance. They don't want to be spun out of their "inner doggy map" since they feel most comfortable when they know where the doors are, etc. so they can find their way around and not lose their independence. I often see dogs prefer vertical positioning—standing, sitting. An incredible amount of trust is needed to get them to lie down for you comfortably. Don't be discouraged if they won't do it for you for the first time! Keep building trust, and it will happen.

Hearing Impairment

Dogs who have hearing impairment will probably get you into canine sign language. Ask the pawrents how they sign to their dogs, what their dog understands, so you will be aware of general expressions and can communicate with the dog better. Letting the dog smell you and your touch will be crucial elements in communication, so master the most gentle stroke that exists so that you will be less likely to scare or surprise the canine in front of you. You can always ask the pawrents about the dog's preferences. How do they practice at home? What kind of positions the doggy likes, so you can cut to the chase and build trust faster and be more effective.

Keeping one hand on them is immensely helpful to keep them comfortable, aware of where you are at, what you are doing, what you are about to do. Let them use their even more heightened sense of smell to "meet and greet" with you and the tools you'll use. If you remove your hand and want to put it on again, be super gentle so you won't startle the dog. Very similar to human massage therapy.

Summary

These methods and "good to know" are meant to give you a general idea about the options to choose from. You are more than welcome to develop your processes, let it be lying on the couch or the bed.

As the primary guideline, the dog staying below the threshold is way more important than what position you put the dog into as long as you can reach the nails and get a good grip and look to trim nails. So let your creativity loose and try out new positionings!

When the Dog's Smell is Gone

Doggies that lost their smell can be handled almost identically to those that still have a sense of smell. At the initial meet and greet, make sure the dog recognizes you, and you are good to go. You can still use food as a reinforcement; they'll surely enjoy the taste of it.

Temporary, "One Time - Quick Fix" Methods for Dogs in Dire Need of a Nail Trim

I suggest these solutions be a one-time, temporary solution only. They are reserved for cases where the nails are causing discomfort significant enough to be worth it to work at or over the dog's threshold.

Doggies who act in a way that it is harder for care providers to trim nails means that the dog is not trained and is not comfortable in that given setting. So our task is to work on getting them back under their threshold as much as possible.

Letting pawrents know about their dog's behavior is crucial. Starting a conversation and discussing options will build trust in all participants. When everyone agrees to go about the nail trim regardless of the dog's behavior, and they decide on the least emotionally invasive method, the likelihood of cooperation from pawrents and dogs later down the road will be significantly greater. After you described to the owner and made notes about the dog's behavior, you all will have a reference point to go back to and see progress in either direction from then on. I find it incredibly useful to provide tips and tricks or refer pawrents and dogs to a trainer if I don't find it safe for pawrents to practice at home alone without professional help due to the high risk of injury to the untrained participants.

Note For Care Providers

Your skin is in the game! If your clients are regular clients, and you are not pointing out the need for help as soon as possible, you will be the one who will need to deal with the dog, and it will be harder and harder and more and more dangerous as time goes by and no one does anything.

When everyone is in total agreement upon the nail trimming method and the upcoming work for the pawrents after it, I proceed with one of the solutions (or more combined) provided below.

In my practice, I have a detailed follow-up series with pawrents between nail care sessions to see how much progress they made and what we can expect for the next appointment. It helps them to stay on track, opens up a space to resolve roadblocks, and provides a significantly better chance to get a calmer client.

I only use these methods on doggies who show early discomfort signs or mild or moderate late discomfort signs.

If you use these methods on dogs who already showed severe late discomfort signs, like growling for approaching or trying to lift feet, you getting bitten is almost a given, sooner rather than later.

To succeed on dogs who showed late sensitivity signs, you will need highly skilled assistance and probably the use of sedation, cones, muzzles, etc., or a combination of these.

It takes a skilled care provider to tell whether to use a muzzle, or it is safe to proceed with bare hand support. It is surely a risky business, so proceed only when you have a solid training background, have extensive knowledge and experience in restraint, and you know what you are doing and getting into. Mistakes can mean severe injuries and weeks out of work/business, so an oopsie here will quickly result in stitches or even surgeries.

Belly Rubs

Belly rubs are an excellent way to keep doggies more comfortable and to keep them from sitting down.

Sitting down is natural for doggies when they are surprised or need some time to figure out what's next. You can see it especially often in puppies. They suddenly sit down in a new or overwhelming situation, and you can see it on their faces that they're "loading" information and asking: Now what?

Dogs who would like to avoid nail trims use sitting down as a way to let us know they are not that comfy.

You may need another person to "spoil the doggy client rotten" with belly strokes while doing nail care. I don't like this phrase, though, but I still use it for now, because often this is how staff and pawrents will describe the need for extra help. And since we are talking about it, I take that chance to translate it to the Giraffe language. When we use this method, we try to use the least triggering solution to comfort the dog. Often the technique itself is triggering to the dog, yet the need for nail trims and the discomfort the dog is living without a nail trim desperately cries for a solution.

Gradually make the transition from the belly strokes to fewer and fewer belly strokes once you feel that the dog is comfortable enough to make the next move. Try to motivate the doggy to stand up with a piece of a treat if the pawrent left you some or the dog is allowed to have some of your doggy goodies. (See the treat chapter about the most popular dog treat recipe!)

Note: I always give only treats that the doggy pawrents bring/approve ahead to avoid tummy upset for the doggies. If your dog has a sensitive stomach, bring along his treats (a lot) for the nail trim/vet/groomer appointments to help with the experience!

Side Support

Side support for sitting on the table - top view

This position is also a last-resort position. I do not recommend it as a #1 go-to position to try out since it is pretty hard on the care provider. It is incredibly useful, though, when a doggy is not that comfy around nail care but will stay still if he can lean on someone. (It is only for cases when we desperately need to proceed due to constant discomfort caused by long nails.) I like to hold my upper/lower arm (depending on their size) against their sides so they'll lean on my arm and stand/sit more still for me. Often it works beautifully, and we can transition the dog to free-standing within a few meetups. Most of the time, even sooner when the pawrents are practicing daily at home.

Belly Hug (Forward/Backward)

Belly hugs work great if your doggy client wants to move about and play fetch instead of the pawdicure session and wiggles more than you can handle with side support. Again, it is for cases when there is a desperate need for shortening nails. And after the nail trim is done, a serious "action plan" talk is implemented with the pawrents to get the help the dog needs (most likely by a trainer) for a rapid solution, so next time, there'll be much improvement.

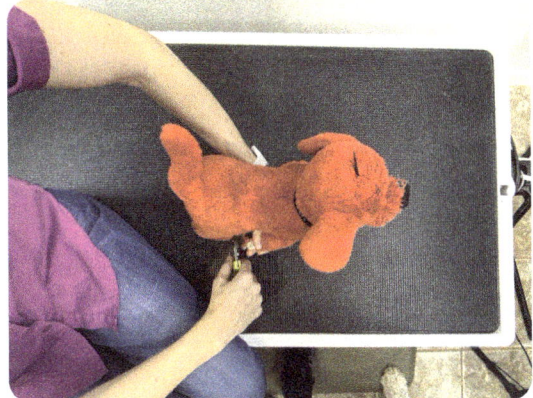
Belly hug forward

Belly hug backward

Since I am right-handed, I like to use my left arm to cross it under the belly, between the legs. I want to keep my arms around the rib area so that the doggy can be more comfortable, and if he is super wiggly, I can lift him 1" or 2-3 cm (if I can), so the doggy will focus more on balance than on the pedicure itself.

Being in the Arms

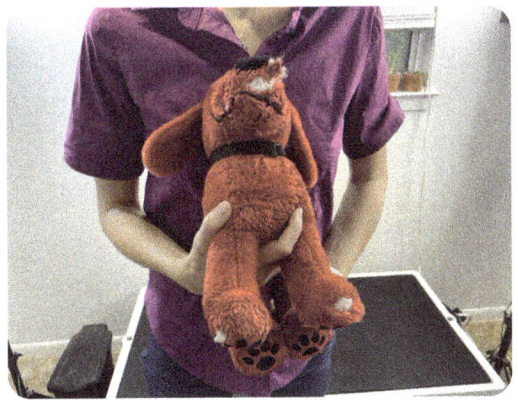
Being in the arms - back to belly

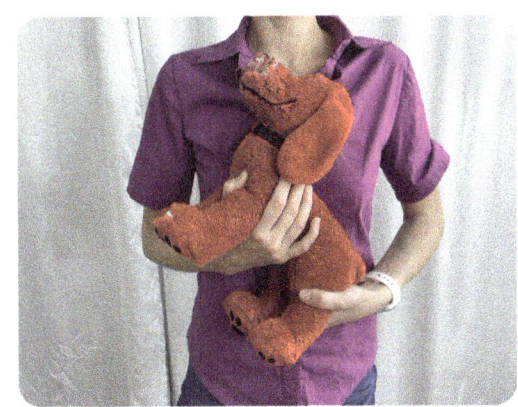
Being in the arms - side to belly

I do not suggest this position, since a much larger human surface is presented for the dog to bite if he is so inclined. Plus, the more participants involved, the bigger the chance for errors. Especially if it's the pawrent who is holding the dog. It can bring considerable comfort for anxious dogs in some cases, though. So it often does worth experimenting with.

This position is often wonderfully beneficial for special needs dogs, who have a missing limb, are visually impaired, or have impaired hearing and need extra support and familiarity.

Avoiding errors! It is crucial to educate the pawdicure participants on which movements are okay and which need to be avoided before doing anything. e.g. quick movements, talk, touch, food, and gestures depending on the dog's temperament are essential points to discuss. Settling on who is in charge is also extremely important. The "captain" will decide when to talk, the next step in the dog's best interest and the participants' safety, and announce every step before performing them.

Personally, if I give this position a try, I dedicate a couple of minutes before doing anything to the dog to outline the positions to the other care providers/pawrents. I want us all to be aware of the dog's personality, positioning preferences, the nail care steps, rules such as not to talk, how to sign when they need a break, etc. so they will be familiar with my signs, I will be familiar with theirs, the upcoming steps, and instructions. After this talk, I will let/ask them to pick the dog up and start the nail care session.

Straddle

The straddle position is for both large and small pups who show mild sensitivity signs. It is also for dogs who are fanatics of this position combined with belly rubs or foot massage. It can be performed on the ground with excellent efficiency. It supports both sides of the dog, and I can get a pretty still and steady doggy out of this human/doggy yoga position.

It is not that comfy on your back in the long run, though, so keep that in mind if you have back issues or want to avoid them.

As always, there is no such rule that you have to finish the dog's nail care session in the same position that you started in. Most of the time, I change positions at least two to three times throughout a nail trim session and implement mini-breaks as well.

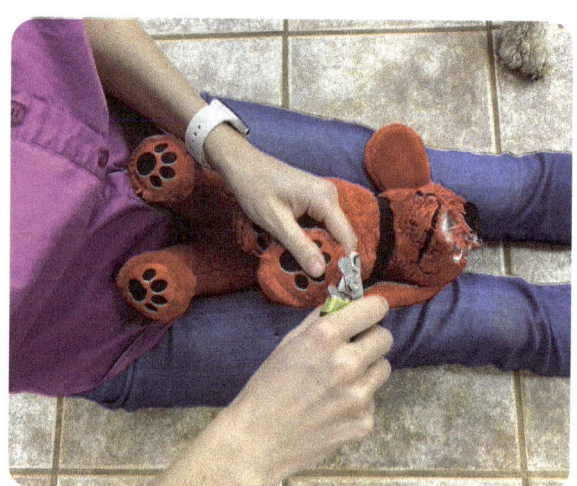
Straddle on the ground - on the thighs version

Chapter 9

Holding Techniques of the Canine

The Goals of Holding Techniques

Our main goal is to keep the dog comfortable and to be able to see the nails from the paw pad side. Many positions allow us to meet both needs. The position I like best is very similar to when horses get a new horseshoe!

Let's take a general look at how to hold the feet, dewclaws, and toenails comfortably for all participants! Then we will break down how to hold the toenails and dewclaws for trimming and filing.

I am right-handed, so please let me explain this the way I have experience with. To help left-handed learners get the hang of it, I created a post for left-handed people to share tips and tricks on their holding techniques in the Nail it! community. Hearing it from people whose left hand is the dominant one will be much more effective.

Holding the Legs

Dos and Don'ts

Experiment with your dog's comfort level without the intention to trim nails at the same time so that both of you can adjust to the other one's preferences, physical limits, and body language.

When we try to do a movement that the doggy's body can't handle or needs to adjust to, we are creating a murky ground that aid injury. A hopping doggy is the last thing we would wish to deal with since we need to make precise movements while cutting nails.

Rotating the leg outward, pulling legs outward, and pulling legs too high up are the most common mistakes that make doggies adjust their balance with a hop or react with mild discomfort signs to let you know it's out of their comfort zone. Sudden hopping and adjusting positioning can result in injuries or sweaty episodes and rapid heart rate for the care provider when not expected.

Flexing/Bending the Legs

Dos and Don'ts

Our goal for a safe nail trimming experience is to take a look at the nails from the paw pad side, from underneath. We'll need to flex the foot on a standing dog to be able to do so. It is pretty easy to perform. Just make sure you're not pulling the legs outward, or too high up, since that'll result in a doggy who'll adjust its balance, and he'll hop. Know that some dogs are more flexible than others.

When we're dealing with a lying doggy, we' adjust our eye level to the dog's nail level on a sitting dog, we can pull the dog's leg straight upward, toward the dog's nose, as if we were trying to touch the dog's chin with the top of his paws. It's not that comfy position for the dog, and it's especially not a comfy one for the care provider. I only use it as a last resort solution for sitting doggies on the table, which can perform a stable sitting posture even when I move the table up high to protect my back.

Holding the Foot

Lifting the Foot

Lifting the Front Foot

Step 1.

You give the dog a verbal cue or by touch that you'll be working on the leg/foot. You can run your palm down from the elbows to the foot on the inner side of the leg. The thumb goes on the back of the leg, between the carpal pad (that bump on the backside of the lower leg) and the paw pads for now. The other four fingers go on the top of the foot. Once comfortable, get a grip and lift upwards, then bend.

Step 2.

Adjust the thumb to go on the paw pad of the nail you'll be working on. (See image above!) The more pressure you apply here, the higher (closer to you) the toenail will rise. The other four fingers stay on the top of the foot.

I find it very helpful to use a cue word for lifting, so the doggy will eventually connect the dots and will know what will happen and can assist you.

Front foot hold for trimming

You can even go next level and teach your dog to lift up the paws this way to assist you like a boss. It's very similar to the one we teach when teaching a dog to limp, but in a sitting position

A dog that feels the need to adjust or is afraid will put a great deal of weight on the foot you are trying to lift. In that situation, you'll need to let it go and let the doggy adjust the stand; otherwise, your arm, hand, and fingers will fall off in about six seconds. If the reason was the need to adjust, the

Holding Techniques of the Canine 147

dog should let you lift up the foot without putting weight there. If the reason was something else, they'll continue the weight putting there and we'll need to investigate further. (Sticker burrs under other foot, between toes on either paw, injury to either leg/foot, being afraid of nail trimming, not comfortable with the height, or slippery surface or paw pads, etc.)

Lifting The Hind Foot

The same approach can be used for the hind legs, with the exception of there is no bump on the hind leg. I usually just get a hold of the metatarsus first and then adjust to hold the feet a tad above the paw pads with the same technique I explained for the front paw.

The most important thing to keep in mind is to keep the leg as vertical as possible, so no pulling outwards at a 90-degree angle or pulling it up high. These super common positioning mistakes that people make is more comfortable for our eyes and arms to see the nails that way. But since the joint can't handle it, the doggy will let us know while hopping to warn us to adjust our hold.

Separating the Toe Pads and the Paw Pad

Separating the pads is super important to get a bigger space while searching for foreign objects (such as plant parts, chewing gum, sticker burrs, cereal, etc.) and checking for mats and, most importantly, trimming paw pad boomerangs out if present.

You can spread the toes by holding your index finger and thumb on each toe and searching for foreign objects between the two toes you are working on. There is a separate section that shows images of how to do this at the paw hair trim section.

Toenail hold - Version 1

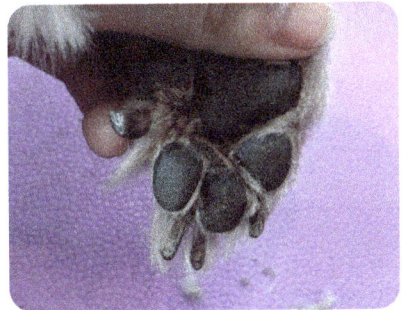
Toenail hold - Version 2

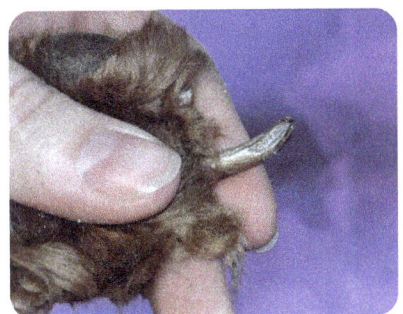
Toenail hold - Version 3

Getting a Good Grip on the Front Feet

1. With your right hand, you stroke the leg down from the elbow toward the feet. You get a gentle grip on the dog's lower leg, the one you are planning to work on
2. You give a cue (verbal, physical) to the dog that you are about to lift the leg, so he can be prepared and adjust with the position he is in if needed
3. Gently lift the leg

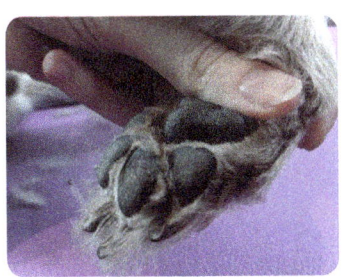
Front lower leg hold - Version 1

4. Our thumb goes right to the base of the paw pad, a bit under where it bends, meanwhile, we make sure the dog is comfortable and he is calm and relaxed
5. Then put two to four fingers of your left hand on the opposite (top) side, and you bend the leg to see the paw pads. We hug the top of the feet with our left hand regardless of whether we are working on the right paw or the left one and irrespective of whether the dog is standing, sitting, or lying down. The top part of the paw is resting on our fingers
6. Then we adjust the "grip" by moving the tip of the index finger down to the tip of the first toenail we would like to trim, to be ready for nail trimming

Toenail hold for trimming - Version 1

Another way I like to hold legs is this one. This is a modified version of the above. (The toenails are facing away from you.) Depending on where your light source is coming from, it might be easier if you ask the dog to move around rather than move the equipment. With flexible dogs, who are happy to move around, you can try this position as well.

Notice how muddy the nails are on the image? Doggies need a paw soak or scrubbing in these situations before the nail trim. With the mud cover, you can't see the layers of the nail, and if you cut too short due to this "blindfolded" guesswork bacteria can get in the bloodstream from the dirt that we desperately want to avoid at all costs.

If there is mud stuck and hardened between the toes, pads, or nails, it needs to be soaked off in warm water before we'd attempt any nail trimming. Those rock-hard balls make the dogs super uncomfortable, so we need to get them off as soon as possible.

Getting a Good Grip on the Hind Feet

Our goal is to see the bottom of the paws/nails. Lifting the leg up high enough to achieve that view yet low enough for the dog to be comfortable is the golden rule. Most dogs are not that flexible as this doggy yogi on the right here, so they will try to disengage their legs when lifted up to this height. That means you need to lower the leg or change positions to keep the dog comfortable and still. Holding the nails is very similar to the above holding technique of the front foot.

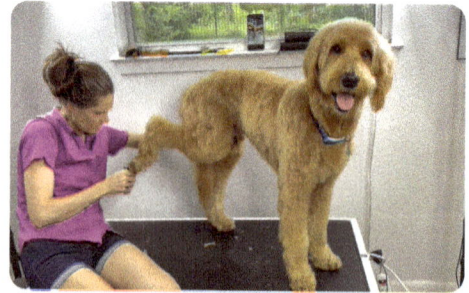

Hind foot hold for trimming - Version 1

Dewclaw Holding Technique

Dewclaws are trickier to hold, so I usually trim them and file them right away as the #1 step on each foot. I'm saving time and the dog's patience with less adjusting and positioning needed by getting a good grip once and doing the trimming and filing back to back.

I use my thumb on the backside and index and middle fingers on the front side to get a steady grip of the paw. Depending on the dog's size, I use the ring finger or the pinky to support the dewclaw from the backside (thick, horny tissue layer). This type of grip enables me to hold the dewclaw still

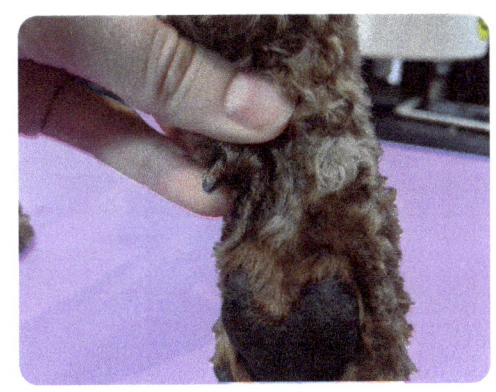
Dewclaw hold - Version 1

and perform precise and safe nail trimming. That is a very comfortable trick for both participants. My middle, ring, and pinky fingers hold the leg's most weight, so the whole leg won't be "hanging on" the dewclaw holding all the leg's weight, causing discomfort for the dog. Dogs appreciate the kindness and will more likely stay still for you as an exchange.

It is much trickier to hold away the hair around the dewclaws when working on a doggy with a longer coat. Keep that in mind, take your time to get a reliable, hairless grip, and readjust with extra patience if you need to give it a few goes before you can master the holding technique!

Toenail Holding Technique

Toenails are relatively easy to hold and position since they are easier to access and in 99.99 percent of the cases they are firmly attached. So we don't have to tiptoe around them. Haha.

To get a good grip on the toenails, we need to make sure we are covering up the part of the nail which we are not planning to work on. We need to block the path that leads down to the base of the nail. If we accidentally open up the clipper wide enough to run down the nail to the nail bed, there will be a roadblock on the nail itself to stop the clipper's motion right by the tip of the nail to avoid cutting off the nail.

What we are trying to avoid sounds much scarier than how easy it is to avoid the tragedy with this roadblock with your finger method. See the three images above to get a closer look at this method!

We also need to make sure that we are keeping the toenail still and the soft tissue parts visible to work on. This is the exact reason why the little "clipper tongue" is not a feasible way to protect the nails. It will prevent the nail from being cut by the base due to the tongue being in the way stopping it from happening, granted. However, it's also in the way for us to see which layer we're working on and how much we are cutting off, so it will not prevent us to cut the nail too short. They have about 3 mm "wiggle room" from the sharp edges. In nail trimming, regardless of the dog's size, that is a huge distance to leave it to chance. Even 1 extra millimeter trimmed off can result in massive bleeding, let alone chopping off 3 mm in the name of "safety" what these tools falsely promise. Now don't get me wrong, the clipper itself can be great, we just need to push the tongue away to see through or unscrew the bolt and remove the tongue completely. We'll detail this later with images and with a video on how to do it yourself.

To make sure we are cutting the parts we want (and not more and not less),

1. we need to see through between the jaws of the clipper—need to move to the side or remove the little tongue thing out of the way and
2. we need to run our index finger on the "back" of the nail. (Horny tissue, on the top of the nail, when the dog is standing.)

To keep the nail still, we need to put our thumb on the toe pad, where the toe we are about to work on resides. I like to run my fingers upright to the tip of the nail, so I can guide the nail clipper to make a more precise cut, without risking cutting more off than intended or even the whole toenail in one snap. Your finger is the best roadblock to keep in there. It might sound crazy, but we are wired in a way that our brain tries to avoid hurting us and knows the location of our body parts intuitively better than we think. It is much less likely to trim the nail too short if your toe is right by the tip of the nail. If you don't feel comfortable leaving your toe right by the tip of the nail and in front of the clipper, you are not yet ready to make precise enough cuts so don't attempt to do nail trims just yet. Make sure your dog is comfy and still enough, and you understand and can identify the nail layers perfectly.

Some may find that trick worrisome, saying they could hurt their fingers "being in the way." Once you put together the four major elements of nail trimming, you'll get the confidence you need to proceed safely.

1. Understanding the layers of the nail
2. Practicing the nail trimming movements on cashew nuts
3. Training your dog before nail care to be comfortable with paw handling and holding techniques so he'll stay still
4. Exercising him right before the trim so he'll stay still

Once we have mastered these, we'll be able to put our knowledge and experience together and the confidence will miraculously appear.

If you do not have that confidence yet, but your dog needs a nail trim sooner than the time you need to practice by yourself or with your dog, I recommend leaving the job to a professional for one last time if nail care is urgent.

We will discuss all four sections separately in detail here and in the videos as well.

We discuss roadblocks in the Nail it! community, so feel free to ask your questions, share videos and images there with us! I'll be happy to help you get the answers you need!

Chapter 10

Nail Care Preparations Way Before Trimming

Finding Possible Triggers

What makes dogs react? Once we know the answer to that question we can come up with way more efficient solutions. Sometimes a quick fix like changing locations or using nail file instead of nail clippers is enough. In other cases the doggy needs customized training and desensitization. Either way, knowing the dog's triggers are the pillars of the solution.

Paw Sensitivity Assessment

As the first step, I determine the body parts I can touch with my hands that the dog can tolerate without showing early or late sensitivity signs! I don't use treats for this test, I want to see how the dog interacts in the situation "raw". I usually gently run my fingers on the coat from the back, hips, thighs, lower leg, foot, toes, toenails.

I go with this order especially if I don't know the history of the dog. This gives me more wiggle room and time to move my hands if the dog shows late sensitivity signs. On the front legs, I go in the neck, shoulder blades, upper leg, lower leg, paw, toe, toenail order. I like to know whether the dog knows to shake so we can do that as well for fun.

If the dog shows no sensitivity at all we can go to the next step.

Tool Sensitivity Assessment

I like to see how dogs react to the tools before I attempt to do a nail trim or file. Sometimes they're absolutely fine with the touching part anywhere on their bodies, as long as there are no nail clippers in sight. Dogs with traumatizing past experiences around nail care (they got quicked, experienced lots of restraint, etc.) will have a significantly tougher time adjusting to the sight of the clipper, so we can expect them to react more when they see one showing up.

I usually check three tools—the paw hair shears, nail clippers, and the nail file. I show the tool, let them sniff it, then move it along the parts I did with the touch. If they are okay with this, I'll lift up the paws and imitate a nail trim by touching the clipper to their nails. If this still goes well, we're ready for a nail trim. This way, you'll be less likely to get surprised by a late sensitivity sign "out of the blue" while doing a pawdicure.

Getting clear signals for these tests means we work in an emotional state below the threshold and we can expect a cooperative dog under our care.

Once you know the triggers (touch/tool/location/severity), go back to the Training the Dog Mind chapter and work with your dog until he is comfortable with your touch.

Test Conclusion

If the dog shows early or late sensitivity signs at any point of these two tests, we'll need to stop and come up with an action plan based on the dog's reaction to the location of the touch, the tool, the nails' length, and the dog's reaction to counter conditioning and desensitization.

Some dogs (can expect it more with seeing early sensitivity signs) do fabulously just after a few tries and we can do magic within like five minutes. Some have been so traumatized, it'll take weeks to see significant improvement with the involvement of a trainer as well.

The tests are critical steps to come up with the best fitting care plan. So is telling/showing the results to the owners and staff so they'll be on board about the current situation and will understand better the level of training involvement you will suggest if necessary. It is easier for owners to see the need for training when they see it in reality, so a video or an in-person demonstration can go a long way. Some owners will still say things that disregard the safety of the dog or care provider, so be prepared to respond in alignment with respect and the need for safety for the dog and care providers.

See the action plan section later in the book to come up with strategies to resolve the case and to make the nail trim and filing happen!

Determining Your Dog's Nail Types

We will need to figure out two things. Whether your dog has dewclaws or not and what type of nails (taco or hot dog) are the toenails and dewclaws he has. The first is fast; you can palpate the inner side of the legs a tad higher than the paws and feel whether there are any nails there. If there are, you found dewclaws.

Toenails are easier, you will find them right by the tip of the toes. Some dogs lose some due to injury or infection, but generally speaking, you can expect four toenails on your dog.

To better understand what kind of approach you will need to get your dog's nails shorter, the second step I suggest is to determine what nail type your dog has on each nail.

One of the best ways to understand what you will be dealing with as a whole is to **take images of all of your dog's toenails and dewclaws from the paw pad side**. See the chapter for reference if needed! Also, there is an exercise chapter at the end of the book to practice differentiating between taco and hot dog nail types. Once you can tell whether it is taco or hot dog nail type precisely on your dog, you will know the upcoming steps, how to do the first cut, the rest, and filing.

For the first time, if you want to go wild, you can organize your images by foot, by the side, and see the progress on the pictures. It's fun! I do this with my clients when the nails are too long, and they understand the process better and are more satisfied to see the nails getting shorter over time. Especially when the live part, the quick has grown down together with the nails, and it takes multiple sessions and home practice to get the quick recede. And in cases when they don't bring the dogs in soon enough, they see the nail growing even longer. So it is a great way to convince pawrents about regular nail trims and celebrate the milestones together!

Determining Your Dog's Nail Length

We have a specific chapter about this topic, so refer back to that part to determine whether your dog needs a nail trim or not yet. Remember! When one nail is longer than it should be, the dog needs to get that trimmed. We should not wait for the other nails to "catch up" and grow longer. Some nails might get worn off more efficiently due to body build, etc. and some nails would never grow as long as the "one long nail". So when a single nail or a few needs trimming, we need to work on those that need trimming only. It's not a must to cut all nails at nail care time. I often see dogs with perfect back nail length. I don't even need to file them. There is no room for that. Dogs who like to dig wear off their front nails amazingly, oftentimes even their declaws. Dogs with activity-heavy jobs or lifestyles and with a great build can take care of all their nails without any assistance. Think about farm dogs or dogs who are companions of hikers. They walk so much, sometimes they'll need boots just to protect the pads from the ground.

Take images of your dog's toenails **from the outer and inner sides** (dewclaws inner side is enough), from the same level as the paws are (phone on or very close to the ground for toenails). And determine whether the nails need to be trimmed based on the drawing in the relating chapter!

Toki's Adventure with the "Nail File" by the Pool

My boy, Toki has two outer nails on the front and back that used to grow longer than the others. He likes to fetch and fun runs, but it was mostly done on dirt or grass and the walks on a leash did not do the trick. So I was cutting and filing those nails. After we moved into our new-to-us home with a pool, running around the perimeter of it wore off the long nails to normal length, and the short ones became extremely short. Not so fun fact, dogs can wear off their nails to the point of bleeding. Toki did that a couple of times and I did not even notice it. He did not show any sensitivity signs, just wanted to play more and get the toy out of the water. Crazy Malinois mindset. I just noticed the blood spots on the ground. We did a few days with the pool being off-limits, and it healed up well. The nails adjusted, the quick to receded even farther, so now he has tight little nails.

Determining Your Dog's Nail Tip Types

You can most likely reuse the images you took to determine the nails type (from the paw pad side) for this part. Take a look at the nail tips and determine their type!

A Plan for Way Before the Nail Care Session

There are a few things I'd like to cover that aids both of your experiences for nail trimming. Here is a summary of what I like to do before nail care sessions.

1. Get the knowledge (and confidence) of canine nail care, nail anatomy, and necessary canine behavior to be able to trim nails without hurting the dog or getting bitten
2. Practicing positionings with the dog
3. Tire out the doggy (You or the owner. Care providers! Ask for it from the owner. Most of them will be happy to bring a tired do to your practice!)
4. Earn the pup's focus and trust and ease into the "let's get pampered" mood with some treats and playtime (paw touching, paw holding, butt rubs, ear rubs, mix & match, etc.) in advance
5. Evaluate comfort and confidence level while playing
    a. Being touched
    b. Lifted up
    c. Holding paws
    d. Equipment around feet (without using it)
    e. Balance
    f. Any Pain
    g. Energy level time frame he'll cooperate, (more exercise needed to get a doggy tired)
    h. Fingers among paw pads
    i. Patience Credit—timeframe he'll cooperate (=energy pups/elderly)
6. Figure out the dog's Favorite Positions
7. Point out the dog's strengths and areas you all (owner, groomer, vet, dog) need to work on
8. Have the most appropriate equipment for the dog's comfort level. Plier-style clippers and nail files work well
9. Make a training/desensitizing plan for the future according to the dog's needs (if necessary)
10. Desensitize, train, practice positioning and comfort the doggy in advance (if possible)

Practicing Without the Dog

The safest way to prepare ourselves to trim dog nails is to gain some confidence by practicing clipper handling, angling, and making actual cuts on a steady object without a pulse and more importantly, nerve endings.

The easiest way to do it is to practice on cashew nuts with a small size Safari nail clipper. The cashews are nail-shaped, so they make fantastic dog nail models. You might have some at the back of the cupboard that will be perfect for practice. (Try to use the unsalted kind so that the salt won't eat up the metal part of the clipper.)

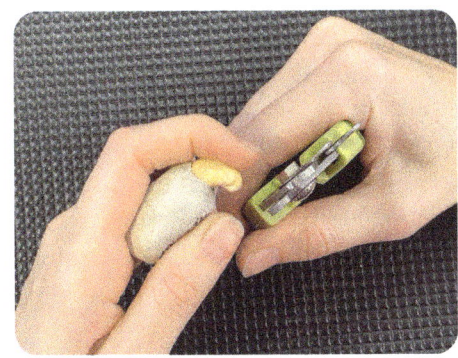

Cashew nut embedded in clay for practicing nail trimming

You can pick similar shapes to your dog's nails and start practicing safely. Cashew nuts are a great way to learn how to position the nail, your fingers, how to hold the dog's paws, how to angle the nail clipper, know how much to cut off, and trim off tiny nail flakes.

Cashews are softer than toenails, they won't make your clippers dull like chopsticks. Given they have no blood vessels and their softness, they are the perfect material for some playtime and safe practice.

Drawing lines where you anticipate trimming would be ideal to stop and making cuts on them, kind of sculpturing the nail to reach the line you marked is a great way to build nail trimming skills and confidence rapidly. See the nail trimming techniques to practice in Chapter 12 for full details on this!

Chapter 11

Nail Care Preparations Right Before Trimming

There are a few preparation steps to nail trimming, which I would like to cover before the nail trimming itself. Seeing the dog's eyes and the dog's ability to see the care provider well is essential for a smooth experience and comes sooner in order in the pawdicure session as well. If your dog has a lot of hair around the eyes and paws, we need to trim the hair in those spots first for comfort and safety for all.

Eye Area Trim

To make sure everyone is the most comfortable, I highly recommend trimming the eye area hair if the dog has a hard time seeing. It will be beneficial not only for the dog's general comfort but also for you to pick up on the dog's reactions. Bonus for the dog's everyday life as well.

The hair around the inner corners can be trimmed off with a few snaps, and the bangs can be shortened as well to the point where the dog will be able to see.

For more info on how to do the eye area trim, even a full FFF, aka the Face, feet, fanny trim, check out my online course on my website! https://bit.ly/3kVZrHF

Same dog, before and after eye area trim

Paw Hair Maintenance

The first step in finding paw pad boomerangs and keeping dogs comfortable on all fours (in general and for nail trims) is to keep their paw hair in check and trimming it short when it covers the pads and prevents the dog from getting a good grip. You will get a much better view of the area between the pads with less hair around the pads and will be able to find and remove paw pad boomerangs easier. Take a look at this white pup's paws. The left image shows before the paw hair trim. The right photo shows the paw hair trimmed short and the paw pad boomerang removed. Which paw hair length will make doggies get a better grip on the ground? Paws down, it'll be the length on the right.

Paw before paw hair trimming - paw pad side

Paw after paw hair trimming - paw pad side

I was shocked to see whole communities who cherish the excess paw hair on dogs and cats. They share images of so called "paw feathers" and adore how they look. All I can see is the discomfort the poor souls go through every second of the day for not being able to get a good grip, and the spraining and other injuries that come with the deal. Jumping is impaired and injury is much more likely with paw feathers present.

I'm very glad though, that now, one more person—you—understands the implications of paw feathers and though they might look cute, I'm sure you'll prioritize the comfort and safety of your dog or cat and get those paw feathers trimmed short as needed.

Dogs with active doggy lifestyles can wear off their paw hair themselves. It is especially true for larger breeds when more weight is involved. Puppies and elderly dogs need help with them.

Trimming the Paw Hair

To start building up trust for nail care and to make sure the doggy we are about to work with (not on, with! ;-) can stay balanced even on three legs, I suggest **checking/trimming the paw hair short** on the paw pad surface and between the pads.

Some super high energy level dogs who get to spend time outdoors enough wear off not just their nails, but also their paw hair on the surface of the paw and toe pads. They can't wear off the hair in between the pads though.

I prefer trimming the hair with the shears you have seen above on the surface of the toe and paw pads and in between.

Paw hair trimming on the paw pad surface

They are called ConAir Pro rounded tip shears and those shears are the perfect tool for this task. See the tools section in the book and the videos for more detail on them, how to use them, safety, etc.!

Keeping the paw hair short is a great way to help doggies get a good grip on the ground, even on hardwood floors. Before trimming the paw hair is an excellent opportunity to check for toe mohawks and paw pad boomerangs as well and trim them out if they are present.

When the dog has multiple, large mats on their paws either between the pads or between the toes, I try to keep them in a lying position to avoid any extra pressure on their feet. After the paws have been trimmed and freed from mats, they can stand up again, and we go about the grooming in a standing position.

Paw hair trim is relatively easy to accomplish. You take a look at the dog's paw pads and trim all the excess hair on the surface, which prevents you from seeing all the pads. Keep close attention to see where the skin ends and the hair starts!

> **Fun Fact**
>
> I like to trim the hair right by the side of the nails, so they won't grow under the nail sort of a tiny layer of cushion between the dog's nail and the surface under it. It's a weird thing, but hair between the tip of the nail and the surface makes it significantly harder for the dog to wear off the nails.

I rather use the ConAir Pro rounded tip shears than a clipper because dogs tend to favor the shears. Clippers make a lot of noise; they vibrate intensely, and since doggy feet are a susceptible part of canines, they tend to react a lot when the loud, vibrating thing is used among the toe pads or around them.

We can get them used to it, but I much rather use a pair of ConAir Pro shears with rounded tips to trim hair there.

This is the only brand I feel comfortable suggesting since it has the perfect balance in sharpness and size to keep the dog's skin safe. Other shears are either too dull, too sharp, too big, or a combination of these.

The areas between the toes are less sensitive compared to the soft skin between the pads. The top of the toes and feet are even less sensitive, and it is less likely the doggy will get injured.

> **Good to Know**
>
> Depending on the dog's age and amount of rough use of the pads (working farm dog vs. walks on grass) dogs paw skin can be softer or rougher. The softer the skin, the easier it is to cut it. The thicker the skin, the harder it is to cut it.

On elderly dogs, even the skin of the pads can be ultra-soft and super thin so I suggest being triple careful and taking your time trimming hair on elderly dogs with thin and soft paw pad skin.

Knowing this, paw hair trim on the paw pad surface on an average, adult doggy with medium-soft skin is a pretty safe way to start practicing trimming hair on dogs. That was the first thing they taught us at the grooming school and I have to agree on this, it's a pretty great way to get the hang of trimming with shears.

Generally speaking, I suggest skipping the clipper among the pads and learning to use the shears around the pads. I use clippers only for the "poodle paw", and even before that I trim the hair on the paws solely with shears between the pads and do a pre-trim between the toes.

Searching for Paw Pad Boomerangs and Foreign Objects

The feet holding method below is for dogs who are standing or sitting.

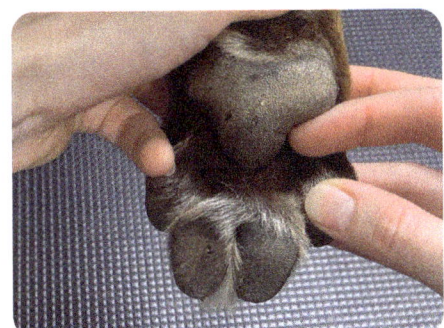

Paw checkup - holding technique 1

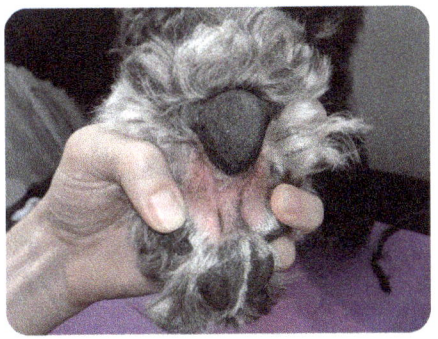

Paw checkup - holding technique 2

Taking a look among the pads is critical to make sure no foreign objects or mats are present to keep dogs comfortable. Practicing this also helps to get them used to be touched on the paws so you're scoring comfort and trust tokens for nail trimming as well. Win-win.

You'll need to get a good view of the paw pad side to do your search effectively. If you put pressure on the toe pads on the sides (toward the outer side at a 45-degree angle), it will open up the pads beautifully.

You will see a large, firm, banana or boomerang-shaped bunch if your dog has shorter hair. If they have long hair, you will probably see a pile of hair, and the pads might not be even visible at all. Stick your finger in the boomerang-shaped gap and feel for yourself whether there are mats, foreign objects, or mud present. If you can feel the skin on the sides, and nothing extra is in there, great. If there are paw pad boomerangs, excess hair, foreign objects present, they need to be removed immediately.

Paw pad boomerang in the paw before trimming

Unfortunately, there can be severe cases like the one on the right. This poor doodle had three!! Rocks stuck in his paws and over two dozen!! Individual mud balls (between the pads and toes) hardened enough to be mistaken for stones. This is incredibly uncomfortable.

Imagine how you feel when a tiny rock or a twig gets in your shoe. You want to get it out instantly, right? This poor dog lived with these for days and days. All four feet were like this one. It took me a long time to calm myself enough to talk to the pawrent in a civilized and professional way after seeing this. I got triggered big time, so I had to do some counter conditioning on myself before talking to the mom at the pickup time.

If the dog has a lot of paw pad boomerangs and possibly foreign objects, do the hair removal while the dog is on his side/back to avoid pressure on the other three unlifted feet while you work on a paw.

The most severe case of paw mats I've seen so far.

Trimming Out Paw Pad Boomerangs

Removing the paw pad boomerangs by cutting them out is the only comfortable way to go about paw pad boomerangs. They cannot be untangled. It is a speedy procedure and brings much-needed relief for dogs. You can see the relief, comfort, and joy in the dog's eyes after they try out the new landing gear while standing on them.

After trimming the paw hair on the surface, I cut the mats out with a pair of pre-haircut shears. Dogs can get a better grip, will be more still, and more effective nail care will happen.

Many groomers use clippers with very short blades (#10, #30) to clean the paws. I prefer shears because, in my opinion, it is significantly easier to nick the dog's paw with a short clipper blade or irritate soft skin there. Plus dogs hate the sound of it, let alone the intense vibration on their feet. They'll wiggle more, multiplying the chances of an injury. So I stick with a particular type of shears to stay safe as I mentioned before. See the tools chapter on which one!

Paw hair trim between the pads

Check out three images below about before and after paw hair trim to get an idea of how a well-prepared paw pad looks like and check out the resources for videos on how to do it.

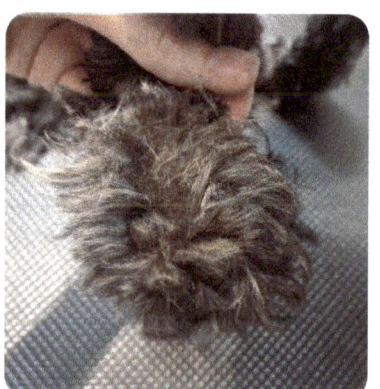
Paw hair before trimming hair - dog 1, paw pad view

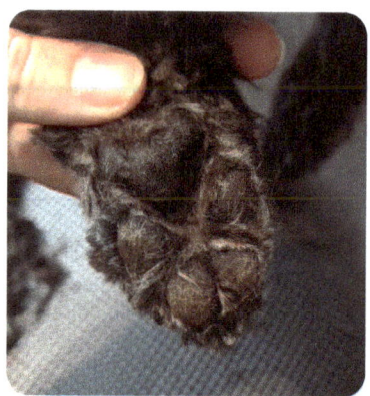
Paw hair after trimming hair - dog 1, paw pad view

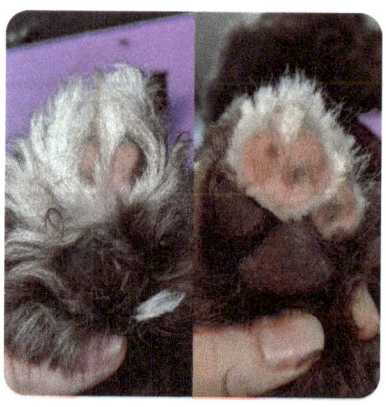
Paw hair before/after trimming - dog 2, paw pad view

Since this step has multiple aspects, check out the online course on how to do this on your dog, hold the paws and toes to make it a comfortable, safe, and quick step of the Paw-di-cure™ path.

Extreme Situations on Everyday Dogs

Yes, that is the paw pad side of the feet, though you can't see a thing of the pads. Now imagine how hard it must be for that poor pup to get a good grip while standing up, running, or just walking on hardwood or any other slippery surface. Let alone when walking in wet grass or mud. All that rock-solid mat bunch means pure suffering. And this is only the paw pad hair and paw pad boomerangs side.

There are other places where mats can hide. See the next session to see where else they can be found!

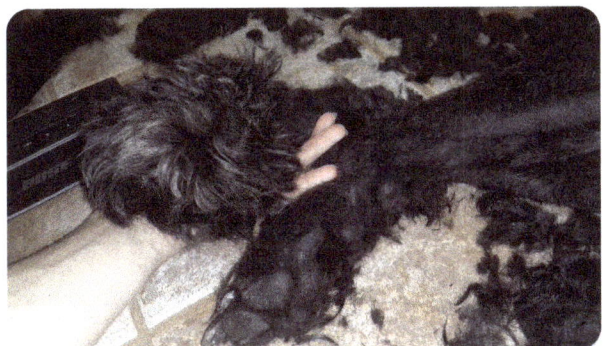

Extremely matted paw hair, paw pad side

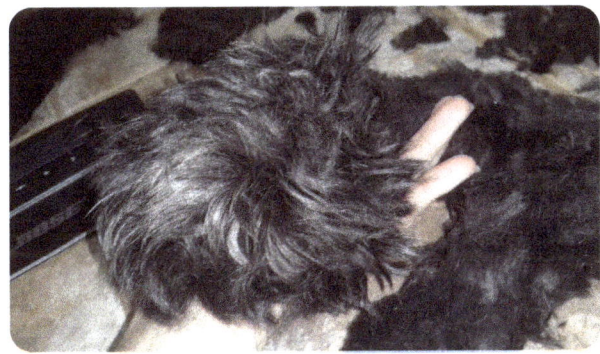

Extremely matted paw hair, paw pad side

How Can We Remove Toe Mohawks?

Cutting out the toe mohawks is the only comfortable way to get rid of them once they're present.

We separate the toes, and using a rounded tip shear (link in the equipment section), we trim them out, holding the shears parallel with the toes. See the image on the right and see the section in the course about this step to get the hang of it!

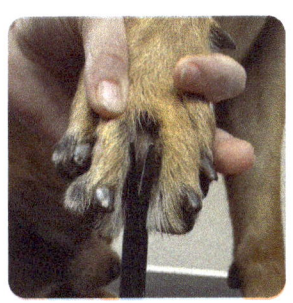

Trimming out toe mohawks

Toenail Socks Search and Trim

Finding toenail socks is relatively easy. If we can't see a particular nail due to fluff tightly encircling it, chances are you just found a toenail sock. To trim it out, I like to try to trim the hair that connects the sock to the nail base. If you can go around the nail there, that'll make it much easier to remove the sock.

Since the nail itself is horny tissue, so you won't be able to cut into it, as long as you can palpate and make sure you are working near the nail, not the skin, you can trim off the thickness of the sock on the sides holding the shears parallel with the nail.

If you can feed the tip of the shear through the thickness of the sock and cut the hair without the nail (or skin) being between the jaws of the shears, that's another great way to go. Removing toenail socks is most cases a repetition of cutting in the mat (not in the nail or skin), pulling, loosening it up, cutting again, pulling apart, loosening again, etc.

Critical to keep in mind! Only cut when you are 100 percent sure after palpating that it's hair only, not skin, nor horny tissue.

See how I remove toenail socks in the Nail it! course!

Nail Care Goals

1. **Physical comfort and safety for all participants**
   - Zero or minimally restricted position for both dog and care provider
   - Eye area and paw hair trim before nail care
   - Emotional support team: If the doggy is not that comfortable being alone with a stranger, have a pack member present; another (low distraction) doggy or owner's presence can sometimes help as well. Furry pack member or groomer's dog. My dogs saved the day on so many occasions and brought the boost my clients needed to start and finish the nail care session

2. **Sensation-free trimming method** (next chapter sneak peek)
   - No pressure or tiny pressure on the quick
   - Sharp nail clipper
   - Scissor type nail clipper
   - Clip tiny by tiny - no/low-pressure angling of the nail clipper
   - Holding the paw to get a perfect view of the nails from the paw pad side
   - Supporting each nail with hold while working on it
   - Foot/nail soak (getting a bath with the tub stopper in, bowl, playing fetch in the creek/lake, etc.) if necessary before nail care

3. **Distraction-free environment**

A Plan for Right Before the Nail Care Session

1. Pick nail care environment (Choose a well-lit area. Use a super bright headlamp.)
2. Prepare all the equipment and strong treats, keeping them handy
3. Tire the doggy out
4. Pee/poop break for both of you :)
5. Clean the eye area from hair so you can see the doggy's reaction and vice versa
6. Playtime warm-up for nail care (feet touches, paw holdings and release, couple of seconds on-off only)
7. Clean paws, paw hair, and toenails, rinse/wash as needed, gently brush if necessary
8. Paw hair length evaluation (foreign objects, "matted mohawks" and "matted noodles")
   a. Search for foreign objects (ruling out discomfort)
   b. On top of the feet
   c. Paw pad surface (hair covering the paw pads, so you can't see the paw pad skin)
   d. More profound among paw pads (matted paw pad boomerangs, mud, etc.)
   e. Between the toes (matted toe mohawks)

9. Nail length:
    a. Is the toenail touching the ground?
    b. If so, are they lifting the paw pads?
    c. Are the inner curves of the nails touching the tip of the toe pads?
    d. Dewclaw evaluation
10. Nail care equipment need (clipper/file or both)
11. Determine the dog's favorite and most comfortable positions
12. Determine triggers for the doggy
13. Trim off paw hair (bottom and top), paw mohawks, and toenail mohawks (comfort and better grip on the surface while balancing)
14. Trim the dewclaws first on the paw
15. File the dewclaw right away (Remember, it can be hard to position it, so once you've got the best grip, it is preferable to do the trimming and filing so there won't be a second grip needed=saving time and patience credit for you all)
16. Trim the other nails on the paw
17. File all the nails on the paw
18. Reinforce the doggy frequently (as needed) throughout the nail care (depending on the dog's training and comfort level)
19. Do the steps on all four paws
20. Paw hair shaping on all four, evening up the hair
21. Nail trim evaluation
22. Future treatment plan (if needed)

Nail Care Workflow

1. Pick nail care environment (well-lit area. Use a super bright headlamp.)
2. Prepare all the equipment and mighty treats
3. Playtime
    a. Satisfying the dog's needs = Happy Puppy **Tire out**
    b. **Pee - Poop break** at home and right before walking in the grooming shop
4. Play groomer - warm-up for nail care (treats, round-tip shears)
    a. **Trim eye area hair** if your doggy can't see you or you can't see the doggy's eye. (You want to see the dog's reactions. Eyes tell a lot; you want to see them.)
    b. Gentle **feet touch, holding paws** and release, a couple of seconds on-off only
    c. **Check for foreign objects** among the paw pads
5. **Paw hair check and trim**
    a. Check for foreign objects amongst paw pads (gently with fingers)
    b. Trim hair on the paw pad surface
    c. Trimming the paw pad hair or "paw pad noodles"

d. Trimming out "toe mohawks"
6. **Feet and nail wash**
   a. Paws, paw hair, and toenails, rinse/wash as needed, gently brush if muddy/necessary
7. **Foot soak** if the doggy is sensitive for nail care to make nails softer (after a foot soak, they feel less pressure to trigger the pooch. If the dog gets a haircut as well, the bath will replace the soaking time; just make sure the dog's paws are underwater for most of the bath time)
8. **Paw hair length evaluation** (foreign objects, "matted mohawks" and "matted noodles")
   a. Search for foreign items (ruling out discomfort)
   b. On top of the feet
   c. Paw pad surface (hair covering the paw pads, so you can't see the skin of the paw pad)
   d. More profound among paw pads (matted paw pad noodles, mud, etc.)
   e. Between the toes (matted toe mohawks)
9. **Nail length**:
   a. Is the nail touching the ground?
   b. If so, is it lifting the paw pad?
   c. Dewclaw evaluation
10. **Nail vs. paw pad relations**
    a. Nail touches the paw pad
    b. The nail is farther away from the paw pad
11. **Choosing nail care equipment** (clipper/file or both)
12. Determine **the dog's favorite and most comfortable positions**
13. Determine **triggers** for the doggy
14. **Trim paw hair short** (bottom and top), paw mohawks, and toenail mohawks (comfort and better grip on the surface while balancing)
15. **Trimming the dewclaws**
16. **Filing the dewclaw** right away (It is hard to position it, so once you've got the best grip, it is preferable to do the trimming and filing so there won't be a second grip needed=saving time and patience credit for you all.)
17. **Trimming the toe**nails on the paw
18. **Filing all the toenails** on the paw
19. **Reinforcing the doggy frequently** (as needed) throughout the nail care (depending on the dog's training and comfort level)
20. **Doing the steps on all four paws**
21. **Paw hair shaping/styling** on all fours, evening up the hair
22. **Nail trim success evaluation**
23. **Future treatment/training plan** (if needed due to long quick or behavior)

If the dog is in desperate need of a nail trim, but he doesn't want to cooperate, I do the following steps:

1. Determine the trigger point
2. Make a plan to avoid the triggers if possible and to get done with the nail care ASAP.
3. Belly hug hold works most of the time for wiggly dogs who show early signs of discomfort only
4. A grooming loop (sometimes combined with a muzzle) is a last resort for dogs who show late discomfort signs (biting, growling, etc.). (If you are using a muzzle, I highly recommend that you use it along with grooming loops; better yet, have another experienced care provider around for safety and speed up the procedure.)
5. A plan for desensitization is vital in these cases to ensure that the canine and care providers are all comfortable and safe in the future

In general, I prefer not to use muzzles, leashes, and crazy restraints for dogs that are not in desperate need of a nail trim. Earning trust won't make those necessary. If it is needed to use restraint and safety equipment because the nail trim is urgent due to comfort or health, it is also **essential to let the owner know what to practice at home between nail care appointments to desensitize a dog to nail care**. Home practice is critical to ensure the doggy will be more comfortable by the next time. That's the way to make the nail care experience better and better for all participants. No such thing as a "bad dog", but ones that need a bit more focused attention to get comfortable do exist.

Desensitizing a dog is a process that won't happen overnight. Appreciate every small step toward the goal and communicate with the owners how they are doing—i.e. whether they got stuck at some point, etc. offer your help/ask for help to turn the dog's behavior around the fastest possible way.

Chapter 12

Nail Trimming

This section is the essence of comfortable and joyful nail care experiences. We will learn to provide not only an injury-free but also a sensation-free cutting experience for dogs, so they will truly enjoy the pawdicure. This section is the heart and soul of recovery for dogs with painful nail trimming experiences.

Holding Tricks for Precisely Trimming Toenails

With a proper holding technique, we want to keep the nail we are working on supported by our other finger(s) for nail trimming, so it won't bend or wiggle away when we are trimming or filing it. Plus with a finger around combined with opening the clipper just enough to cut a corner, not wide enough to run down to the base of the nail, we can make sure the clipper won't go too deep.

Clipper holding method - paw pad view

You can get different grips on the dog's feet; here are a few suggestions from my favorites.

My thumb supports the toe pad in most position types. The index finger is either bent and hugs the toenail you are working on from the pads' opposite side (top) -see the first image below or it is running through the top of the nail like on the second image below.

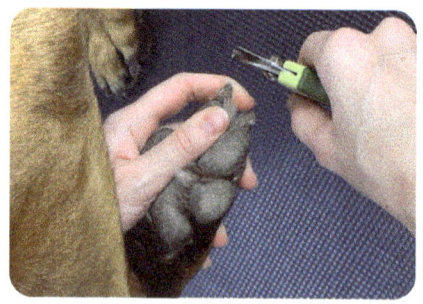
Clipper holding method - paw pad view

Clipper holding method - side view

With my index finger, I get to adjust the depth of the cut by moving it higher or lower on the nail. By controlling how wide I open up the clipper's jaws, I can make a double barrier to avoid cutting too deep. With these two safety measures, we can reliably and systematically avoid injuries.

Move the Tongue out of the Way

In the tool section, we touched on why the little tongue is so unnecessary and even harmful. Here is a demonstration of the difference in view when the tongue is blocking your view of the nail (first image below) and when it is moved out of the way (second and third images below).

You need to see exactly what you are doing and which layer you are working on to stay safe. We discussed the additional method to keep you from cutting the whole nail off, so I think we are on the same page by using common sense to move the tongue out of the way. You can even remove it from your clipper, there is no situation that it can be useful for in the nail trimming process. When the tongue is blocking your view it is like doing surgery wearing a blindfold out of fear of cutting too deep. We can prevent that exactly by making sure we see what layer of tissues we are working on.

I removed the tongues from my daily clippers, only kept it on this display tool to show you how it looks on the clipper and why it is so dangerous to use.

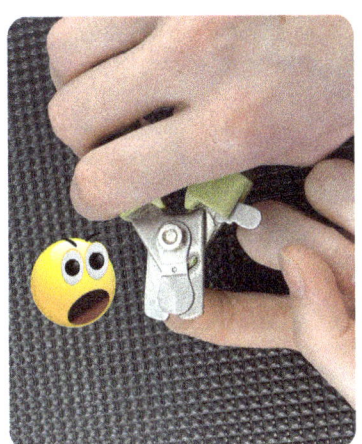
The clipper's tongue is in the way, you can't see which layer you are working on and how deep you are cutting

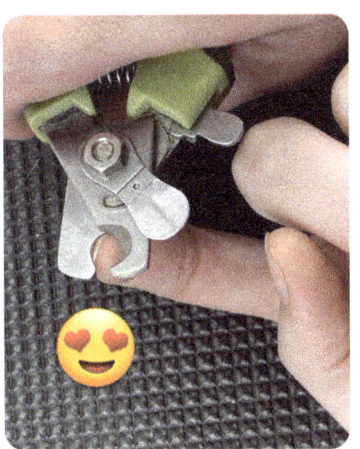
The clipper tongue has been moved to the side to see which layer you are working on

The clipper tongue has been moved to the side to see which layer you are working on and how deep you are cutting

Top Tip

If the dog is super sensitive to nail clipping, you can soak the feet in warm water for a few minutes to help soften the nails enough to make nail trimming work. The best is to time the paw care around bath days so it will soak even more before nail trim. After a good fun run, post-bath zoomies, and shake-shakes, the doggy will be ready for the pawdicure.

Holding the Clipper for Pressure-Free Clipping

One of the biggest triggers for dogs is the pressure of cutting with a bad clipper holding technique. (Or a dull clipper, but let's say ours' is new or sharp enough, we checked already.)

Dog nails have an oval or rounded tube-like shape, and when we squeeze even the surroundings of the "stuffing" (the soft tissue), the dog will freak out, thinking we will cut the live part of the nail.

We can influence the amount of pressure they feel and even eliminate it by angling the clipper. It is an incredibly essential step for dogs (especially with painful past experiences) in the desensitization phase and for beginners to set the joyful tone for nail care from the start.

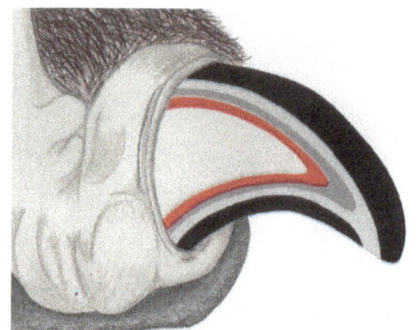

Layers of the nail

The horny tissue is the thickest throughout the top of the nail length, to protect it from the elements around the top of the paw. (Compare the two black layers, top and bottom, on the drawing to the right.)

The horny tissue on the sides of the nail and on the bottom closest to the ground is significantly thinner on both nail types. Most often the bottom is fused on the hot dog nail types (first image below) and open in case of the taco nail types (second, third images below). Either way, it still protects the nail just fine.

Regardless of the nail type, when we squeeze the nail's sides while trimming, it has the same consequences, a wiggly or snappy dog because of the squeezing sensation on the soft tissue in the best, or seeing bleeding as the worst scenario.

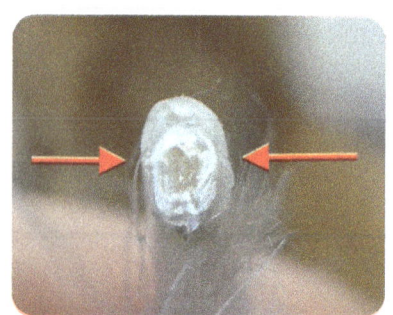

Pressure on the soft tissue of a hot dog nail type from the sides, when we position the clipper's jaws to encircle the outers sides of the nail.

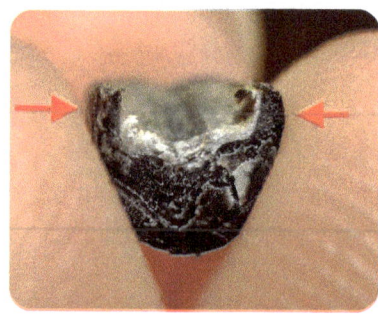

Pressure on the soft tissue of a taco nail type from the sides, when we position the clipper's jaws to encircle the outers sides of the nail.

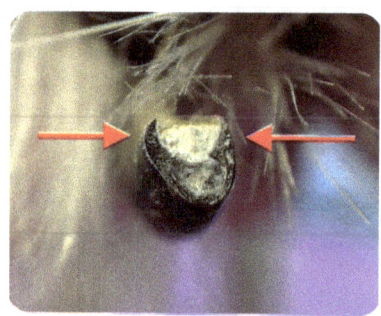

Pressure on the soft tissue of a hot dog nail type from the sides, when we position the clipper's jaws to encircle the outers sides of the nail.

The **first image** above shows a hot dog nail type. Notice the top horny tissue is the thickest, the sides and bottom are significantly thinner. The bottom is fused.

On the **second image** above, you see a taco nail type, shot from the cut line closer toward the dog's side (the tip of the nail is looking away from the viewer). The bottom is unfused, opened.

On the **third image** above, you see a unique hot dog nail type with an unfused bottom. Notice how thick the powdery sole layer is. Fascinating, isn't it?

Nail Trimming 169

Pressure-free positioning of the clipper on the soft tissue of a hot dog nail type from the bottom side, when we position the clipper's jaws to encircle the top and bottom sides of the nail.

Pressure-free positioning of the clipper on the soft tissue of a taco nail type from the bottom side, when we position the clipper's jaws to encircle the top and bottom sides of the nail.

Pressure-Free Clipper Holding Technique

The angles above work great for the first cut for both nail types, and for the follow-up cuts on the top of the nail (where the horny tissue is the thickest.) Remember, that the thicker top will be located on the bottom when you are turning the feet upside down to get the paw pad view like above.

The clipper can start cutting smoothly in the thinner tissue and will result in a pressure-free experience for the dog.

(The holding technique to trim the sides is coming up below. This method detailed here is not designed for trimming that nail part.)

The clipper putting pressure on the soft tissue of a hot dog nail type from the sides, when we position the clipper's jaws to encircle the nail from the outer sides of the nail.

The clipper putting pressure on the soft tissue of a taco nail type from the sides, when we position the clipper's jaws to encircle the nail from the outer sides of the nail.

The top left image shows a pressure-free clipping method on a hot dog nail type, hence the emoji with heart eyes. The right image above shows a pressure-free clipping method on a taco nail type, with the same emoji.

Notice how the outer curve of the nail nestles in the inner curve of the lower jaws of the clipper. That will enable a sturdy grip and will make a smooth cut on the nail, starting by the thinner edges of the nail, by the clipper's upper jaw.

This is the magic in action that will reassure dogs that it is a pain-free method that they can enjoy.

The Pressure Sensation Generating Clipper Holding Technique

This is how not to hold the clipper, especially not on a clipper-sensitive or "recovering" dog. Remember, the clipper's jaws cut smoother when they can "bite" in a thinner edge of the nail first! When we hold the clipper's jaws angled like above (when the outer side of the clipper's jaws meet the neighboring nail), we will squeeze the softer tissue by squeezing the horny tissue on the sides before the cut, regardless of how sharp the clipper is or what nail type we are working on.

That is a guarantee for a reacting dog since they feel the pressure around the soft tissue, and they will think you will cut into the layers with blood vessels and nerve endings. So they will protest big time against the suspected ouchie outcome for them (and for you as well).

Pressure-Free Trimming of the Tip of the Nail

Here is a demonstration about making that initial cut on the tip of a nail. I keep my pinky in this instance as a guide to the clipper and as a shield to avoid the clipper running too deep. The clipper is parallel with the imaginary line between the two outer pads. That way the clipper's jaws will start cutting the dog's nail by the bottom and will make the cut smooth, squeeze, and pressure-free.

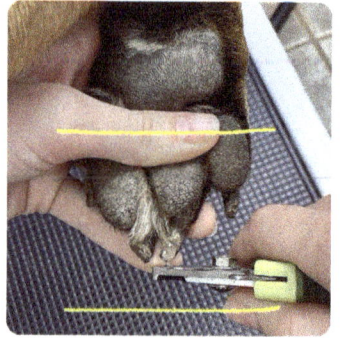

Pressure-free positioning of the clipper on the soft tissue of a taco nail type from the bottom side, when we position the clipper's jaws to encircle the top and bottom sides of the nail.

(Ignore the dirty nails, Toki got a paw soak before trimming, it was just an impromptu photo shooting and a good reminder for us all to soak and scrub those nails before the pawdicure itself.)

Pressure-Free Trimming of the Sides of the Nail

For the side trimming, you can hold the clipper at a 30-45 degree angle and trim the sides (and even the thick horny tissue) as seen on the image to the right.

Make sure to keep the clipper's jaw that cuts from the tip less than half from the middle section of the nail at the tip to avoid generating the pressure sensation.

Keep in mind, the horny tissue on the side is very thin, so the other jaw of the clipper should not go too deep down (I'm thinking about 1-2 mm only), otherwise, we are risking injury. Do this 30-45-degree angle on both sides, left and right.

You can also do this angle or a modification of it on the tip of the nail. We will detail this alternative method in the section where we will learn how to help the quick to recede, by cutting out a little triangle from the tip section of the nail.

If you are unsure how deep the soft tissue is below the surface, scratch the top with your fingernail very gently and it will tell you what layer you are seeing and whether there is a Jelly layer close by. If it comes apart, it is a powdery layer, you can cut further. If you see the Jelly layer popping up close under the powdery layer, stop and file only.

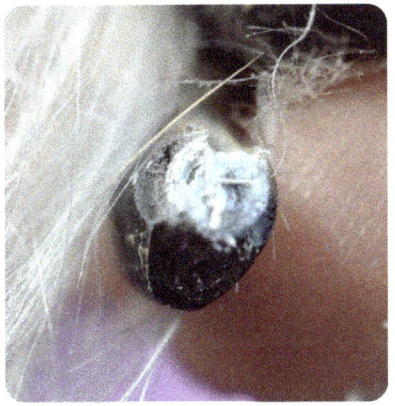

Angled side cuts to slowly explore the nail layers to find the stop sign without squeezing the soft tissues underneath the horny layer

Paw-di-cure™ Method - Clip the Tip, Bit by Bit

You can see a sample of nail flakes in my palm below. Notice how tiny and thin they are? This is what I mean by bit by bit. The second image is made with a 20x zoom lens so you can really see the details of the "cutlings". Don't worry, we're not here to learn how to trim nails under the microscope! I just included it here for fun and a deeper understanding of what I mean by tiny.

Nail flakes or "cuttings"

Nail flakes or "cuttings" - close up

Advantages of the "Clip The Tip (Or Edge), Bit by Bit" Method

- We put almost no pressure on the dog's nails when cutting
- We can stay safe because we can see the layers on time, before hitting sensitive layers, unlike when we cut a more massive chunk off at once.

These two are the cornerstones of a calm and cooperative canine to work with. If any of those get compromised, we'll be facing a not so relaxing and fulfilling nail care session, to say the least.

Holding the Nails for Nail Trimming

Dewclaws

- Hold the sides of the dewclaw with your thumb and index finger
- or run your index finger lengthwise on the top of the dewclaw,
- or combine the two above

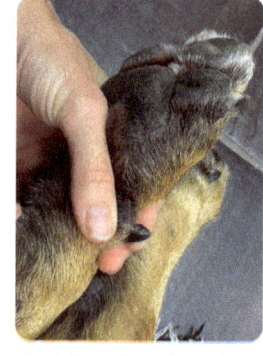
Holding the dewclaw for trimming

Toenails

- Embed the nail in the crack of your index finger joint
- Run your index finger on the top of the nail lengthwise until you cover it with your index finger up to the tip of the nail
- Combine the two above

Holding the toenail for trimming

Holding Tricks for Trimming the Dewclaws

Holding the Firmly Attached Dewclaw

Getting a good view and a stable hold on the firmly attached dewclaws can be tricky, especially on the front legs of a fluffy dog. My routine goes like this: I always start with the dewclaw and do all the nail care steps (haircut around nail if needed, nail trimming, and filing) right after one another. I like to keep one grip throughout the whole thing to keep the dog patient and get done the fastest possible way. If you can get a comfortable grip and you are not pulling/pushing on the dewclaw, dogs don't really mind holding the position.

I trim the hair around the nail if needed, like matted hair around, or if a short haircut is desired. Sidenote: It is much easier to cut the hair shorter than to position the hair away from the dewclaw for the time of nail care on a wiggly/beginner dog. If a long haircut is desired, then try to get a secure hold of the hair, keeping it close to the skin, and try not to adjust the grip since it takes a long time to herd all that hair away from the nail and the doggy's patience is not unlimited.

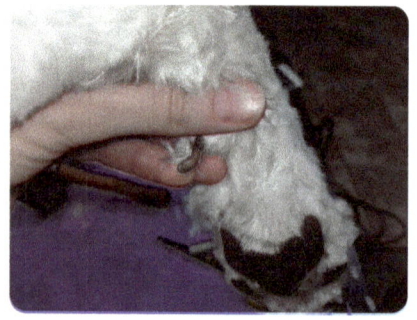
Dewclaw holding technique version

I keep my pinky finger as a guide at the top of the nail (see image to the right) to help the clipper stay right where I want it to be and to perform multiple, tiny, and precise cuts. When I reach the stop sign, I do the filing right away so I don't need to perform that hard to accomplish grip again.

After finishing the dewclaw on one paw, I go to the rest of the claws on the same paw, and then I repeat it on all fours. This method works great for me since the dewclaws are located a tad "away" from the rest of the nails and are often small and covered in a bunch of hair.

> **Top Tip**
>
> When the dewclaws enjoy a priority pawdicure, I can make sure I won't forget them. So I highly recommend a helpful routine to adopt for yourself so it'll be second nature to get them done without forgetting about them.

After you have moved the hair out of the way, try to keep your ring and pinky fingers close together and position the dewclaw in the crack between them. Your fingers will adjust pretty fast to these seemingly crazy positions. Often you may find that your whole body is twisted, so don't forget to adjust to a more comfortable position! Holding the dewclaw can usually be done while the dog is standing or is on his side/back. Sitting is not the most comfortable position to get to dewclaws, especially with smaller breeds. There is just not enough room to fit hands, tools, and see what you are doing under the belly there.

Holding the Loosely Attached Dewclaw

The loosely attached dewclaw is very easy to get a hold of in most cases. You can gently squeeze the sides between the two legs and even move it toward you a bit to get a better view and reach the tip with the clipper. The clipper is best held just as for toenails, at the same angle to avoid that squeezing sensation. When I trim, the clipper is right behind the dog's leg facing either toward my right or left. (Avoid the clipper facing directly toward the ceiling or ground on a standing dog so you won't squeeze the soft tissue while cutting!)

You have more wiggle room to twist a loosely attached dewclaw as opposed to the firmly attached one. Still, be gentle and see what is comfortable for the dog!

Trimming Step-by-Step

Step 1. Making the First Cut - Clipping the Tip of the Toenail's Tip

Making the first cut was probably one of the most frightening steps to imagine before you got this book. I believe we domesticated this "monster" pretty well by getting a better understanding of nail layers in previous sections. Still a bit worried? Check out the nail anatomy chapter to get that confidence boost you need! We'll go through the trimming sections in the nail types' order since nail types need custom attention to bring out the best experience.

First Cut on a Taco Nail Type

After making the first cut on a taco nail type, **we will get three anchor points** to keep an eye on.

Thin Nail Tip

In the case of the thin nail tip, we first determine the line where the soft, sensitive layer ends, and the horny layer starts. It is incredibly useful to take the opportunity and trim as many flakes off of this section as possible. You can go from the tip of the nail toward the base of the nail and stop at least 1-2 mm before the sensitive layer to leave some room for filing and to avoid any pressure for the dog.

Note that I am not saying to cut as much off of the nail as possible!

Once you are more experienced and the dog is cooperating well, you can trim thicker pieces off as well. Or if you are working on a feet-sensitive dog, and you have to speed up to finish nail care, you can also do this "shortcut" to trim a bigger chunk off.

Use this method only in those special cases and only on the taco nail type!

First Cut on a Hot Dog Nail Type

After making the first cut on a hot dog nail type, **we will get four anchor points** to keep an eye on. Let's take a look at nail tip types of the hot dog nail type!

Pointy Nail Tip

In a hot dog nail type with a pointy nail tip, the quick is either pretty close to the tip of the nail or resides farther back on the nail. The wisest way to go about it is if you observe the nail from the paw pad side first and see where the quick is. On the image to the right, the middle nail has a very thin tip and there is virtually no room for the quick to be there. Confirm your educated guess by actually checking it from the bottom side at all times! After

Pointy nail tip

confirmation, we can trim that super thin and long part short even with one first clip and follow it up with filing. On the nail closer to us though, the pointy tip is thicker. I'd definitely go with evaluation from the bottom and tiny by tiny cuts to make sure I won't go too short. When the nail is thicker, we need to assume the quick is there and explore by sculpturing the nail cutting tiny by tiny.

Nail Trimming 175

Rounded Tip

With a hot dog nail type with a rounded nail tip, the quick is often super close to the nail's tip. Be very cautious to determine where to make the first cut! I usually start with a super thin layer on the upper edge of the nail, since the horny surface is most of the time thicker on that side, which enables me to see the layers better underneath and to be able to safely determine the angle of the second cut at the same time.

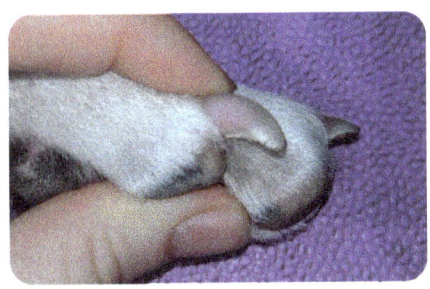
Rounded nail tip

Rectangular Tip

A hot dog nail type with a rectangular nail tip often times has a quick that is not too close to the nail's tip. Most dogs with this nail tip type often have a powdery layer and you can trim the nail to the proper length. But don't take that for granted!! Explore instead of gambling! I usually start on the nail's outer tip, away from the paw pad, because the horny layer is thicker there. This method also enables me to see the layers better underneath to safely determine the angle of the second cut at the same time.

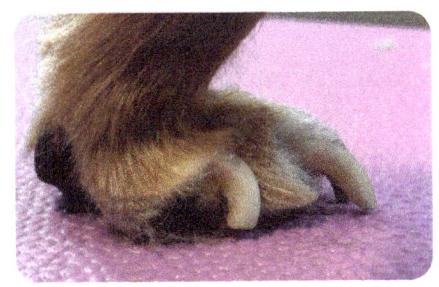
Rectangular nail tip

Anchor Points and Edges

Taco Nail Type Anchor Points

Before jumping into the second step, let's familiarize ourselves with the anchor points and edges we will create after the first cut.

With the taco nail type, we will generate two anchor points and one edge. With the hot dog nail type, we will generate four edges.

Let's take a look at the images below to locate those points!

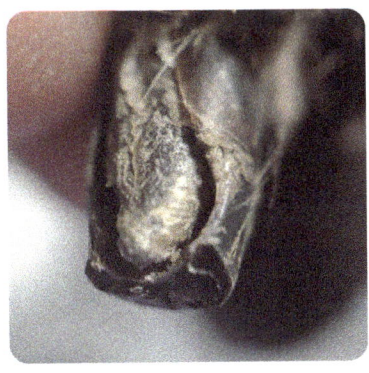 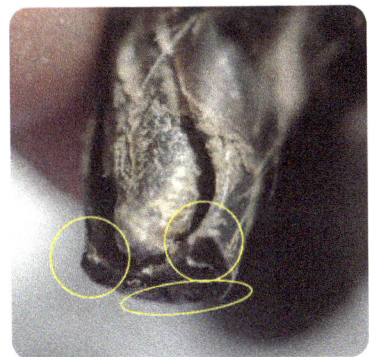 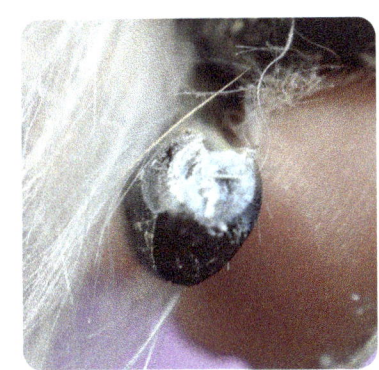

Anchor points on a hot dog nail type   Anchor points on a hot dog nail type   Anchor points on a taco nail type

These images are about the taco nail type and the two anchor points (circles) and one edge (oval) generated after taking the first cut.

In this specific case, we don't need to go any deeper, only to trim one itty-bitty slice off of the edges to make it easier and faster in the filing phase. If the dog shows sensitivity for nail clipping, we can jump right to filing as well.

Hot dog nail type anchor points

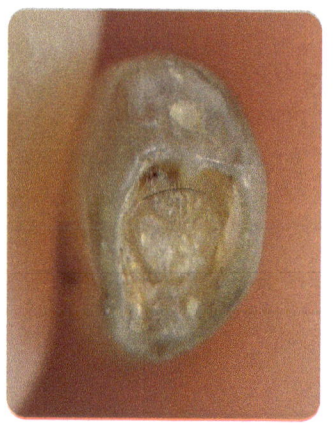
Hot dog nail type anchor points N, S, E, W

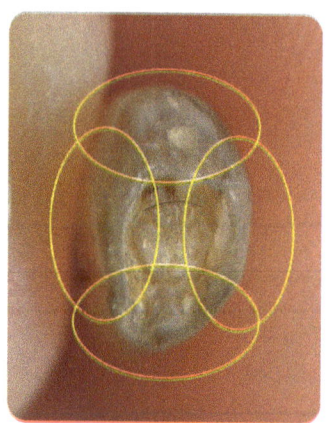
Hot dog nail type anchor points: N on the top (thickest) S on the bottom (small and thin) W, E sides (long and thin)

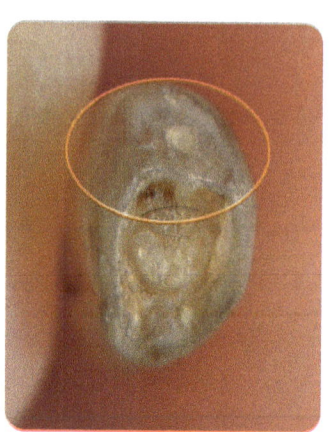
Dog naturally wore off the N edge of the nail

These images with the cream-colored nail on the right show the hot dog nail type and the four edges (marked with yellow ovals) we will need to keep an eye on before and after making the first trim. To make it easier, let's name them after the quarters, N, S, E, W.

There are two edges by the nail curve on the top and bottom N, S, and there are two edges on the sides, lengthwise, W, E. Notice how much thicker the N edge is! That is located on the top when the dog is standing. See how long and thin the W, E, edges are? The S is a tiny, thin part.

When we are trimming nails with hot dog nail types, we are working mainly alongside these edges to form a cone shape out of the nail. We position the nail clipper based on the edges first, then follow up by cutting the corners to make it a smoother surface. This makes the nail file step faster. See the video about positioning and angling the nail clipper in the Nail it! course!

You can see that the dog was filing the tip of the rectangular nail tip off a bit on this specific image. (Image on the right with an orange circle.)

Step 2. Clipping the Sides/Edges

Taco Nail Type

There will be two anchor points, and one edge left after the first clip on a taco nail type. You will see two anchor points by the two ends of the horseshoe and one edge where the horseshoe shape has the curve. Those are the most important parts we need to keep an eye on.

Cutting the tips or edges on those -one by one- and going around (not just cutting on one anchor point) **will help us see the layers very well and stay safe.**

Every cut needs to be **super thin**. When we cut, we need to **put more pressure on the thinner edges** and cut from those ends to put **less pressure on the dog's nails**.

Depending on the dog's nail length at the time of nail care, we will need to do only a few (one to five) very thin cuts on those parts (on each nail) to be able to find the Jelly layer under there or six to ten or more.

Check out the images above of the nail flakes and see the thickness for yourself! Use the cheat sheet at the end of the book to distinguish between the layers you will see! Check out the video about angling in the Nail it! course!

Hot Dog Nail Type

With the hot dog nail type, we will work on the edges we mentioned above. After cutting the North (N) edge—I usually start there, I work my way around the nail, W, E, S, cutting off the same, very thin layers, and I observe the surface. If it is still the powdery layer, I make another round, one layer deeper, still cutting off very thin layers. N, W, S, E edges. I keep this up until I meet the tip of the Jelly layer of the sole. If the dog has a very large and thick nail, I trim the corners as well after doing the N, W, S, E edges.

Finding the tip of The Jelly Layer, the "Stop Sign"

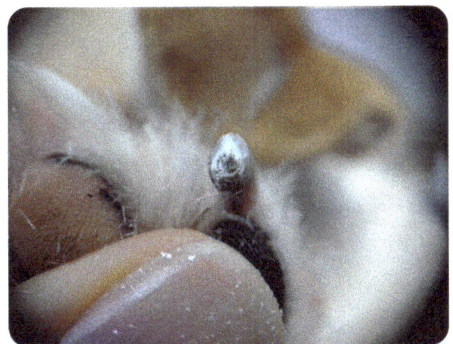

Tip of the Jelly sole, our stop sign - gray dot in the middle

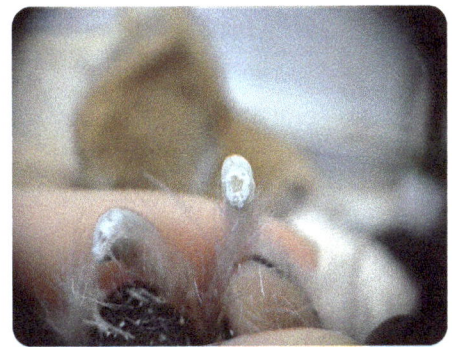

Tip of the Jelly sole, our stop sign - pink dot in the middle

Remember that the hot dog nail type is the type where we are **looking for** that **"bull's eye" dot around the middle of the nail**. Don't bet on it, though. It's not always entirely in the middle. Neither is it always a perfect dot. Sometimes it is more like an oval when the nail is more oval-shaped so that it can vary. The texture is significantly more telling. See the nail layers section for more info if you need to refresh that chapter!

The dot can be anywhere along the length of the nail, but it usually doesn't go higher north than a quarter of the nail. If it does, that usually means the nail is super short.

If the nail is longer than it should be, and the dot is closer to the tip than to where the proper length of the nail would be (short enough to not touch the ground when the dog stands on all fours), that is when we say, **"the quick has grown down together with the nail."**

This is why it is essential to cut bit by bit because we never know where our stop sign (the tip of the Jelly layer, NOT the tip of the quick!) is along the way, and we might end up causing injury.

So cutting very thin, tiny layers off and **keeping a sharp eye out for changes in nail texture** change will keep us safe.

We are cutting into the horny and powdery layers (listing the layers in order from the outer surface inward), and we are looking for a change in texture around the middle of the nail.

Feel free to scratch the middle surface very gently with your nails to feel any texture change. You can scrub the powdery layer with your nails away. Like dust, the powdery layer will fall apart. The Jelly layer will be softer to the touch, won't fall apart, and act and look like Jelly. It's squishy and bright.

If there is no Jelly layer, and the dog is not showing sensitivity signs directly to this scratch test, then it means we are still at the powdery layer, and we can go forward, cutting tiny layers. Or we can file if we or our canine client feels more comfortable with that from this point.

We can safely find the tip of the Jelly layer and the tip of the sole as well with only nail clippers. This does not mean we can skip filing, I always highly recommend filing the edges after a nail trim.

I usually **start with the dewclaw on one foot, trim it, then file it so I won't forget it**. Plus, getting a hold of those dewclaws, especially on a fluffy dog, is a challenge, so I would rather not let it go until I have finished all the steps on them.

I usually **do all four toenails with the clipper, then file all four nails** right away and go to the other foot with the same method. We never know when we need to take a quick break, so following up the trimming with filing latest at one foot is a good idea. If we were to trim all nails on all fours and then the doorbell or phone rings before the nail filing, we could risk injury while we sort those things out and the dog scratches himself or us for a belly rub. If you trim nails on one foot only, even if a distraction happens, finishing those four nails up before answering the door could happen without much delay to attend to those unexpected tasks.

Step 3. Filing the Nail

Filing the nails is usually the easiest part of nail care. Most dogs handle the handheld doggy nail file with a breeze, showing no discomfort at all.

Check the nail filing chapter after the first aid section to learn how to file dog nails to make them smooth and avoid scratches!

> ### Fun Fact
>
> The nails look different when they are dry and when they get wet after trimming and filing. The images on the next page show the difference. After filing, the tip of the nail looks more white and powdery (first image). When they get wet after the pawdicure, they look grayer and Jelly-like. (second image)

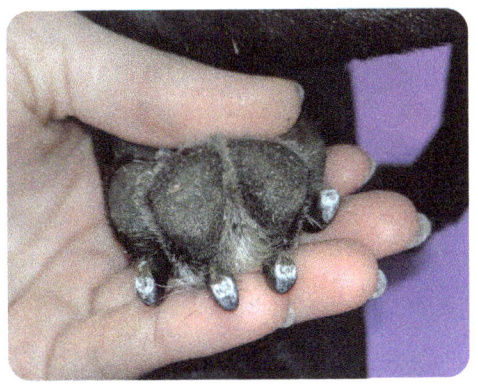
Filed black nails - dry

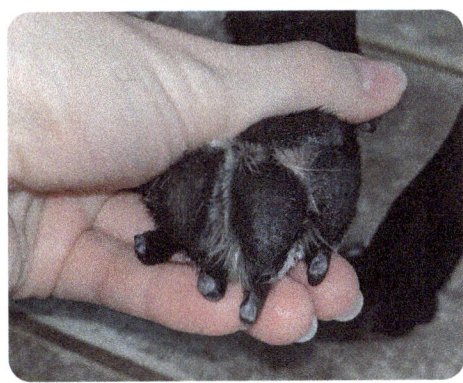
Wet black nails after filing

Trick of the Day

There is a great trick for all doggies, but especially useful for hounds with sensitivity to nail trimming. Soaking the feet before nail trimming is a surprisingly effective way to get a cooperative dog and reduce the sensation on the soft tissue in the nail. I time the nail trimming after the bath most of the time to make the nail softer, just like it is at pedicure sessions for humans at a salon. I make an exception for dogs whose nails are touching the ground; those nails get trimmed and filed before the bath since that is very uncomfortable to stand on.

Room for your Thoughts and Notes

___
___
___
___
___
___
___
___
___
___
___
___
___

Nail Length

From Normal to Severly Overgrown

Nail lengths from normal to severely overgrown
1. Normal – 100 percent comfortable dog, pawrents
2. Normal, a bit scratchy. - 99 percent comfortable dog, 70 percent comfortable pawrents
3. Too long, nail is touching the ground. – 100 percent uncomfortable dog
4. Too long, touching the ground, and lifting up the toe. – 100 percent painful dog
Dog neglect below:
5. Too long, touching the ground and lifting up the toe and about to grow in the skin.
6. Too long, touching the ground and lifting up the toe, and rubbing against the skin on the side.
7. Too long, touching the ground, and lifting up the toe, and pushing against, about to open up the skin due to rubbing and pressure. (Can be trimmed to the proper length in one appointment.)
8. Too long, touching the ground, lifting up the toe, and pushing against, about to open up the skin due to rubbing and pressure. (The quick has grown down together with the nail, it cannot be trimmed to the proper length without bleeding.)
9. **Too long, touching the ground, and lifting up the toe, and nail grew into the skin already.**

Nail Trimming 181

What to do When the Quick has Grown Down Together with the Nail?

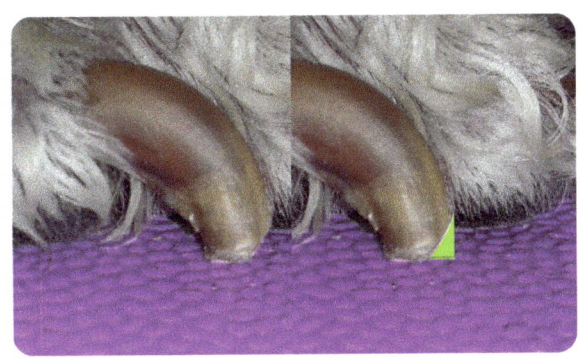

When rounded or rectangular nails grow longer, I like to trim the front part of the horny tissue (green triangle) a tad higher and more in-depth than I usually would. That gives some advantage for the dog to wear the nails down to getting the quick to recede faster. When we do this particular cut on the nail, we trim off a lot of the horny tissue's thickest part. That helps the dog wear the nails down more efficiently by stimulating the soft tissue, which will signal it to recede. All this happens without bleeding. That way,

Triangle cut at the N edge of the nail to make the quick to recede

the doggy himself, the pawrent or I will be able to file a tad more within a week, without bleeding so that the quick can grow back without painful nail care (cutting in the quick to make the nail to the proper length) or injury due to too long nails getting caught in something.

Getting the Quick to Recede

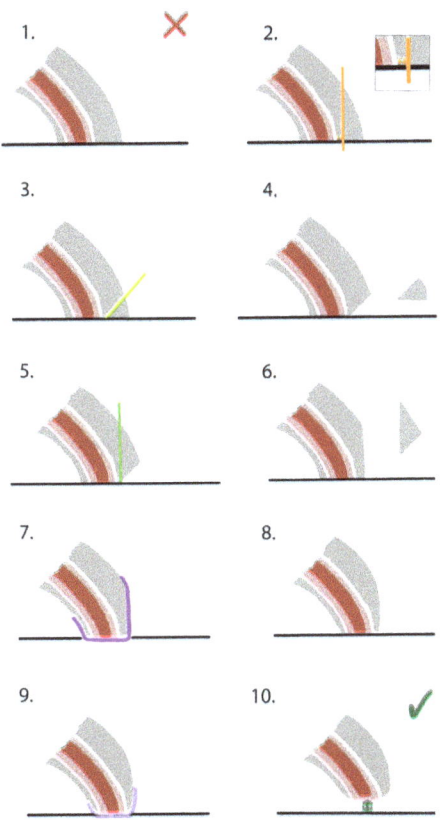

On the drawing to the right, we will detail step-by-step how we can make the quick recede or "go back where it belongs".

1.) In the first drawing, we see the quick has grown down together with the nail. It is right by the tip of the nail. We know the dog is not comfortable (the nail is touching the floor), so we need to do something as soon as possible.

In reality, you get the info about the quick when you look at the nail's bottom from the paw pad side.

2.) On the second drawing, we see how to make a plan for our goal. This drawing shows the final results after multiple cuts, how deep we will reach in the horny tissue (gray surface).

We determine this line between the powdery layer and the horny tissue from taking a look at the nail's tip from the paw pad view and leaving a bit of room to stay safe (see zoomed in drawing on the top right corner)

Workflow of getting the quick to recede

The spot where the soft nail tissue is meeting the horny tissue is your red dot. You don't want to go there. Furthermore, you want to leave a small room to protect it.

The starting point for the orange line (the zoomed-in little rectangle) on the nail will be the spot where you will first put one side of the clipper. Keep in mind; we are taking multiple cuts, not one chunk! Let's see how that looks!

3.) The third drawing shows how to make the first cut. It's the shape of a pizza slice

4.) The fourth drawing shows what's left of the nail after the first trim

5-6.) The fifth and sixth drawings show the second cut. This is the step that helps the dog getting the quick to recede by everyday wear and tear! If the doggy has thick nails, you can do multiple cuts to get this triangle shape off of the dog's nails in the end

7.) The seventh drawing shows which areas you need to file (purple) to get the dog's nails smooth and rounded and avoid sharp edges and scratches to the dogs' skin or yours

8.) The eighth drawing shows the result after filing

9.) The ninth drawing shows which areas the dog wears off while doing everyday doggy business between nail trims, like running, walking, digging, playing, etc. If the doggy is elderly or lives a restricted life for a while from moving due to injury or surgery, etc. we can do this filing ourselves as a follow-up nail care appointment or the doggy owner at home once a week ten to twenty movements on each nail or so. I'm giving out advice for my clients when their nails need a follow-up filing, and they are willing to try/do it at home. You can give it a go, too!

10.) As a result of the filing, the tenth drawing shows how the quick receded due to the stimulation, and the nail is raised from the ground. That results in a comfortable doggy, and the nail will reach the proper length

When done consistently, a doggy who needs some recurring TLC (tender loving care) due to long nails usually gets the nails to the proper length within two to six weeks, including two to three nail appointments or nail filing by the owner at home. No blood, no pain! How cool is that?

If your dog is still responding with wiggles or bites after trying the suggestions in this book, chances are he's got some PTSD and trauma built up, so you will need specialized help from a trainer to find the triggers and resolve the situation with your doggy/client.

I worked with several cases where the dog got so frustrated by only seeing the clipper that we had to split up the appointment. The pawrents agreed and they did several desensitization trainings at home and at my salon to get to the point when my furry client was comfortable enough for me to do his nails. We made it happen!

Chapter 13

First Aid for Nail Trimming

Injury at the Time of the Nail Care (Hitting the Quick)

How Can You Tell the Quick Got Hit?

The most obvious sign at the injury site is going to be a drop of blood or more. Some dogs reach/snap/bite at the tool/care provider at the time of the injury (totally understandable due to pain). Some freeze and don't show any of those signs. Sometimes you just get a bit too close to the quick and there will be no immediate bleeding. The initial bleeding will occur after some wear and tear like a walk when that tiny layer gets worn down by the dog that kept the nail from bleeding. You will find tiny drops/spots of blood in the house/furniture and usually your dog licking the injured nail. Those are signs that something is off.

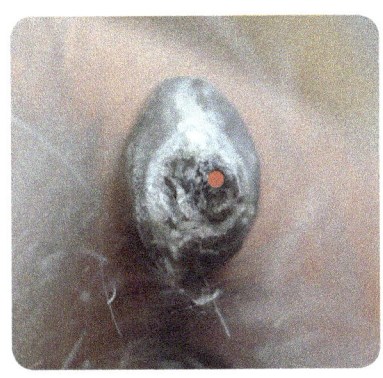

When the quick gets hit and bleeding occurs

What To Do If You Accidentally Hit The Quick?

It may happen in your life that you will meet a dog who had his nails trimmed too short or that you may hit the quick accidentally. It is essential to have a "nail trimming first aid kit" handy BEFORE you start the doggy pedicure, regardless of your level of experience. I keep the quick stop powder with the nail clippers so I have it ready in case I need it.

The Most Important First-Aid Steps

1. Stopping the bleeding
2. Sanitizing the area and keeping dirt and water away
3. Pain management

First Aid Items

- **Quick stop powder** or **Styptic powder** (recommended, preferably with the temporary pain block)
- **Exam or sterile rubber gloves** (to apply the quick stop powder and to avoid infections)
- **Q-tips** (as one way to take out/apply some styptic powder)
- **Sterile gauze pads** or a clean paper tissue (where you place the needed amount of styptic powder)
- **Groomers' glue** (as a last resort, not really recommended)
- **Corn starch** as a last resort if you don't have anything else at home to stop the bleeding. Again, prepare before trimming!

Quick Stop Powder

Quick stop powder

Quick stop powder is a powder that you apply with some pressure to the bleeding nail. It will eventually stop the bleeding. It is yellow and will become red or brown when it gets soaked with blood. Most of the time, you can still see a yellowish/brownish (depending on how severe the bleeding was) tint to the area for days after application. It works well, and because it is a permeable barrier, it lets the nail "leak" in case it needs to clean itself. It is excellent from a healing perspective so bacteria won't get trapped in the wound.

Quick stop powder

How to Apply the Quick Stop Powder?

To stop the bleeding and to keep the area clean, the quick stop powder is a great way to go. Get some powder out on the lid, pinching some powder between your thumb and index fingers, and apply pressure, by gently pressing it against the bleeding spot. If the bleeding was only like a drop, you can release it after five to ten seconds. If the bleeding was severe, you might need to keep the pressure for several minutes and apply more powder as needed to stop the bleeding. Check the nail in a few minutes to see how it is regardless of the amount of bleeding. Sometimes by walking or jumping the dog wears the powdery layer off and then it starts bleeding again. Avoid long hikes for a few days to let the area heal and seal.

Top Tip

I do not like, nor suggest using the quick stop powder dispensers. They are way too deep and wide for small and even medium-sized dogs. You will be much more precise with the application if you see the area you are trying to work on better, not getting it covered by the dispenser. Plus you don't have to spread the toes that much like you have to when using the dispenser. It's also a waste of quick stop powder and the yellow powder will get stuck in the coat on the paws with that large gap to dip the nail in.

Groomers' Glue

Groomers' glue, on the other hand, is like super glue for wound healing. When it gets hard, it becomes a waterproof layer, which is an advantage if you could sanitize the area 100 percent. It's a pretty risky business to seal a wound that is not fully sterilized, so it's not the first thing I recommend using. It will take longer to solidify if the bleeding is intense. With groomers' glue, any bacteria that got stuck underneath will grow under a "shield" as it pleases. That is the biggest reason why I neither like nor recommend this method as a first go-to for nail first aid.

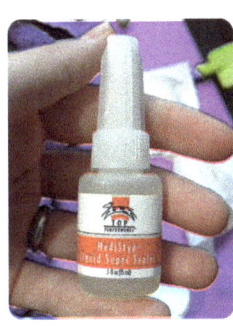
Groomers' Glue

From the dog's safety (and comfort) perspective, I highly recommend doing the nail trimming AFTER the bath. The bath will clean and soften the nails and it'll be easier (and sensation-free) to trim the nails.

If you hit the quick before the bath, splitting the grooming session is desired to avoid infection. All the dirt we wash off of the dog will end up right by the open wound on the nail, and dogs are at high risk for infections in this case.

Note for Vets/Vet Techs

Note for Groomers/Bathers

It can seem pretty disturbing to let the doggy owner know if you hit the quick (and ask the owner to come back again to finish grooming), but it is in the dog's best interest. In general, people appreciate honesty, and the fact is that both of you and the owner want the best for the dog.

If you deliver the happenings with clarity and without using blaming phrases, adding training suggestions/resources, most of the pawrents will take it in a calm manner and will work on their dog if needed.

To avoid postponing the appointment happening again in the future, analyze the situation, and delay the nail care after the bath rather than delaying the bath itself. Offer training nor refer them to a trainer if the dog's behavior requires it!

After the Bleeding is Stopped

1. Analyze what happened and why
2. Learn and grow from the situation

Analyzing What Happened

With clear observation, replay the time you were trimming the nail and describe who was doing what. What position was the dog/you in? How did you hold the clipper? Did the dog move? Did you move? Any distractions that made your dog move? Was the dog "supervising" you? Any other signs of early or late discomfort signs?

For the best learning experience, you can record the nail care sessions and analyze them afterward regardless of the outcome until you get the hang of it. You can rewatch the dog's body language, the way you held the clipper, etc. and come up with better plans for the future.

Learn and Grow from the Situation

After you figure out what was the cause of the mistake, think about other ways you could perform the nail care differently in the past to avoid that mistake in the future!

The Efficacy of the Paw-di-cure™ Method

To give you a general idea of how effective the method you are learning about is I wanted to share with you the statistics of my practice regarding nail trimming injuries. To avoid becoming overwhelmed with data and to turn it into a huge pile of numbers, take a look at my nail trimming statistics for the last three years!

Betty's Nail Trimming Statistics	2019	2020	2021
Total number of nail trimming (toenails & dewclaws)	16,300+	12,200+	17,100+
Total canine blood loss due to hitting the quick	~2 drops	~1 drop	~1 drop
Total human blood loss due to biting the care provider	0 drops	0 drops	0 drops
Muzzles used	0 cases	0 cases	0 cases
Cone, Elizabethan collar, harnesses used	0 cases	0 cases	0 cases
Support picking up a dog in hands	<20 cases	<10 cases	<7 cases
Number of split appointments due to the dog not cooperating	1 case	1 case	1 case

First Aid for Nail Trimming

Summing it up, as long as you can pick the right support to keep the dog comfortable and still for you and you gain the necessary knowledge to trim dog nails, the likelihood of cutting in the quick is very, very low. A rock-solid desensitization plan for dogs with any sensitivity around nail care will save the day and will help you come up with a plan that suits a reactive dog's needs. Split the nail care appointment if needed!

Even when you make a mistake, it will not be like a scene from the ER on a busy day. If you follow the guidelines, you will be able to stay safe and minimize the damage so it will be no more than a drop of blood if you trim the nails a bit too short.

How to Tell When the Quick Got Hit

How can you tell whether a dog's nails have been trimmed or filed too closely (after the bleeding has/ has been stopped)?

Look for the following signs, multiple at the same time. Licking by itself can happen for an incredibly wide variety of reasons, making assumptions just by that might not be accurate.

Signs When the Quick Got Trimmed in

- Yellow/reddish/brownish powder on the tip of the nail (see image to the right)
- Super glue-like feeling on the tip of the nail (groomer's glue) with red, raw-looking nail tip
- Lots of licking on the nail or the feet after the nail care/spa day/ vet visit. Remember, this sign by itself is not enough to determine what happened with certainty, so look for multiple signs from this group to confirm! And as always, take pictures! Dogs can lick their feet when they get their hair trimmed around or have had their skin cut by a clipper or shears, too.
- Favoring the feet, limping, sensitivity when feet touches the ground
- Bleeding from the nail
- The brownish/reddish film around the tip of the nail (see below), indicating a scab on the site (when the quick stop powder wears off or has not been used)

Quicked nail with yellow quick stop powder

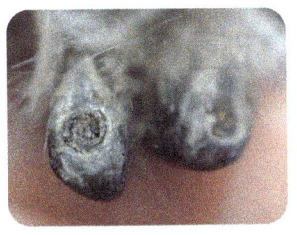 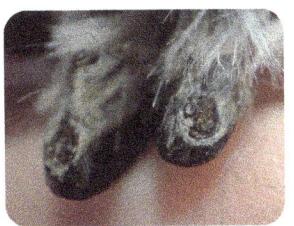 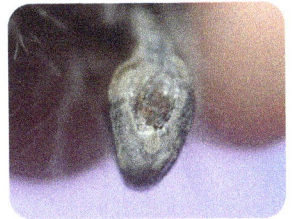 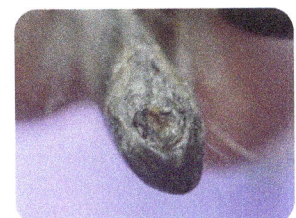

Quicked nails

On the two images below (white paw hair), you see another example of a nail quicked. Notice the nails on the left image! They are naturally worn on the edges, so it's been a while since this dog had a nail trim. The soft tissue (middle of the nail) looks consistent with the horny tissue and the nails' color. In both images, the two nails in the middle are shorter and more straight. The nails on the sides are curved more and are longer.

If you take a look at the nail circled with yellow below, you see a reddish/brownish dot in the middle. That's an indicator that the dog had that nail trimmed to the point of bleeding recently. My guess would be within seven to ten days of this discovery. It can be more if they did a profound injury, and it took longer to heal. The nail care job looks very sloppy; they failed to meet the dog's paw care needs—a very lamentable occurrence.

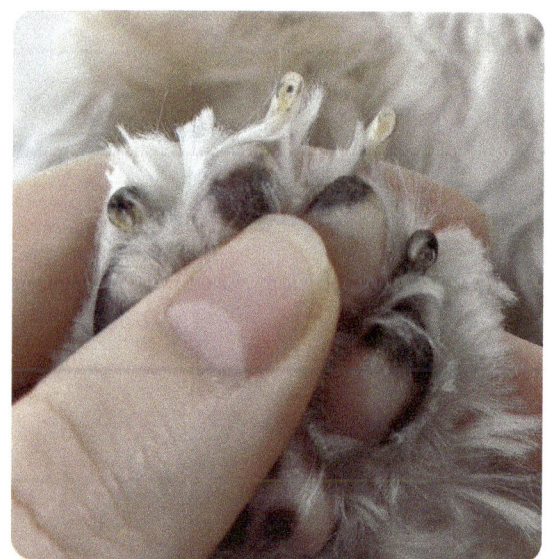

Not quicked nails

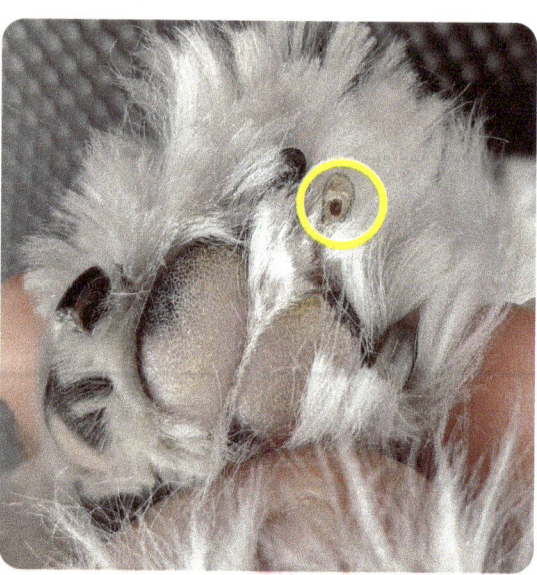

Quicked nail

Chapter 14

Nail Filing

Nail Filing Tools

Dog Nail File

This is my favorite tool to file nails. Safari makes the best one that I came across so far. It's effective, quiet, small enough to work on large and small dogs as well, even works for puppies. It's not vibrating so dogs get used to it way faster. The grit is just perfect for fast work and smooth results. This is my everyday go-to tool for nail filing. Bonus, when it becomes too smooth to be effective, I use it on my own nails since it has the perfect curvature for my taste. Works on dewclaws and toenails as well.

Nail Grinders

They can be an option, but I never use them or suggest them. They are loud, they vibrate, they work super-fast, and regardless of the "safety cap" or using a sock with a hole to stick the nail through to keep the hair away, it is still possible to get hair caught on the drum. That'll tear the hair right out with its roots and that's not something we want dogs to experience. Grinders work super-fast and they are right in the way so we can't see what layer we're working on.

I prefer visibility and comfort over working too fast and risking injury or grinding nails too short or giving the slightest chance for a single hair to get caught in the drum.

For those reasons, nail grinders are replaced by nail files in my practice. Works on dewclaws and toenails as well.

Emery Board

Emery boards alone or wrapped with 150 grit sandpaper can be a budget-friendly way to file nails. There are two minor roadblocks to work through. One is they are flat, with no curvature to keep the nail on the board. As a result, dog nails often slide off of it, making the nail trim longer. The other one is they can be pretty wide or tiny and flexible so getting to the nail is tricky. Works on dewclaws and toenails as well.

Scratch Board

Scratch boards offer some solutions to nail filing, but they're not a 100 percent solution. When dogs file their nails on the board, they usually file the middle two nails faster than the outer two due to the positioning of the nails relative to the board. It's especially an issue when the dog's nail is positioned in a way that they can't file the nails by themselves at all. Nails can be located in a way that the sandpaper won't reach them properly. The sandpaper can wear off the paw pads as the dog is pawing at it or with our help. Works on some toenails but it's hard to reach dewclaws with this tool.

Walk on Hard Surface

It can be a pretty good solution to wear off the edges of the nails for dogs who are still getting used to nail care. Dogs who are getting desensitized can get to the point when they can handle nail trimming but can't yet deal with the nail filing after that, so we can compromise to "file the nails with a walk" and follow it up with a regular nail file afterward to smooth the nails all around.

Timing is critical with it, we really want to go for that walk right after trimming to keep the dog safe from scratches by sharp nails. Works on toenails but won't work on dewclaws.

Holding Tricks for Filing the Tightly Attached Dewclaw

It's the trickiest to get a hold of, but it can be done. You'll need to keep in mind you'll need to see the paw pad side of the dewclaw and that you need to lift the paws in a way that the dewclaw will bear no weight of the leg. I find it easier if you have the dog on his back or on all fours. It'll make it level 10 if the dog is super fluffy and you'll need to dig for the dewclaw in the hair. Take your time adjusting so it'll work out for both of you.

I like to hold the dewclaw in the crack of my finger and move the nail file in one direction only, so I don't have to become a finger yogi and master a holding position that supports the nail from the top and the bottom as well. Hugging the tip of the nail with my finger between two digits will be enough support to keep the nail still when I'm using the nail file in one direction only. See the Nail it! video in the course on nail filing!

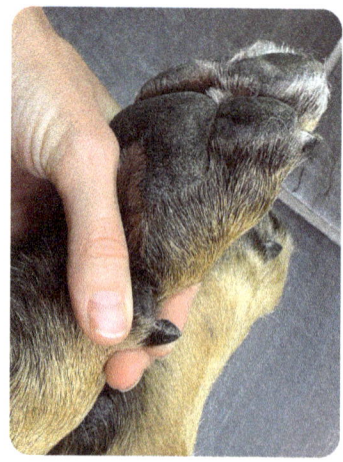

Holding the dewclaw for filing - Version 1

Holding Tricks for Filing the Loosely Attached Dewclaw

The loosely attached dewclaw is the easiest to get ahold of. You do not even have to lift the dog's leg in most cases. You can just gently clamp the dewclaw between your thumb and index fingers and gently twist it in the desired direction. Most loosely attached dewclaws will be loose enough to let you turn them around quite a bit.

Listen to the dog's comfort level and remember that the dewclaw should not bear any weight!

Holding Tricks for Filing Toenails

The process is very similar to nail trimming. The only difference is that we want our fingers to be less close to the nail's tip, and we need to keep the toenails more secure since filing will result in greater force on the nails.

With the nail file, we'll "draw" on a larger area than with the nail clipper. It's a longer tool, and we'll use different angles from trimming, wide and long movements, like a violinist.

Some dogs are fine regardless of the direction you are moving the file, let it be back and forth or in just one direction, then moving the nail file back to the start and file again. For sensitive dogs, one direction is easier to digest, so it's a good place to start!

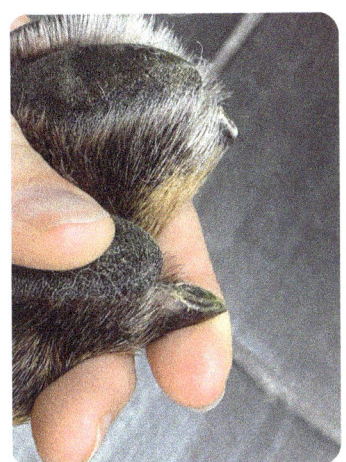

Holding the toenail for filing - Version 1

To keep dogs comfortable, **the single biggest trick is to hold the nail still with one hand and gently file with the other**. Dogs hate when their nails are not supported enough and the filling makes the nail wiggle.

Different positions require different holding techniques. First, we'll discuss the horseshoe holding technique as a guideline so you'll be able to get the idea and modify the hold to your preferred position and to your comfort level.

The thumb is on the toe pad, index finger and middle finger are supporting the toenail from the sides or top.

This will result in a solid grip and a still nail, which results in a still dog.

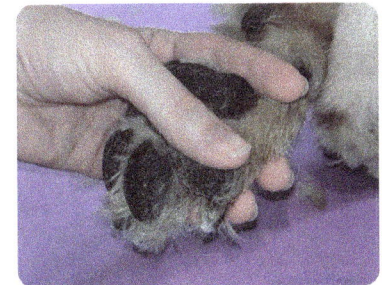

Holding the toenail for filing - Version 2

Holding the Nail File

My favorite nail file is the one that Safari makes. It has a green round handle, so I just call it the cucumber. Depending on the dog's size, you can either hold it with three to four fingers with barely any force on it, or you can get a good strong grip on it if you are dealing with a large dog's nails.

Remember to adjust the pressure you are putting on the dog's nails with the nail file! The more pressure you'll use, the faster the nails get filed theoretically. But some dogs react to a lot of pressure on their nails, so you might not get too far if you want to rush the session.

I like to hold the nail file in a way that the file part of the nail is facing to my thumb, since my index finger and thumb are more sensitive to feedback from the nail file and the dog, so I can pick up on sensations faster with this hold. And adjustments can come faster so I can support the dog's needs sooner.

Holding the nail file

Nail Filing Methods

Filing is usually the easiest part of nail care. Most dogs handle the hand nail file with a breeze, showing no discomfort at all.

> **Top Tip**
>
> When holding any nail, let it be dewclaw or toenail, make sure you're holding it at least mid-length and not farther back toward the base of the nail. We'd want to find the golden middle between leaving room for filing nails like a violinist and making sure that the grip we hold is supporting the nail enough. When we hold the nail too close to the nail bed, it'll wiggle the horny tissue just enough to make the dog very uncomfortable and to react.

So for a still dog, the recipe is to keep not more than about ¼" (6 mm) room on the tip of the nail for filing.

Movements with the Nail File

We can move the nail file **back and forth** on experienced dogs and only in **one direction only** on sensitive doggies (from the top of the feet toward the paw pad side or vice versa).

If we could go close to the Jelly layer's tip with the clipper, our work with the file is super easy and fast. Only about 5-10-15 movements and we are done.

Our goal is to file off the rough edges so the dog won't scratch itself, nor us when pawing at us, for example. Once you have filed the nails off and checked them with your fingers for any sharp edges, you are officially done with the nail care session. Give a jackpot reward to the dog and celebrate!

Angling the nail file

> **Top Tip**
>
> I like to check the nails' softness while I am looking in another direction than the nail itself. Ceiling, the dog's coat, or closed eyes work well. Make sure the dog is still and safe! You can't do this unless the dog is calm and has a trustworthy stay. When I'm not visually focusing on the nail, it is easier for my mind to focus on the surface with my skin and my eye won't fill in the gaps. I get much more "raw data" and it'll be easier to find a pokey spot.

Filing Dewclaws

When it comes to filing dewclaws, we'll need to keep in mind the limitations of the location of it and our need to get the tip's surface smooth where we were clipping.

When I'm filing dewclaws, I hold the nail file 90 degrees related to the leg. I try to reach half of the surface I need to work on from the inner side of the dewclaw where it is closer to the leg, and from the outer side.

I find it easier than trying from the inside-outside directions.

You'll see that you have more room to do long strokes with the nail file if you let it run on the side of the nail, by the leg than when you'd do it on the top and bottom side of the nail, toward the dog's leg. The leg would be in the way so you'd be able to do only tiny strokes before the tip of the nail file would hit the dog's leg.

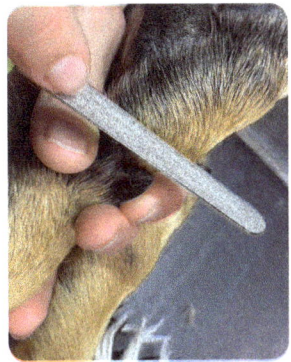
Filing dewclaws

With the side strokes, you can round the top and back while doing 45-degree angle strokes just by the front and the back of the leg.

Filing Toenails

It's fantastic that we have the most space to work on nails in the case of toenails, so we can get to them easier. I like to separate the nails a bit farther to aid the comfort for both of us. It allows me to get a better hold on the nail and more room for me to play the nail file violin.

On the side nails, we'll have more wiggle room than on the middle two nails. We can easily access all four toenails for filing from the top, bottom, and sides even. We can move toenails not only toward the sides to spread the toes but up and down as well to separate them even farther.

Make sure the hair is out of your way since it's significantly trickier to file nails with hair between the nail and the nail file. You may laugh, I certainly did at first, but you'll see it's true! :P

Rounding the edges up is a breeze given the toenail mobility and can be done in a half-circle or almond-shaped motion as well.

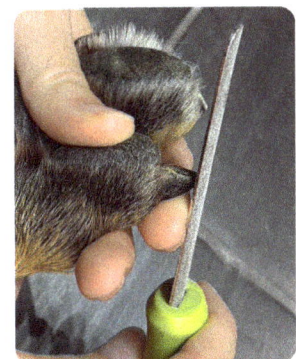
Filing toenails

It's important to know that when you're filing nails on brittle, dry nails sometimes the sides have bigger, dryer chunks falling off. They're thin, but can be 1/4" (6 mm) or even longer and about 1/8" (3mm) wide or larger. Don't be alarmed! The more you practice, the more you'll be able to spot the possibility for this so you can even gently peel the loose part off before filing. Move the nail file slowly until you get the hang of it so you won't give the chance to tear off a bigger chunk on a brittle nail!

Here is another advantage of why I prefer the more "intimate" nail file, not the rough and tough nail grinder. We don't want those loose pieces to get caught between the drum and the "safety" cap. Gentle observation and gentle tools will go a long way.

See the video in the Nail it! Course to learn more about nail filing positions and techniques!

Differentiating Among Worn Off, Trimmed, and Filed Nails

It's handy to know why exactly nail filing is worth the extra effort. It's also good to learn to tell whether our pet got a nail trim, nail file, both, or none!

Worn Off Nails

You can see naturally worn nails below. You also see extreme levels; hopefully, your dog won't go this far with the project.

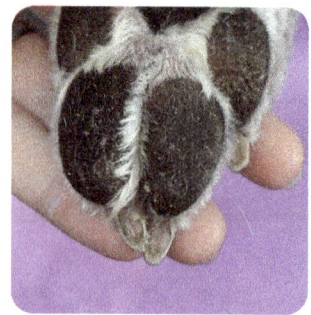
Naturally worn nails

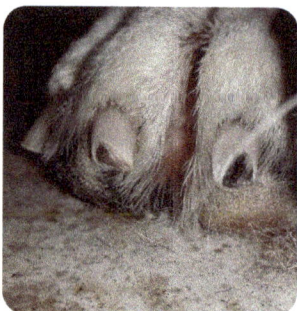
Excessively worn down toenails

Excessively worn down toenails

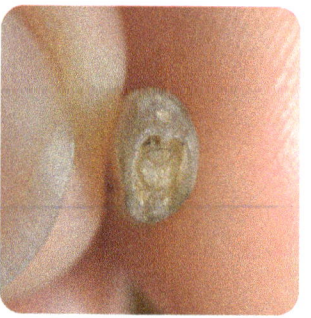
Somewhat worn nail, but not short enough

The first image shows a Standard Poodle girl's naturally worn nails. She does not need nail care on these toenails; she does all of it herself.

The second image shows a French bulldog's nails. You can see that the two nails in the middle are worn down shorter, even on the top.

The third image shows a bird's eye view of the same dog's nails. From that angle, it might look like the dog's nail was trimmed too short, but it's not the case. This dog's powdery layer is absent due to excessive wear. (You see it fairly often with this particular and similarly built breeds.) You can see a very thin layer of Jelly, and the quick is hiding right behind it, super close to the surface. If these dogs get a longer hike in rough terrain, they can make their nails bleed, so a good quality doggy shoe is highly recommended for longer hikes.

The fourth image shows a segment of a dog's nail. You can see this dog, too, wore off its nail on the top (left side, where the horny tissue is thicker). However, you can see the soft tissue, the powdery layer in the middle. It's dry, not Jelly-like to the touch, and works as a protection to the nail's soft tissues. This dog's nail was longer than the proper length, however, it shows that dogs wear off the nails on the outside and you can observe the differences between stages of this.

Trimmed Nails

On the images below, you see nails that have been trimmed, but not filed. These images show why nail trimming alone makes dog nails sharper than when left long. When we trim nails without filing, we run the risk of injury to the dog's skin (dog scratching itch, ears, etc.), the cornea (dog trying to remove hair from the eye), or the risk of injury to us, or our kids and their cornea (dog jumps up, scratches the skin, the kid's cornea, etc.)

If you take a look at the images below, the red arrows show where the nail is the sharpest and those edges make most of the damage. I think it's clear to see the dangers that sharp claws promise and the benefits of a quick nail file to make the nails rounded.

By cutting those edges (red arrows) farther with clippers, we can make the nails less sharp, but they will still injure skin and cornea without filing. See the third image and compare it with the first two images! Better, but just not quite there yet.

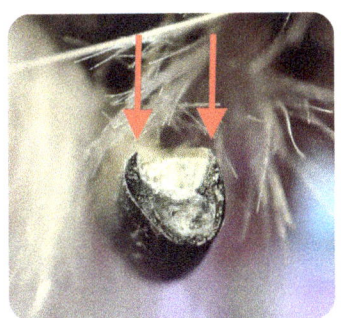
Trimmed, but not filed nail

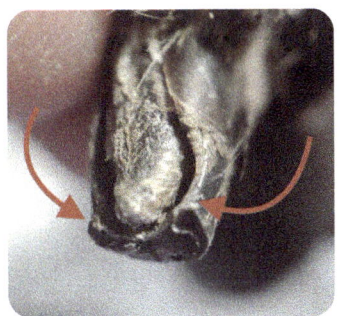
Trimmed, but not filed nail

Trimmed, but not filed nail

Filed Nails

Let's take a look at filed nails! You see a young dog's healthy nails rounded up with a handheld nail file on the first image below. It's obvious how smooth the edges are, how rounded they look and soft they feel when you check them! These nails won't make tights torn when touching them to ask for a belly rub at prom night or wedding!

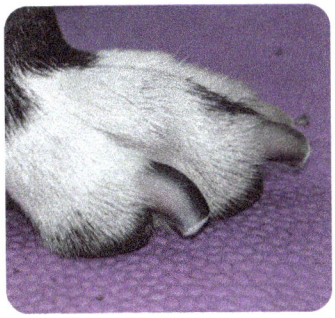
Trimmed and filed nails

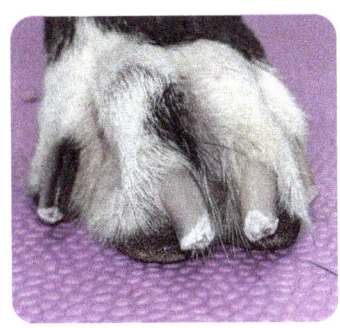
Trimmed and filed nails

Trimmed and filed nails

The second image is of the same dog, but from a different leg, the frontal view. Nice and rounded, no sharp edges.

The third image shows an elderly dog's nails filed from the side view, shot closer from the ground.

I think we can agree that it is unequivocal; the filed nails are way safer for everyone. Let's take a look at how we file nails!

Comparison of Worn Off, Trimmed Only, and Trimmed and Filed Nails

Excessively worn down toenails

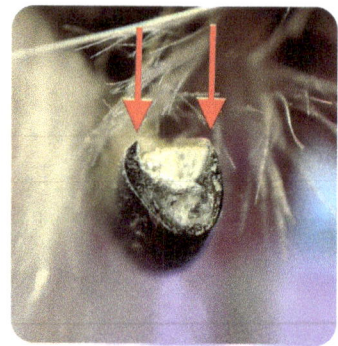
Trimmed, but not filed nail

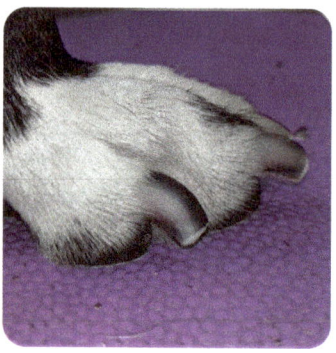
Trimmed and filed nails

I think it's safe to say that we all agree to trim and file together gets the safest and softest results.

Chapter 15

Nail Care Plans After Pawdicure

Depending on the dog's nail length and behavior for nail trimming, they might need some TLC after the nail trim to get the nails to the proper length. If the quick has grown down together with the nail or the dog's behavior needs to be addressed and remedied, or the combination of the two, we need different action plans to be able to get the dog in a comfortable stage paw and heart-wise.

First, let's talk about what influences the need/frequency of nail care!

Circumstances That Influence the Need (or the Frequency) of Nail Care

Let's say the nail care went perfectly. The next question usually is, when does my dog need another nail trim again? There are a lot of things that influence the frequency of nail care, so let's take a look at the list!

- Dog's Age
- Energy Level
- Amount of hair around paws and nails
- Activity/Lifestyle
- Leg structure
- Paw Structure
- Nail Structure
    - Type of Nail
    - Location of the nail (feet and dewclaws in general)
    - Position of the nail
    - The shape of the nail
- Surfaces the doggy is exposed to (living environment)
    - Rugs
    - Carpet
    - Tile
    - Laminate
    - Hardwood floor

- - Concrete
  - Dirt
  - Grass
  - Dog bed in the crate for extended hours daily
- Weight
- Dog's Breed (size, built)
- Disability
- Injury
- Surgery
- Genetics (tiny dog inherits larger nails from a parent)
- Etc.

Take a look at the Nail Length poster in the attachments section to determine when your doggy needs a pawdicure session.

Behavioral and Trimming Success Assessment

I like to do a behavioral assessment for my clients from the meet and greet to the final goodbye at the end of the spa day so the pawrents will get a better understanding of the dog's reactions regardless of how cooperative or reactive the dog was.

You can take a look at the spa day summary I fill out with my clients to help them thoroughly understand how their doggy did. https://bit.ly/3r9DdG5 Scan the QR code on the right to go to the pdf version of the spa day summary!

Let's say the nail trim did not go as planned, so we'll need to make an assessment of the things that got done, the things that didn't, the dog's behavior, energy level, triggers, so we can come up with a plan to keep the dog comfortable and still enough so we can trim and file all nails that need it.

Success Assessment
Download QR code

Steps of Resolution

1. **Energy level – exercise balance assessment** (calm or wiggly dog due to energy)
2. **Behavioral assessment** (nail care step – reaction)
3. **Trimming and filing success assessment** (note nails that got trimmed and filed and nails that still need trimming or filing)
4. **List triggers the dog reacted to** (early sensitivity signs – late sensitivity signs)
5. **Separate the triggers and practice them one by one!** See the training the dog's mind chapter again if you need to refresh the notes on CCDS!

6. **Join us in the Nail it! Community for customized help** to come up with an action plan for your dog's unique case !

Still Too Long Nails After Trimming

There are cases when even though we went as short as possible, found our stop sign, and stopped on time, at the final assessment we still saw that the nail was too long. In the section where we detailed the steps of how to getting the quick to recede, we demonstrated the technique, but we did not talk about any timelines.

When I see dogs with super long nails and I can't get them to the proper length, I initiate a discussion with the owner on the situation to see what works best for them that is in alignment with the dog's needs. **Usually, I suggest a nail file session at least biweekly** at home or at my doodle spa **to stimulate the quick** fast enough, but not too fast to get results without bleeding or discomfort for the dog.

That usually gets the results we want in about two weeks or a month. It might be a tad more for very severe cases.

If the dog doesn't get a nail file in two weeks, by week three or four, there will be probably enough room to trim 1-2 mm off the nail and do another filing. This is a slower way, but it can work as well.

More frequent, smaller stimuli closer to the quick will result in a faster process.

Chapter 16

Exercises

Toenail or Dewclaw?

Determine the followings about the images below:

1. Toenails or dewclaws?
2. Needs nail care or not?
3. Why needs nail care? Why not?

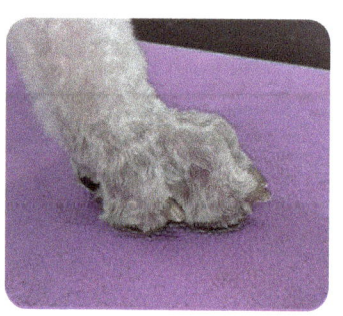

Image 1.

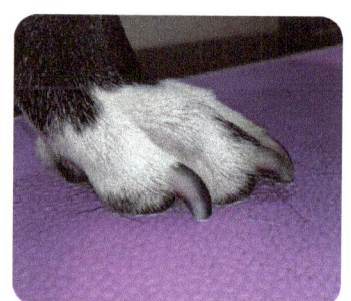

Image 2.

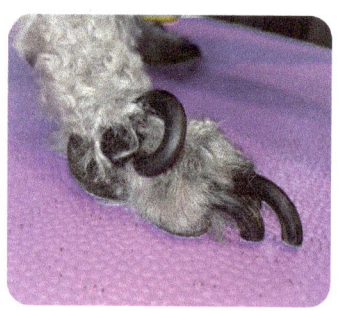

Image 3.

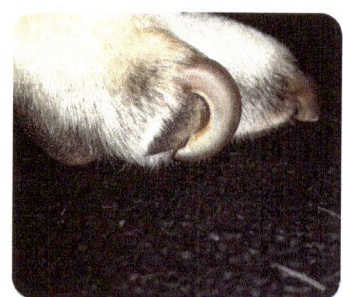

Image 4.

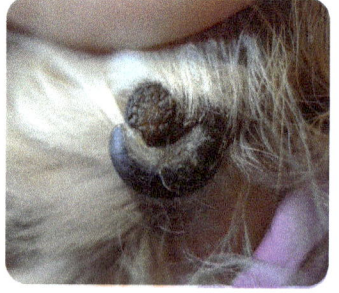

Image 5.

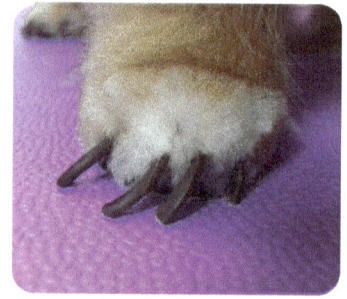

Image 6.

1st image

1. It is an image of cream toenails.
2. If you wrote down, "No, this dog does not need a nail trim," we agree that this dog has the perfect nail length.
3. The tip of the nail does not touch the ground, and neither does the paw pad. The inner curve of the nail does not touch the paw pad either.

Sidenote: I like to check for rough edges and file them off with a nail file, but sure thing, this dog does not need nail trimming at all.

2nd image

1. It is an image of black-white-clear toenails.
2. If you wrote down, "Yes, this dog needs a nail trim," we agree.
3. This dog needs a nail trim because the nails touch the ground, especially the one closest to the camera.

3rd image

1. It is an image of black toenails.
2. If you wrote down, "Yes, this dog needs a nail trim," I agree!
3. This one is tricky, so let's explore a little bit. You can see the dog's other front leg in the background. We can conclude we see the right front leg. Dewclaws are located in the legs' inner side, so the nail, which is the closest to us, is a malformed toenail, not a dewclaw. However, since it is not touching the ground but is curling back like a dewclaw, we need to apply the dewclaw rules on this nail.

4th image

1. It is an image of light brown-cream toenails.
2. If you wrote, "Yes, this dog needs a nail trim," we agree.
3. The nail's tip touches the paw pad, the toenail is curled back, and when the dog is walking, he puts his body weight on the nail, which puts pressure on the toenail. This stage is super uncomfortable for the dog.

5th image

1. It is an image of a black-cream dewclaw.
2. If you wrote, "Yes, this dog needs a nail trim," I agree.
3. The dewclaw's inner curve is close to the skin, and the tip of the dewclaw is curling back to the skin. If left as is, it'll grow into the skin, causing the dog a great deal of pain and discomfort and placing him at risk for infections at the site of the wound under the tip of the nail.

6th image

1. It is an image of brown toenails.
2. If you wrote down, "Yes, this dog needs a nail trim," we agree.
3. The nails touch the ground, and they are twisted sideways due to the pressure this poor fella must endure while walking on these gigantic nails.

Taco or Hot Dog Nail Type?

Image 1.

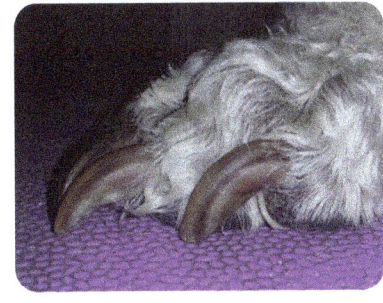
Image 2.

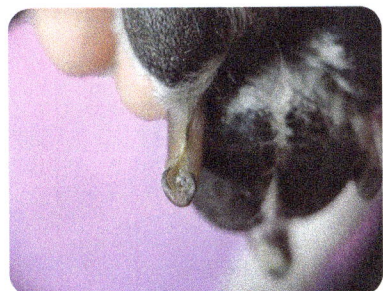
Image 3.

Image 4.

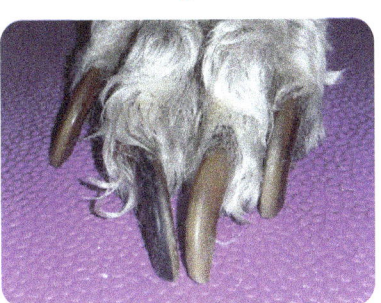
Image 5.

Image 6.

Image 7.

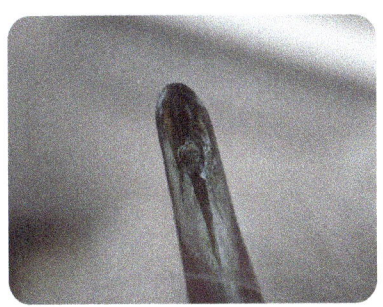
Image 8.

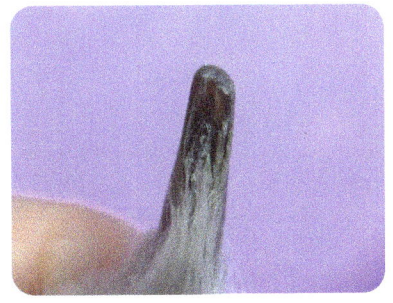
Image 9.

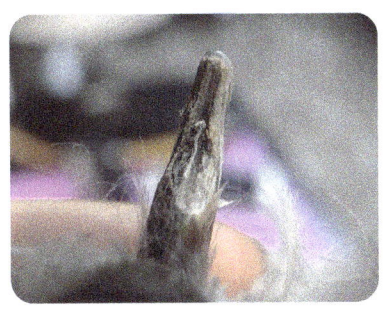
Image 10.

Answers to Taco or Hot Dog Nail Type?

Image 1. Hot dog

Image 2. Can't see from this angle

Image 3. Hot dog

Image 4. Taco

Image 5. Can't see from this angle

Image 6. Hot dog

Image 7. Taco

Image 8. Hot dog

Image 9. Taco

Image 10. Taco

For more games and nail quizzes, join us at the Nail it! course!

Attachments

Guidelines - Before Trimming the Nails

- Collecting information about the dog (general fitness, previous experiences, sensitivities, previous/ongoing pain, injuries or surgeries, etc.) to figure out the best place and practice for the dog for nail care
- Figuring out the best motivation/reinforcement for the dog (food, toys, ear/butt rubs, break needs, etc.)
- Positioning the dog (floor, table, in arms, lying, standing, sitting, etc.) depending on age and physical capabilities (elderly, disabled dogs, dogs in pain, etc.)
- The position depends on age, physical strength, disabilities, injuries, weight, comfort zone, etc.
- Letting the dog eliminate (pee, #2) RIGHT before nail trimming
- Playing with tiredness (tired, but not too tired, not hyper either)
- Trust toward the owner, care provider (walks, playtime before a pedicure, food, toys, self-confidence, etc.) (recently rescued dogs with a tough life, new pups) Recent vet visits with trying experience
- Toe pre-soak the nails for pressure-sensitive dogs or for dirty nails
- Trim the hair by the eye area and around the paws before the nail trimming so that the doggy can get a good grip on the floor for better balance on three feet. Plus, it is easier to get to the nails and trim and file the nails with less hair around. The same thing applies to the dog's ability to file his nails
- Positioning to what is comfortable for the care provider (straight back, knee pads, headlamp, bright lights, etc.)

Checklist for Nail Trimming

- Moderately tired doggy
- Doggy (and care provider) with empty bladder and rectum
- Calm and relaxing environment
- Comfortable, non-slip surface for the doggy
- Treats - Toys
- Rounded tip shears (scissors)
- Nail clipper
- Hand nail file (No nail grinders!)
- Bright headlamp
- Disinfectant spray or liquid for the equipment
- Leash or muzzle **if** the doggy is not happy about nail care **and** immediate nail trim is critical to the dog's health and comfort
- Kwik Stop or groomers' glue as a backup plan. With this technique, it'll just expire on you, untouched :) ;-)
- Knee pads/towels—under your knees or butt, for working on the floor, and for the doggy if the floor is too cold (thin coated dogs can be too cold and not so cooperative because of it). Note for pawdicures performed outside: Watch out for ants and other insects around. Don't sit in ants, and take mosquito repellent with you

Nail Tissue Cheat Sheet

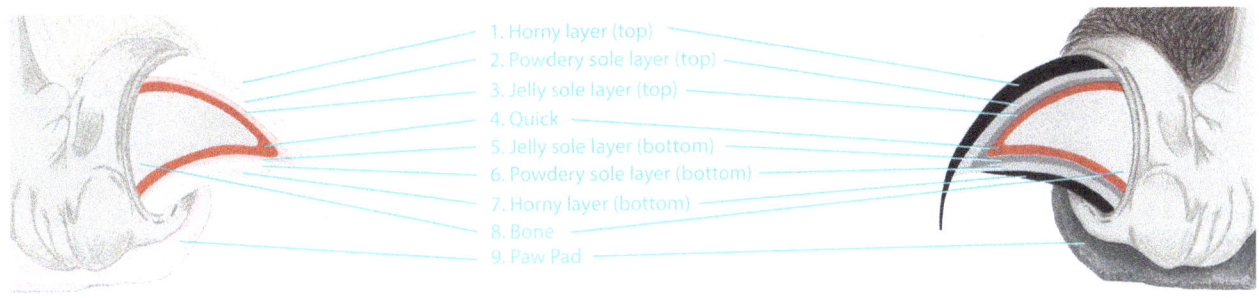

Taco Nail Layers

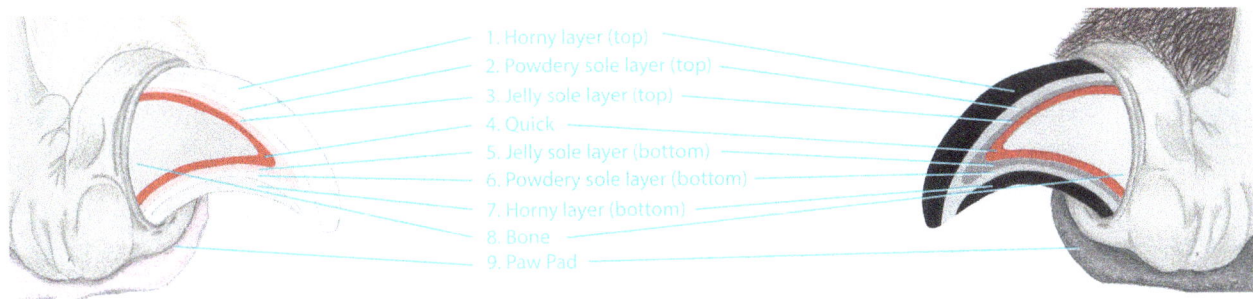

Hot Dog Nail Layers

Horny Tissue

- Texture: Hard, Shiny
- Shape/Location: Outer surface, circle, or horseshoe-shaped

Sole

Has two types: Powdery and Jelly layers

- **Powdery Layer**
    - Texture: powdery.
    - Shape: Circle or horseshoe
    - Location: Right below the horny layer. Sometimes, it is so thin that it is barely visible; sometimes, it does not develop, so it is absent
- **Jelly Layer**
    - Texture: soft and shiny
    - Shape: Dot
    - Location: Under powdery layer

Quick

- Texture: soft and bleeds when you hit it, so can't see much, other than blood
- Shape: Dot
- Location: Under the soft sole layer. There are blood vessels in the bone as well

Nail Types

Taco

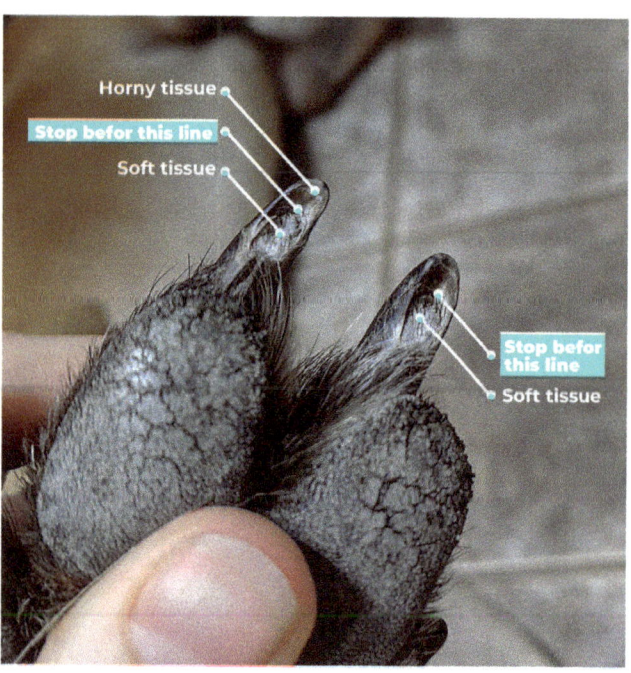

The horny tissue **partially** encircles the soft tissue

Hot dog

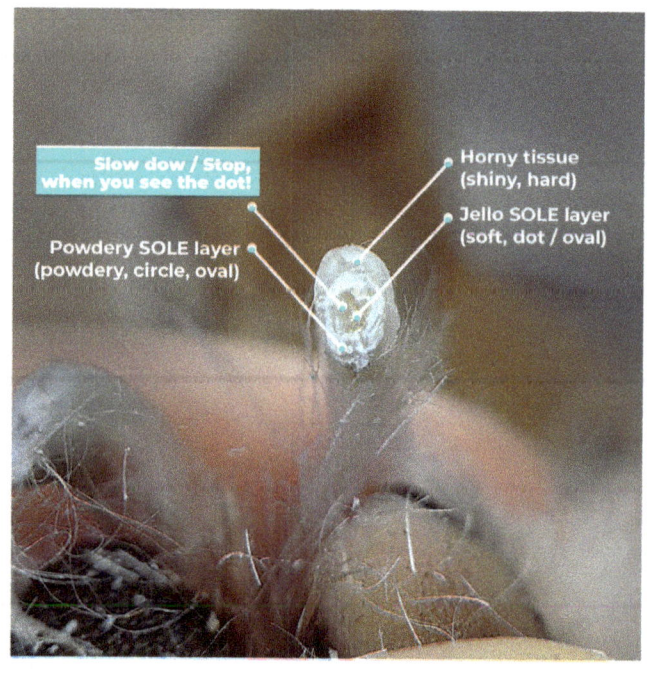

The The horny tissue **completely** encircles the soft tissue

Nail it! A Step-by-Step Guide To Wholesome Dog Nail Trimming

Nail Layers

Taco Nail Type

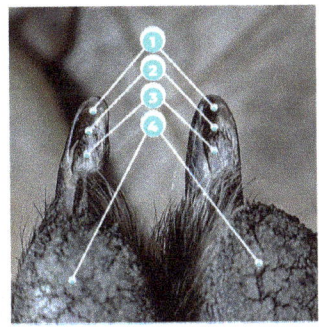 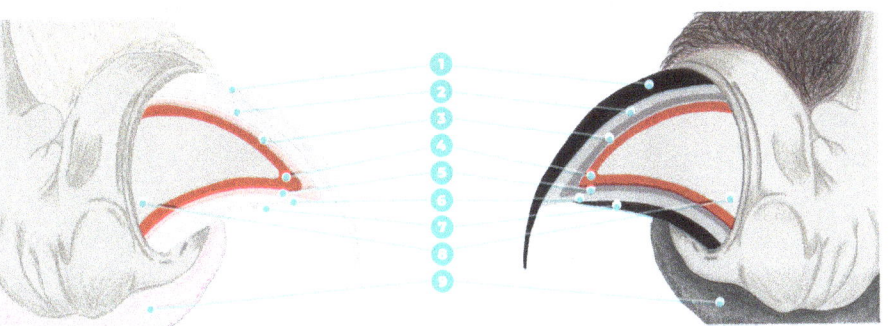

1. Horny tissue
2. Stop sign (soft tissue meets horny tissue)
3. Soft tissue
4. Toe pads

1. Horny layer (top)
2. Powdery sole layer (top)
3. Jelly sole layer (top)
4. Quick
5. Jelly sole layer (bottom)
6. Powdery soe layer (bottom)
7. Horny layer (bottom)
8. Bone
9. Paw Pad

Hot Dog Nail Type

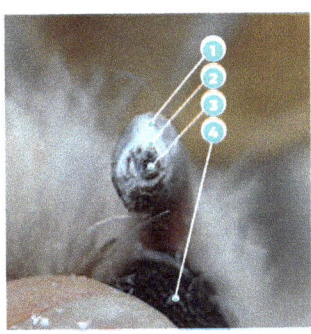 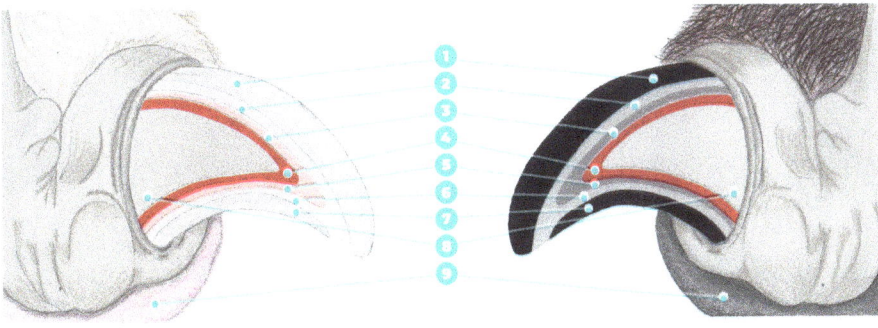

1. Horny tissue
2. Powdery sole layer (soft tissue)
3. Stop sign, Jelly sole layer (soft tissue)
4. Toe pads

1. Horny layer (top)
2. Powdery sole layer (top)
3. Jelly sole layer (top)
4. Quick
5. Jelly sole layer (bottom)
6. Powdery soe layer (bottom)
7. Horny layer (bottom)
8. Bone
9. Paw Pad

Nail it! A Step-by-Step Guide To Wholesome Dog Nail Trimming

BETTY PETO

Nail Length

From normal to severely overgrown

NORMAL

100% comfortable dog, pawrents

NORMAL,

a bit scratchy.
99% comfortable dog,
70% comfortable pawrents

TOO LONG,

nail is touching the ground.
100% uncomfortable dog

TOO LONG

touching the ground, and lifting up the toe.
100% painful dog

TOO LONG

touching the ground and lifting up the toe and about to grow in the skin

TOO LONG

touching the ground and lifting up the toe, and rubbing against the skin on the side

TOO LONG,

touching the ground, and lifting up the toe, and pushing against, about to open up the skin due to rubbing and pressure. (Can be trimmed to the proper length in one appointment.)

TOO LONG,

touching the ground, lifting up the toe, and pushing against, about to open up the skin due to rubbing and pressure. (The quick has grown down together with the nail, it cannot be trimmed to the proper length without bleeding.)

TOO LONG,

touching the ground, and lifting up the toe, and nail grew into the skin already

1 2 3 4 5 6 7 8 9
NORMAL TOO LONG SEVERELY OVERGROWN

Nail it! A Step-by-Step Guide To Wholesome Dog Nail Trimming

Paw Positioning
for Trimming and Filing

Error-prone view

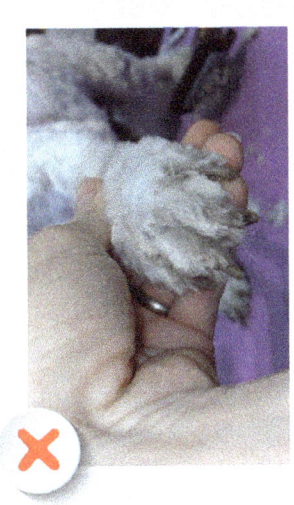
The horny layer is in the way of seeing the soft tissue layers

NEVER CUT NAILS FROM THESE ANGLES TO AVOID TRIMMING THE NAILS TOO SHORT!

Paw pad view

Position the canine to see the bottom of the nails!

Positioning that enables you to see the nail layers

Close up of the nail layers (taco nail type)

Close up of the nail layers (hot dog nail type)

Nail it!
A Step-by-Step Guide To Wholesome Dog Nail Trimming

Top 10 Nail Secrets

Secret #1
White or Clear Nails are Not Easier to Trim Than Black Nails

Secret #2
The Safe Holding Technique to See the Layers is the "Paw Pad View" Holding

Secret #3
Quick Stop/Styptic Powder Helps to Stop the Bleeding, But it Won't Eliminate the Pain

Secret #4
Most Dogs are Sensitive to Nail Care Because the Method is Uncomfortable or Painful for Them

Secret #5
You CAN Desensitize a "Feet Sensitive" Dog

Secret #6
Dogs Need Their Nails Trimmed and Filed Customized to Their Needs

Secret #7
One Nail Trim Appointment, in Some Cases, Might Not Be Enough to Get the Nails to the Proper Length

Secret #8
Tiny-tiny Cuts on Nails are the Safest, most Comfortable, and Fastest Way to Trim Nails

Secret #9
Dogs Can Be in Any Position They Want for Nail Trimming, as Long as You Can Get a Paw Pad View, Enough Space to do a Safe Angle for the Clipping

Secret #10
Dremels or Grinders Might Promise a Fast and Safe Alternative to Make Nails Shorter but at the Expense of the Dog's Comfort and Safety

Secret +1
The Scratchboard Will Not File All Nails Evenly

Secret +2
The Safety Guard on the Nail Clipper Will Not Keep You from Hitting the Dog's Quick

Secret +3
Using the Quick Stop Finder Type Clippers and Nail Grinders Will Not Keep You From Making Your Dog's Nail Bleed

Secret +4
Trimming the Nails Needs to be Followed up with Filing Them

Nail it! A Step-by-Step Guide To Wholesome Dog Nail Trimming

References

Nonviolent Communication by Marshall Rosenberg

Connecting Across Differences - Finding common ground with anyone, anywhere, anytime - giraffe book by Dian Killian and Jane Marantz

https://drjwv.com/wp/2013/11/24/nail-trimming/

https://www.shorthairsandshotguns.com/post/the-art-of-nail-trimming-part-1

https://groomwise.typepad.com/smartstyling/2009/12/canine-nails-101.html

https://caringhandsvet.com/trim-dog-nails/

https://www.fenzidogsportsacademy.com/blog/operant-conditioning-and-classical-conditioning?fbclid=IwAR1nys9AGEgJ-jRG30psHCGhsKSTVC3EaC-7sZwZZy6tGcxVbAfWikMjZv0

https://kimpikespositivepaws.wordpress.com/2014/11/05/what-is-a-cer-and-why-do-i-care/

https://www.facebook.com/groups/nail.maintenance.for.dogs/

https://veteriankey.com/disorders-of-the-claw/

https://epub.ub.uni-muenchen.de/8246/1/8246.pdf

https://www.magonlinelibrary.com/doi/epub/10.12968/coan.2013.18.4.165

Resources

FREE Nail it! Course

WholesomeGroomingAcademy.com/page/nail-it-book/
Coupon code: nailitbook

Free Printable Downloads

Get the pdfs from WholesomeGroomingAcademy.com/page/nail-it-book

- Giraffe formula sheet
- Doggy feelings and physical sensation list
- Doggy needs list
- Human feelings and physical sensations list
- Human needs list
- Behavioral assessment checklist for before the nail care session
- Preparation and tool list for right before the nail care session
- Assessment list for after the nail care session
- And more

Recommended for Further Education

Canine Nail Education

The Art of Nail Trimming - Part 1. By Shorthairs and Shotguns (bird dog training)

https://www.shorthairsandshotguns.com/post/the-art-of-nail-trimming-part-1

Nail Trimming - by Dr. Jeff Vidt

https://drjwv.com/wp/2013/11/24/nail-trimming/

Disorders of the Claw by Veteriankey.com

https://veteriankey.com/disorders-of-the-claw/

Claw Disease in Dogs: Part 1 – Anatomy and Diagnostic Approach by Sarah Warren BVetMed MSc

https://www.magonlinelibrary.com/doi/epub/10.12968/coan.2013.18.4.165

Microanatomy of the Canine Claw by Ralf S. Mueller*, Anj A Ssterner-Kock & Anthony A. Stannard

https://epub.ub.uni-muenchen.de/8246/1/8246.pdf

Canine Body Language and Training

On Talking Terms With Dogs: Calming Signals - by Turid Rugaas

Doggie Language: A Dog Lover's Guide to Understanding Your Best Friend - by Lili Chin

DogMantics.com by Emily Larlham for training, desensitization with a clicker, and positive reinforcement

How Stella Learned to Talk: The Groundbreaking Story of the World's First Talking Dog - Christina Hunger

Whole Dog Journal - canine care, training, grooming, nutrition

Compassionate Communication

CNVC.org to learn more about the Giraffe language

Nonviolent Communication by Marshall Rosenberg

Connecting Across Differences - Finding common ground with anyone, anywhere, anytime - giraffe book by Dian Killian and Jane Marantz

Punished by Rewards - book by Alfie Kohn

Unconditional Parenting - book by Alfie Kohn. Though it's about kids, I highly recommend this book for furry kids as well.

Attachment Parenting - http://www.attachmentparenting.org

Puddle Dancer Press - http://puddledancer.bookstore.ipgbook.com

More About the Wholesome Grooming Method

WholesomeGroomingAcademy.com

Nail it! Community - https://bit.ly/312TsK0

Places to Purchase Tools

Amazon.com for nail trimming equipment (fast shipping, easy returns)

Ryanspet.com for wholesale pet supply, nail clippers, tables, etc.

PetEdge.com for wholesale pet supply, nail clippers, tables, etc.

More About the Author's Work and Philosophy

WholesomeDoodleSpa.com Dog spa of the author of Nail it!

DoodleGroomingAcademy.com Coat care courses for Doodle Pawrents.

WholesomeGroomingAcademy.com Grooming and coat care courses for Pet care providers, from pawrents, through groomers, vet techs, and veterinarians.

Appreciation

Dear Reader,

I admire your dedication to searching for new ways to improve the nail care experience for canines and care providers. I am very grateful to you for reading through this book.

I thank you in the name of doggies on Earth for your curiosity and persistence.

You now have the knowledge and tools in your hands for a safe and joyful Paw-di-Cure™ journey!

Please share your nail care experience with me and this new knowledge of yours with others to help them gain the confidence they need to succeed.

I would like to invite you to join the Nail it! community to share milestones, resolve roadblocks together, and answer any questions you have!

You are the change. We are the change! Let's make this world a better place together!

One dog nail at a time!

Belly rubs to your doggy, hugs to you!

Betty :)

Afterword - Be the Change!

Letter To Veterinarians, Veterinary Technicians

Whether you are already a practicing or a student veterinarian, veterinary technician, I admire your work and all the time you put into getting your degree. All the knowledge you gained and all the care you put into saving lives every single day, whether it rains or shines.

Nail care is a tiny part of veterinary care that has a huge impact on the dog's behavior. I would like you to realize that you all are the hub of change. You can make a difference in dog nail care for your clients, peers, and yourself. You have the knowledge, the respect, the power to make rapid change around yourself.

Every one of you has the power to write, rewrite the rules in your facility and make suggestions. You can choose to be an advocate for a more comfortable and cooperative nail care experience.

You are a role model for the other professionals and facilities around. If you pay attention to the tiniest detail you can make the nail trimming sessions a wholesome one for all.

Clients will notice it and will appreciate your new approach so much.

I encourage you to talk to your staff members and bosses to accommodate for a gentle pawdicure session. If you need in-person training on-site or a live one online, I am happy to provide that for you.

I wish you a joyful nail care journey!

Hugs to you and belly rub to your dog(s)!

Letter to Groomers, Bathers

Fellow groomers and bathers! We do way more than pampering pets. It's not like we're giving out ear and butt rubs all day long as people imagine. Our work is physically demanding even when the dog cooperates.

Nail trimming is a crucial part of grooming and doing it in a way that your clients will stand still for you and help with paw lifts is an idea that gives me butterflies. No more struggling, no more pulling. You can balance out the situation and transform behavior.

I encourage you to give this method and approach a try! Share it at your dog spa! Bring in the book and have discussions about it!

A word on the tricky cases.

Dog owners want the best for their pets, but sometimes their own need to focus on something else that they find more important gets in the way. I find it very useful to talk to my clients about their dogs' behavior, nail care needs, connect with them about what kept them from fulfilling their dog's needs for nail care, training, etc. After the connection is there, so they will be less likely to take it as a lecture, we can suggest a few tricks to practice at home for a more fun vet appointment or spa day. Most of them are even open to getting a few private lessons, just about nail trimming to keep everyone comfortable.

All I had to do is start a conversation with them and explain how their doggy was feeling and what were his needs. It is surprising how often the only thing we need to modify a pattern is to share what's in us in a compassionate way.

Keep in mind, when a client is not at all cooperative, and no change will happen, you can always decline service and suggest they go somewhere else. Or report neglected dogs to the authorities. After a while, they will get the idea that they either do something about their pets' behavior or won't get stuff done, and they have to deal with the authorities as well. Neglecting dogs is a serious issue, and we, professionals, need to stand as one to help dogs get the care they need.

We need to keep our safety just as important as the dog's need for shorter nails, so make sure you are taking care of safety not only for your furry clients but also for yourself and your staff as well.

Know, that even though the corporate world might pay for your work, you have to stand up for yourself and do only what you feel comfortable with!

I wish you a joyful nail care journey!

Hugs to you and belly rub to your dog(s)!

Letter to Pawrents

If you are a dedicated pawrent of a dog or more and are looking for a way to prevent and get the best outcome for your pets, I hope you find the info in this book helpful. If you have/had a dog who is/was not comfortable around his feet, and you will get him a nail appointment until you get the confidence you need to do it yourself, I encourage you to find a practitioner who lets you be in the same room for the nail trims.

Often all we need to do is ask. Nail clippers and nail files are mobile equipment, so is the staff. Remember! If you are not comfortable in a situation, there is always an option to stop whatever procedure your dog is getting and leave. Sometimes we forget it, and we just freeze and quietly listen to our dogs screaming, and it is traumatic for all.

Keep in mind; training is much easier and faster than rehabilitation or desensitization. So if you are uncomfortable, ask to stop, compensate for whatever task got done, and leave. It's okay to leave in the middle of anything if you or your dog don't feel comfortable.

Training and desensitization are critical, so I recommend you do preparation and prevention at home by yourself. In severe cases, especially with powerful breeds who show late sensitivity signs or have a history of biting equipment, humans, or pets, you need to go to a dog trainer to help overcome the challenges with your dog's behavior and stay safe.

If you feel like training yourself for the task, with this book, especially with the tutorial videos as an addition, you will have what you need to perform safe and comfortable nail trimming at home.

I wish you a joyful nail care journey! Hugs to you and belly rub to your dog(s)!

Letter to Breeders

I admire the dedication that breeding dogs requires. All the time, effort, training, socialization, feeding times, and staying up at night when a dog is in labor, no weekends, no holidays.

The work you put into picking the right parents to breed and the love and care you offer for raising the puppies, through finding the right home for all of them is remarkable.

I see what you do and I respect your work.

I wanted to ask you a big favor. I'd like you to refuse dewclaw removal unless it is medically necessary. Dogs after birth need to focus on learning to feed and grow and removing the dewclaws causes pain and cuts into their comfort.

Dogs will be less likely to be reactive for nail care if their dewclaw is left alone. It's less work for you and it'll be no pain for the puppies. Win-win.

Pawrents are realizing this and say no to mutilation in rapidly rising numbers.

I hope you can take my request to heart and approach this issue with compassion in your heart. Changing habits is hard. I am confident you have the power within you to make it happen for happier puppies, pawrents, and groomers.

I appreciate your contribution to having amazing dogs on this planet!

I wish you a joyful nail care journey! Hugs to you and belly rub to your dog(s)!

Letter to Dog Trainers

Last, but not least, I wanted to address a few words to trainers, to come full circle. The dog's health, mind, and comfort. I enjoy so much working in collaboration with trainers because your work is essential to keep dogs still on the grooming table.

Introducing them to sounds, sensations, building the bond between dog and pawrents, teaching them to do recall, and shake-shake, and stay, and turn around, and jump, etc. are not only necessary for everyday life but at the groomers as well.

I am glad to see that more and more trainers expand their knowledge about grooming steps and help their clients to prepare their fur babies for spa days at home and at the groomer as well.

Your contribution to calm canines in society is invaluable and much needed.

I hope this book helped you gain a new perspective on how to help reactive dogs to nail trimming!

Thank you for what you do!

I wish you a joyful nail care journey!

Hugs to you and belly rub to your dog(s)!

Your Notes

Glossary

Canine feelings
Feeling that the dog feels at any given moment.

Canine needs
General canine needs that continuously need to be fulfilled to balance the dog's mind, body, and soul.

Classical conditioning (CC)
It is a type of learning (first described by Ivan Pavlov) in which a stimulus elicits a response. In classical conditioning, two events are getting linked as they happen, regardless of what the learner is doing. Dogs trained with this method learn to associate a tool or sound with a biological need (food). Associations can happen between any two elements in the environment that are noticed/experienced by the learner, in our case, the dog. This method is one great way to help dogs learn how to be just as excited when seeing the nail clippers as when seeing a bag of treats, their dinner ready, or their leash.

Counterconditioning and desensitization (CCDS)
Combination of the two techniques to reach the best results the fastest.

Counterconditioning (Cc)
We replace an undesirable or maladaptive response with a more desirable response with a stimulus, utilizing customized conditioning steps.

    Example: Dogs who previously were shaking or hiding when you grabbed the nail clipper start to drool (ready for food), wiggle, maybe even do the zoomies when they see the nail clipper due to counter conditioning.

Desensitization (D)
It's a technique very often paired with counterconditioning. We keep the dog below the threshold (relaxed and alert) and exposed to fears in an increasing hierarchy of intensity to diminish the fearful response over time. We keep the scary thing at a comfortable distance and at a low enough intensity that the dog can stay relaxed during the entire training session. Over multiple sessions, the frightening thing/situation can move closer or be more intense, resulting in a comfortable and cooperative canine.

Desired dog grooming – "working with" method

When we include the dog's perspective, feelings, and needs along with the grooming tasks at hand, we come up with compassionate strategies that help the dog to stay below threshold and cooperate willingly.

Dewclaw

Nail located higher up the inner side of the lower leg.

Dewclaw pad

Cushion of the dewclaw.

Getting the quick to recede

Stimulating the quick to shorten to achieve optimal nail length.

Hitting the quick

Cutting in the quick, the live part of the nail with clippers causing bleeding.

Horny tissue

The hard, most outer layer of the nail that protects the soft tissues below it.

Hot dog nail type

The nail type when the horny tissue completely encircles the soft tissue from the nail bed to the tip of the nail.

Jelly sole

The deeper layer of the sole, right before the quick. This is the layer we need to stop at to avoid bleeding.

Nail color

Color combination of the horny tissue and the soft tissues below.

Nail flakes (cutlings)

Nail slices we cut off when trimming nails.

Nail socks

Matted hair in shape of a sock on the nail. Can form on toenails and dewclaws as well.

Operant conditioning (OC)

Operant conditioning is a type of learning where consequences modify behavior. You change dog behavior by planning which consequence applies for each behavior, and you do it with precise timing and consequently. Keep in mind, the environment around us conspires to use some consequences of

Glossary

its own, as well. In operant conditioning, there are four kinds of consequences. There are two major groups. See the Training Dog Minds section.

Pawdicure
Nail care for canines expressed in a humorous way.

Paw-di-cure™ method
Betty's error-free nail trimming method.

Paw pad
The biggest cushion of the paw.

Paw pad boomerang
Matted hair among the toe and paw pads.

Powdery sole
Type of a nail layer, between the horny tissue and the Jelly sole.

Pressure-free clipping method
A method that is designed to position the nail clipper in a way that it won't put pressure on the horny tissue that results in pressure on the soft tissue underneath to keep the dog relaxed. The method covers holding and cutting techniques at the tip of the nail and on the sides to provide a comfortable, sensation-free nail trimming experience.

Quick
Type of a nail layer, full with nerve endings and blood vessels. It's the "live part" of the nail.

Sensitivity signs
Dog's reactions (body language, vitals, etc.) to triggers that put them around or over the threshold. There are early sensitivity signs and late sensitivity signs.

Sole layer
Type of a nail layer that has two sup layers, Powdery sole and Jelly sole.

Taco nail type
The horny tissue partially encircles the soft tissue of the nail.

The quick has grown down with the nail
The quick has grown longer than the normal nail length within the nail.

Threshold
The threshold is the point at which your dog is starting to show sensitivity signs of getting triggered. When the dog is below the threshold, the dog's body language shows the dog feels relaxed. When the dog is at the threshold, the dog is starting to show early sensitivity signs. When the dog is over the threshold, the dog shows early or late sensitivity signs, and everyone is at a higher risk of getting injured.

Toe mohawk
Matted hair between the toes.

Toe pad
Cushion under the toe.

Toenail
Nails at the end of the toes.

Triggers
Distractions that dogs respond to with discomfort signs.

Undesirable dog grooming – "doing to" method
When we focus on the task at hand so much we exclude the comfort/perspective of a living, feeling canine. We are doing things to them, not working with them.

Acknowledgments

I will always cherish the memory of a tenish-member dog pack in the suburbs where I grew up who attacked me and helped me develop the biggest fear of mine at the age of eleven. Yep, after that, I was terrified of dogs.

I am thankful for all the pups I grew up with or got to know even for a brief ear rub time or a quick snap. Without you cheering me up and challenging me, I would not have transformed my fear into compassion and understanding and would have no idea why you reacted the way you did. Let alone have tricks up my sleeve to help all of us feel more comfortable so you won't feel the need to use your teeth.

Special thanks to my furry clients who let me take tons of images about their pawdicure sessions and were bearing with me when their spa day lasted three times longer due to the puparazzi photos.

I appreciate my clients' patience and willingness to support me and be flexible about the pickup times due to me taking images of their dogs' nails. And for listening to me being blown away by their dogs' natural stripes on their nails and other details, which mesmerized me about their dog's feet. Turns out I might have developed an obsession.

Extra belly rubs to Töki, my Belgian Malinois, who watched me rubbing countless doggy butts and refused to disown me for not rubbing his instead. Buddy, I wish I could tell you that I earn money for your home, toys, and dinner by rubbing dog butts. Sorry that I chose to write when you pushed my elbow up with your nose (so hard I punched the screen a few times) while I was working on the manuscript. I am almost done, and we will take more hikes together and we'll do more pool time, I promise!

Special thanks and a handful of treats to Moose and a massive hug to Kathleen Gomez for taking the extra time with me in the evenings to make the cover of the book happen as adorable as it turned out.

To my parents, who did their best, they knew how in every situation. Without my upbringing, my fairy tale would not have started on a new continent with "Once upon a time, in a land far, far away..."

To my husband, who was waiting for me in a land far, far away, and who encouraged me to accomplish many of my dreams, including the publication of this book. His support, patience, and guidance made me pull through the challenges.

To Évi! Thank you, sis, for being there for me when I was a jealous little brat growing up. I had a hard time sharing attention with you and I took every chance to make you pay for it. Your compassion toward others, even me regardless of my actions fueled me and mom in the hardest times. I am pleased to see that since then you have learned to give without being selfless and you are sharing your attention keeping others and yourself in mind as well, as a self full, Giraffe speaking individual. I am trying and I hope I can make it up for all the trouble I caused you growing up someday! We are resolving so many generational challenges, I am glad to know we are walking together on unexplored territory and making a difference for our future while supporting each other.

To Zoltán Pető, who tirelessly analyzed the manuscript, who gave me invaluable suggestions in a gentle yet clear and distinct way about all parts of the work, let it be the text, cover, or how could I let my readers know that it existed.

Shannon Bailey! I am so delighted you kept searching for the right groomer with the best fitting approach for Gwenevere! I am the happiest that you gave me a chance to do your girl's nails years ago. I am humbled that you found the method you saw working on Gwenevere precious and fell in love with it so much that you offered your support with grammar, editing, proofreading, encouragement, and emotional support for this book becoming a reality. I am beyond happy to care for Pixel and your new family member, Stella, and enjoy our talks while doing some pawdicure work in action.

Brigitta Szabo, your talent in arts is a crucial element in displaying my nail trimming method. My artsy side does not go beyond cutting dog hair and nails. Your work made it possible so the concept looks professional and clear. Those potatoes, shall I say more like little wee-wees (meant to be dog nails with a paw pad) I came up with initially were not doing much other than making people blush or laugh. Sometimes both.

Brent Spears! My deepest appreciation for designing the interior of this book in print and ebook formats! You became my rock and you were there for me when the first designer folded on the project and you took on this massive challenge and helped me publish Nail it!. Your attention to detail, expertise in your field, speedy work, and genuine kindness made a huge difference not just for me in the process of getting the book printed but also for the readers with the stunning result. I will be forever grateful to you for helping me make my dream come true, listening to me being unusually particular about my taste in details in the book's design and withstanding it all with compassion and understanding. I appreciate you guiding me through it all. You made a long and bumpy road of getting this book out there not only bearable but fun and fruitful.

I am in awe of all of the workshop and course participants, and forum fans who asked questions and helped me fine-tune details for a better understanding and a faster learning experience, even for beginners.

I will be forever grateful for the late Marshall Rosenberg's work. His books and courses about the Giraffe language helped me see the world a better place, ease my pain about my past and create a joyful present, regardless of the circumstances for me and those around me. With your help, Marshall, I found meaning in life. I am doing my best to keep your work alive and let dogs and doggy owners experience a fundamentally different approach compared to the traditional grooming experience out there. I am heartbroken that I could not meet you in person, but I see you on the living-room wall every day and will keep your legacy alive!

To Dr. Aviva Romm, who dedicated her life to helping women and children thrive! I appreciate you taking me as a client years ago! Regular doctors could not figure out why I felt so crappy and you did and helped me support my thyroid to get my life back. How fascinating is that that you have the knowledge and power to do that kind of transformation for people?

You gave me the proof that I am a badass MTHFR (genetic condition) and the tools I needed to work with this gene mutation. And a joke I can share with people, haha. Your work always inspired me from the get-go and kept my spirit up when I almost threw in the towel while working on this book.

Tim Dockery and Judit Bodor! We will be forever grateful for your tireless help to get our first house just before finishing this book in the craziest market ever. It makes a huge difference to live in a home we adore and enjoy to bits. Recharging here will make life sweeter and many more books will come way faster than this one made it to the shelves.

To Edit Gajdács! You helped me to get on the path of grooming dogs and I will be forever grateful for you to open up possibilities that I could not see myself in. I thought grooming was doing haircuts, and bows, dying hair, and painting dog nails and I did not agree with the last three at all. You helped me see how I could merge my philosophy, training skills, and doggy haircuts together and how to embrace the elimination of the ones I did not agree with and how to create a method that became incredibly popular in a snap. I think befriending a spouse's ex is an underrated pleasure. It sure worked out for you, Levi, and me! We appreciate you giving us Pupák, our kitty cat to join the furry family as a companion for our first cat, Mr. Chips.

A huge thanks to my three cats, who proved I am a crazy cat lady, too, not just a crazy dog lady. Mr. Chips and Mr. Pupák, I appreciate you helping me take care of my body and get up from my desk to prepare and give you all some yumms way more often than you needed it or I found efficient from a writing progress perspective. Thank you for your company while writing this book in bed, slightly sick, or just way too tired to sit by the table. Your company, warmth, and purring made all the emotional boo-boos I came across during the birth of this book much more bearable.

My cuddliest "cat-kitten," Luna, who beat all odds with her heart murmur, keeps on living the wildest cat life, chasing doggy tails and giving away free nose boops. Who tirelessly sat on, lay on, sneezed on me, the keyboard, and the top of my laptop while I was trying to make this book happen. You are my mobile body warmer when I'm sitting in front of the laptop. You were my tear catcher when I was struggling to digest I missed another deadline of the book; or when I was facing harsh feedback from tired and angry groomers, and I could not take it anymore. Appreciate your protests at the beginning (NONAILTRIMSFORLUNA!! GRRRR) and your cooperation later on after the desensitization for letting me trim your nails, too!

To Mr. Pupak, who keeps the monsters at bay under the bed (favorite hiding spot for the day, our little alley cat) and who gently wakes us up with chest compressions and face taps when his belly becomes urgently hungry.

Last but not least, to Picúr, our maltipoo, the newest addition to the family. I specialized in doodles years ago and finally got my hands on one in 2021. I appreciate you being the doggy model representing the small woofers of the world (and sometimes the feisty ones) and showing off your little nails in the tutorials for others to learn from. You are the biggest cuddle bug in the family and we appreciate the new perspective on life you brought to us!

232　　NAIL IT!

 I want to thank everyone who contributed to this project listed here or not in any way, let it be helping me which way to go or not to go. Your opinion helped me get where I am today and I am grateful for the lessons and the experience.

Betty Peto
Georgetown, Texas, USA - January 2022

";lkdcgvhbjnjhjgfchvjbhbnjjhbghvjbhiiiiiiiiiiiiiiiii"

~Luna

Luna

"FHOHOSTHIJHrpijlSGNj/GIJ"GRnrg"

~ Mr. Chips (Csipesz)

Mr. Chips

"kjuh;iygluvjhbkjnlaefFAEqkopde"

~Mr. Pupák, Töki & Picúr

Mr. Pupáak

Töki

Picúr

About the Author

Betty Peto was born in Hungary, Europe in 1987, and always felt a calling for working with animals, especially with dogs.

She got her grooming diploma in 2010 in Hungary and has been combining her grooming methods with dog training ever since.

Betty specialized in grooming dogs only with a restraint-free grooming method. She owns the Wholesome Doodle Spa near Austin, Texas.

She is the president of Wholesome Grooming Academy and Doodle Grooming Academy and is on a mission to teach compassionate grooming methods to pawrents and professionals in the pet care industry.

Betty Peto

Betty came to the US with a big dream to meet with Cesar Millan, the dog whisperer in 2010. She not only met him but also got an autograph and a tour around the Dog Psychology Center in Santa Clarita. Dream fulfilled. Most importantly, she met the love of her life, Levi. Funny enough, he was also born in Hungary and they met in Los Angeles.

After a nineteen-month wait for the fiancé's visa to clear, Betty finally moved to the US in 2012 to marry Levi, barefoot in the sand on the beach in Newport Beach, CA. She became a US citizen in 2016 and is beyond grateful to live in the United States of America and enjoy what it has to offer.

In her free time, Betty likes pool time, gardening, reading, and DIY projects around the house.

Check Out Betty's Other Book

Available Wherever Books Are Sold

Learn More On

WholesomeGroomingAcademy.com

Joyful Spa Days
for all participants

For Pawrents

Coat care at home from the basics to a full-body trim.

For Breeders

Help your puppy pawrents prepare for smooth grooming expereinces!

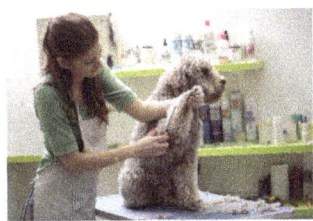

For Groomers

Specialize in Wholesome Grooming! Get free handouts! Get certified!

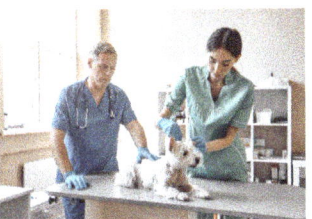

For Vets, Vet Techs

Learn to trim and file nails with 100% accuracy!